1973
The Supreme Court Review

197.

Th

"Judges as persons, or courts as institutions, are entitled to no greater immunity from criticism than other persons or institutions . . . [J]udges must be kept mindful of their limitations and of their ultimate public responsibility by a vigorous stream of criticism expressed with candor however blunt."
—*Felix Frankfurter*

". . . while it is proper that people should find fault when their judges fail, it is only reasonable that they should recognize the difficulties. . . . Let them be severely brought to book, when they go wrong, but by those who will take the trouble to understand them."
—*Learned Hand*

THE LAW SCHOOL

THE UNIVERSITY OF CHICAGO

Supreme Court Review

EDITED BY

PHILIP B. KURLAND

 THE UNIVERSITY OF CHICAGO PRESS

CHICAGO AND LONDON

JH
1561
.S8
1973

INTERNATIONAL STANDARD BOOK NUMBER: 0-226-46424-5

LIBRARY OF CONGRESS CATALOG CARD NUMBER: 60-14353

THE UNIVERSITY OF CHICAGO PRESS, CHICAGO 60637

THE UNIVERSITY OF CHICAGO PRESS, LTD., LONDON

© 1974 BY THE UNIVERSITY OF CHICAGO. ALL RIGHTS RESERVED. PUBLISHED 1974

PRINTED IN THE UNITED STATES OF AMERICA

TO
SUSAN AND EDWARD

Friendship, of itself a holy tie,
Is made more sacred by adversity.

—John Dryden

CONTENTS

GERHARD CASPER

APPORTIONMENT AND THE RIGHT TO VOTE: STANDARDS OF JUDICIAL SCRUTINY

I

In March 1964, in *New York Times v. Sullivan*,[1] the Supreme Court of the United States adopted the "Meiklejohn interpretation of the First Amendment." Professor Alexander Meiklejohn viewed the First Amendment as a necessary predicate to the right to vote, the "external expression" of the self-governing activities of the people.[2] Three weeks before its decision in *New York Times v. Sullivan*, the Court in its first major substantive reapportionment case, *Wesberry v. Sanders*, had described the fundamental status of the right to vote in these terms:[3] "No right is more precious in a free country than that of having a choice in the election of those who make the laws under which, as good citizens, we

---

Gerhard Casper is Professor of Law and Political Science, The University of Chicago.

[1] 376 U.S. 254 (1964), as interpreted by Kalven, *The New York Times Case: A Note on "The Central Meaning of the First Amendment,"* 1964 SUPREME COURT REVIEW 191. Kalven's interpretation was confirmed in Brennan, *The Supreme Court and the Meiklejohn Interpretation of the First Amendment,* 79 HARV. L. REV. 1 (1965).

[2] Meiklejohn, *The First Amendment Is an Absolute,* 1961 SUPREME COURT REVIEW 245, 255.

[3] 376 U.S. 1, 17 (1964). Although Black's formulation has a poetic rather than an analytic ring, I take the reference to "illusion" to mean that on the right to vote depends some measure of representation in lawmaking. Most, if not all, "operational details" have remained unclear. See text *infra*, at note 5.

must live. Other rights, even the most basic, are illusory if the right to vote is undermined."

While the hierarchy of rights has thus become well established and has since been confirmed in an avalanche of voting rights cases which suggest that the right to vote is the First Amendment right par excellence, it remains one of the most peculiar facts of American constitutional history that this "preservative of all rights"[4] has suffered from neglect for prolonged, though interrupted periods. We still are ill equipped analytically to deal with most contemporary questions pertaining to the electoral process and its effects upon the right to vote.

These issues relate even to "ordinary" apportionment, not to mention multimember districts and gerrymandering. The laws governing the internal structure of political parties, campaigns and their financing, voting in primaries, the powers of national party conventions, access to the ballot, and other related matters have received little scholarly attention. These variables, as well as others, structure and limit "the people's choice" and thus supposedly affect the right to vote. Their status in constitutional law and theory is far from clear. As a matter of fact, it remains unclear to this day, the labors of the United States Supreme Court notwithstanding, what, if any, right "to be represented" is entailed in the right to vote.

Reapportionment cases have mostly been treated as right to vote cases and have focused "on something called individual voter weight"[5] without any detailed analysis of the concept of representation. Supposedly the voter should be more interested in being represented than in a mathematically equal vote. The goal of voting, representation, continues to be a treasure hidden somewhere in a maze of slogans. The fault is not entirely that of the Supreme Court. As has been noted by Professors Prewitt and Eulau, despite the proliferation of representative governments over the past century (they offer a figure of about ninety thousand different political units in the United States), "*theory* about representation has not

---

[4] Yick Wo v. Hopkins, 118 U.S. 356, 370 (1886).

[5] Dixon, *The Court, the People, and "One Man, One Vote,"* in POLSBY, ed., REAPPORTIONMENT IN THE 1970s 7, 18 (1971).

moved much beyond the eighteenth century formulation of Edmund Burke."[6]

In part at least, this state of affairs may be attributed to the fact
that the franchise in the United States, since 1920, has been universal except for Southern blacks, for whom the right to vote remained more fictitious than real until the changes brought about in
the 1960s. The right to vote has been universal, not only in terms
of adult suffrage, but also as to opportunities to vote. Except for
Switzerland probably no other democracy provides as many chances
to vote on candidates and issues from the local to the national level
as does the United States. Not until recently have the Civil Rights
movement and other challenges to the legitimacy of American government in the 1960s led to widespread questioning of the effectiveness of the vote.

Scholarly and popular neglect of the right to vote may also be
due to the circumstance that, as a consequence of the political conditions prevailing at the time of the Constitutional Convention,
voting rights and representative government were left almost entirely within the jurisdiction of the states, where they were subject
to an infinite variety of arrangements. With the exception of constitutional prohibitions of certain types of discrimination and
congressional protection of the state-granted right to vote in congressional elections,[7] the right to vote did not receive explicit recognition as a status right of a United States citizen until the decision
of the Supreme Court in the reapportionment case of *Wesberry v.
Sanders* in 1964.[8]

The original constitution did not guarantee the right to vote nor
did it provide for direct elections, except for the House of Representatives. Senators and Presidents were to be elected indirectly, the

---

[6] Prewitt & Eulau, *Political Matrix and Political Representation: Prolegomenon to a New
Departure from an Old Problem*, 63 Am. Pol. Sci. Rev. 427 (1969).

[7] 376 U.S. at 46 (Harlan, J., dissenting).

[8] *Id.* at 17. Its constitutional stature remains precarious. As late as last Term, Mr.
Justice Marshall could state: "Yet it is clear that whatever degree of importance has
been attached to the state electoral process when unequally distributed, the right to vote
in state elections has itself never been accorded the stature of an independent constitutional guarantee." San Antonio Independent School District v. Rodriguez, 411 U.S. 1,
101 (1973) (Marshall, J., dissenting). Except that I do not know what an "unequally
distributed state electoral process" is, I think the observation is a technically correct
summary of the law. It does not take account of the symbolic significance and implications of the Court's jurisprudence.

former by the state legislatures, the latter by the electoral college, the members of which were to be "appointed" in such a manner as the state legislatures saw fit. To this very day, the right to vote for presidential electors seems to be based on no more than the brute fact that all states have chosen to "appoint" the electors by means of popular election. The House of Representatives was to be popularly elected under the original scheme, but it was left to the states to determine who should have the right to vote. As far as the United States Constitution was concerned, the states were given control over voter qualifications in both state and federal elections. To be sure, by the middle of the nineteenth century the right to be a voter had generally been granted to all white adult males, but this was the result of state, not national, command. The rather feeble attempt by § 2 of the Fourteenth Amendment to make it costly for the states to deny voter status to "male citizens, 21 years of age" collapsed quickly owing to the unforeseen consequences the provision had in the Northern, rather than the Southern, states. When, in 1913, the Seventeenth Amendment made popular elections of senators mandatory, voter qualifications were again left to be determined by the states.

Formally, the history of federal protection of voting rights is a history of protecting the franchise, not so as to make it "effective," but against particular types of "discrimination" and abuse. Substantively, it is a history of progressive enfranchisement of classes of citizens without explicit recognition of the franchise as a matter of federal government jurisdiction. The right to vote has achieved its current status as a "fundamental right" in a piecemeal manner, which cannot be fully appreciated if one reads only modern pronouncements on the hierarchy of values. Beginning in 1870 the United States Constitution set out to protect the right to vote against discrimination on account of race (Fifteenth Amendment), then followed sex (Nineteenth Amendment, 1920), poverty in federal elections (poll tax abolition by the Twenty-fourth Amendment, 1964),[9] and finally, "age." The Twenty-sixth Amendment lowering the voting age to eighteen was adopted in 1971 after an attempt to accomplish the same goal by federal antidiscrimination legislation had failed as far as state elections were concerned.[10]

---

[9] Extended to the states by the Supreme Court in Harper v. Virginia Board of Elections, 383 U.S. 663 (1966).

[10] Oregon v. Mitchell, 400 U.S. 112 (1970).

While the Nineteenth, Twenty-fourth, and Twenty-sixth Amendments met with virtually automatic and complete compliance, the same cannot be said of the Fifteenth Amendment. The fact serves to illustrate the rather limited nature of the original federal effort. Grandfather clauses, white primaries, and literacy tests have all been used by the states to deny the right to vote. While eventually these techniques were recognized as federally impermissible, the most formidable of the hurdles, literacy tests, was found to be valid by the Supreme Court of the United States as recently as 1959.[11] It is fair to state that effective protection of the right to vote free from racial discrimination began only when the Congress stepped in (Civil Rights Acts of 1957, of 1960, of 1964, Voting Rights Acts of 1965 and 1970). The Voting Rights Act of 1965 was by far the most drastic and the most effective of these enactments, with its suspension of literacy tests and its provision for federal control of the election machinery in certain states.[12]

Enforcement of the right to be a voter has thus largely been accomplished by means of constitutional amendments and congressional legislation. The role of the courts in this area over the past ten years has mostly been restricted to marginal addenda to the voter lists (such as soldiers in Texas or new residents in Tennessee). It has not been the question of access to the ballot box, but rather the weight of the ballot cast, which led the Supreme Court to establish the right to vote as a "preferred freedom" under the Equal Protection Clause of the Fourteenth Amendment. Once the jurisdictional barriers had been overcome in *Baker v. Carr*,[13] no great dose of legal realism was required to recognize that the right to vote of, for instance, a citizen of Hartford, Connecticut, could reasonably be considered to be worth much less than the right to vote in Union, Connecticut, since the 383 inhabitants of Union had the same representation in the Connecticut House as had the 162,178 citizens of Hartford. It was also reasonable to conclude that in this situation—where Union had an "amount" of representation about 425 times that of Hartford—some problem of equal protection ex-

---

[11] Lassiter v. Northampton County Board of Elections, 360 U.S. 45 (1959).

[12] While voter registration is not to be confused with actual voting, the progress in voter registration has been impressive. Cf. STATISTICAL ABSTRACT OF THE UNITED STATES 1972, 374.

[13] 369 U.S. 186 (1962).

isted. As Mr. Justice White put it last Term, recounting the 1964 example in a case involving Connecticut's 1972 reapportionment, the variations were "enormous."[14]

To be sure, the critics of the Supreme Court reapportionment decisions were quick to point out that representation was more than a mere numbers game. Yet given the fact that the representation issue was first presented in terms of rather egregious contrasts and also given the elusive nature of the concept of representation, it is understandable, if unfortunate, that the Supreme Court has concentrated so much of its effort on policing numbers.

II

Wesberry v. Sanders[15] was the first major case. It concerned malapportionment of congressional districts in Georgia. The *Wesberry* decision opened a line of cases unbroken and unqualified to the present day. It held that the command of Article I, § 2, that Representatives be chosen "by the People of the several States" left no room for classification of people in a way that "unnecessarily abridges" their right to vote.[16] It also held that as nearly as is practicable, one man's vote in a congressional election is to be worth as much as another's,[17] which to the Supreme Court meant equal size districts. Though substantively the problem was treated as one of equality of voters and votes, technically the case was not decided on the basis of the Equal Protection Clause of the Fourteenth Amendment. Since the Constitution leaves voting rights to the states, one might have assumed that, congressional legislation aside, the states could be controlled only by means of the general prohibitions of the Fourteenth Amendment. Mr. Justice Black, however, found a specific guarantee of the right to vote and a specific prohibition of malapportionment in congressional elections flowing directly from Article I, § 2. The technical question of standards of judicial scrutiny under the Fourteenth Amendment was thus avoided as concerns congressional districting. It was faced several months later in the first major state legislative reapportionment case of *Reynolds v. Sims*.[18]

---

[14] Gaffney v. Cummings, 412 U.S. 735, 744 (1973).

[15] 376 U.S. 1 (1964).   [17] *Id*. at 18.

[16] *Id*. at 17.   [18] 377 U.S. 533 (1964).

III

Baker v. Carr had concerned a relatively clear situation: a state constitutional command to reapportion every ten years and no action by the Tennessee legislature since 1901. In light of this, Mr. Justice Brennan sounded persuasive when he said: "Judicial standards under the Equal Protection Clause are well developed and familiar, and it has been open to courts since the enactment of the Fourteenth Amendment to determine, if on the particular facts they must, that a discrimination reflects *no* policy, but simply arbitrary and capricious action."[19] On the other hand, it was clear from the beginning that if the Supreme Court restricted itself to a mere rationality test, as then administered, there would not be very much the Court could do, since, under the test, state statutes benefit from a presumption of constitutionality and stand unless the courts cannot conceive of a rational basis for distinctions and classifications made by the legislature. Some of the state political establishments which were defendants in reapportionment suits, as well as some of the Court's critics, could discover rationality even in rotten boroughs.

The normative equal protection standard established by *Reynolds* was, of course, the holding that "an individual's right to vote for state legislators is unconstitutionally impaired when its weight is in a substantial fashion diluted when compared with votes of citizens living in other parts of the State."[20] This principle has become known as "one man, one vote," though nowadays—with another linguistic bow to women's liberation—it is apparently referred to, at least by Mr. Justice Rehnquist, as "one person, one vote."[21] The standard of review accompanying the one man, one vote, one value rule established the right to vote as a preferred freedom in language reminiscent of Chief Justice Stone's famous *Carolene Products* footnote,[22] though no reference was made to it in the reapportionment cases: "[S]ince the right to exercise the franchise in a free and unimpaired manner is preservative of other basic civil and political rights, any alleged infringement of the right of citizens to vote must be carefully and meticulously scrutinized."[23] Apparently

---

[19] 369 U.S. at 226.   [20] 377 U.S. at 568.

[21] Mahan v. Howell, 410 U.S. 315, 319 (1973).

[22] United States v. Carolene Products Co., 304 U.S. 144, 152, n.4 (1938).

[23] 377 U.S. at 562.

this meant that in voting rights cases the presumption of constitutionality and mere rationality were not enough to uphold state legislation.

Two other aspects of Chief Justice Warren's opinion for the Court in *Reynolds* are important for understanding subsequent developments. (1) Although Warren recognized the dogmatic difference between *Wesberry* and *Reynolds* which the Court had established by treating congressional districting as an Article I proposition, he also emphasized that the normative principle underlying both decisions was the same, namely, "the fundamental principle of representative government in this country": "equal representation for equal numbers of people, without regard to race, sex, economic status, or place of residence within a State."[24] (2) The Court emphasized one consideration as justifying some deviations from a population standard in state legislative apportionment as long as population remained the "controlling consideration," insuring some voice to political subdivisions, as political subdivisions.[25] The Court apparently searched for some reconciliation between the principles of territorial representation and majority government.

IV

The most important of the congressional redistricting cases after *Wesberry* was *Kirkpatrick v. Preisler*.[26] By 1969 the Court had developed a fairly mechanical way for measuring deviations from the "ideal" of "equal representation for equal numbers": take the state population as a whole and divide it by the number of districts, this will yield the "ideal" population per district; then look at the average and maximum percentage variations from the ideal. The average variation from the ideal in *Kirkpatrick* was 1.6 percent, the most populous district was 3.13 percent above the mathematical ideal, and the least populous was 2.8 percent below. Missouri prayed that these variations be considered *de minimis*. Mr. Justice Brennan, speaking for the Court, rejected the plea, insisting instead that "the command of Art. I, § 2 . . . permits only the limited population variances which are unavoidable despite a good-faith effort to achieve absolute equality, or for which justification

---

[24] *Id.* at 560–61.   [25] *Id.* at 580.

[26] 394 U.S. 526 (1969). See also Wells v. Rockefeller, 394 U.S. 542 (1969).

is shown."[27] The state had the burden to show either that the variations were unavoidable or to justify the variation some other way. The justifications offered by Missouri, e.g., the "necessity" to avoid fragmenting areas with distinct economic and social interests and thereby diluting the effective representation of those interests in Congress, were all rejected. The example provided was even considered "antithetical" to the basic premise of the constitutional command,[28] without the benefit of a detailed discussion of the concept of representation. Justices Harlan, Stewart, and White dissented. White considered the insistence on absolute equality an invitation to gerrymander: "Legislatures intent on minimizing the representation of selected political or racial groups are invited to ignore political boundaries and compact districts so long as they adhere to population equality among districts using standards which we know and they know are sometimes quite incorrect. I see little merit in such a confusion of priorities."[29] Mr. Justice White also said that at this "trivial level" he would be willing to view state explanations of the variance with a more tolerant eye.

In 1973, in the Texas congressional districting case *White v. Weiser*,[30] the state apparently believed that the "new" Court might be willing to relax standards. The figuring is by now familiar: take the four Nixon appointees and add one or both of the Warren Court "conservatives" and you may have a majority. This calculation proved to be about 50 percent right and 50 percent wrong. The *Kirkpatrick* dissenters still on the Court decided to honor precedent and unequivocally affirmed adherence to *Kirkpatrick*. In this they were joined by Mr. Justice Blackmun and, of course, by Justices Brennan, Douglas, and Marshall. Justices Powell, Burger, and Rehnquist even made for unanimity by equivocally concurring "unless and until the Court decides to reconsider" *Kirkpatrick*. Mr. Justice White wrote the opinion for the Court.

The case concerned the 1971 redistricting of congressional districts in Texas. Plan A, as enacted but rejected by the District Court, entailed an average deviation from the ideal of 0.745 percent. The largest district exceeded the ideal by 2.43 percent, the smallest district stayed short of the ideal by 1.7 percent. The abso-

---

[27] *Id.* at 531.

[28] *Id.* at 531–36.

[29] *Id.* at 555.

[30] 412 U.S. 783 (1973).

lute population difference between these two districts was 19,275 persons (the ideal district comprised a population of 466,530). Plan B, originally submitted by the plaintiffs, generally followed the redistricting pattern of Plan A. Texas had justified Plan A by a policy aimed at maintaining existing relationships between incumbent congressmen and their constituents and preserving the seniority that members of the state's delegation had achieved in the United States House of Representatives. Plan B did not substantially disturb that policy but made adjustments so as to achieve smaller population variances among districts. Under Plan B, the total absolute deviation between the largest and the smallest district had been cut to 696 persons, the smallest district was overrepresented by 0.086 percent, the largest district underrepresented by 0.063 percent. A few days before the scheduled hearing of the case in the District Court, however, the plaintiffs amended their complaint by submitting Plan C. In this plan, the absolute population difference between the largest and the smallest district was about twice that of Plan B, namely, 1,323 persons. The largest district was overpopulated by 0.139 percent and the smallest underpopulated by 0.145 percent. The District Court found Plan A unconstitutional and adopted Plan C because it was "based solely on population" and was "significantly more compact and contiguous" than either of the other two plans. The 1972 congressional election was held under Plan A because the Supreme Court had granted Texas a stay of the District Court Order. On 18 June 1973 the Court upheld the District Court rejection of Plan A but found adoption of Plan C to have been faulty, since the District Court failed to state a good reason why it preferred Plan C over Plan B, which most clearly approximated the reapportionment plan of the state legislature while satisfying constitutional requirements. Mr. Justice Marshall was the sole dissenter from this part of the Court's opinion.

Expressed in terms of the so-called maximum range measure which is apparently designed to express the maximum "injustice" under an apportionment scheme: the difference between the percentage of underrepresentation of the largest district and the percentage of overrepresentation of the smallest district—the range was 4.13 percent under Plan A (by comparison with 5.97 percent in *Kirkpatrick*), 0.149 percent under Plan B, and 0.284 percent under Plan C. Texas argued that the deviations under Plan A were *de minimis* and should be upheld absent proof of invidiousness. This invitation to change the standard of review for congressional districting was rejected although the Court accepted it the same day as far as state legislative apportionment was concerned.[31] The state's additional argument that, in any event, the 4 percent range was justified by the state policy favoring incumbents was put aside, since Plan B admittedly served this purpose as well as Plan A, while adhering more closely to population equality. The deviation therefore had to be considered avoidable or not necessary.

Mr. Justice White did not spend much time defending rejection of the *de minimis* argument with respect to congressional districting, although the Court now permitted it in state legislative apportionment. There is a reference to Article I, § 2, followed by this sentence: "It is clear, however, that at some point or level in size, population variances *do* import invidious devaluation of the individual's vote and represent a failure to accord him fair and effective representation."[32] This statement can obviously not serve to distinguish the cases because it simply restates the rationale underlying all reapportionment cases, state and congressional. The general statement is followed by one single sentence of substance and another reference to Article I and the command that congressmen be "chosen by the People." The substantive sentence urges us to keep in mind "that congressional districts are not so intertwined and freighted with strictly local interests as are state legislative districts and that, as compared with the latter, they are relatively enormous, with each percentage point of variation representing almost 5,000 people."[33] The first of these two assertions is an empirical proposition of dubious validity. The second makes the equally dubious assumption that underrepresentation by one percentage point is more invidious when that one point represents 5,000 people out of 467,000 as compared with, let us say, a one percentage point variation representing 500 persons out of 50,000.

As to the District Court's choice of Plan C with larger variations than Plan B but with greater compactness, contiguity, and disregard for the Texas policy of favoring incumbents, the Supreme Court urged restraint and held that a district court should honor state policies which are not in and of themselves invidious. Decisions made by the legislature in the complicated process of reapportion-

---

[31] Gaffney v. Cummings, 412 U.S. 735 (1973).

[32] 412 U.S. at 792–93.   [33] *Id.* at 793.

ment should not "unnecessarily" be set aside. Why a state policy favoring incumbents is not invidious is not explained. To be sure, representation is not an isolated phenomenon and must be seen as a part of larger systems (*e.g.*, the Congress with its seniority rules). On the other hand, a "state policy" favoring incumbents often is no more than an euphemism employed by those incumbents for perpetuating themselves as a power elite unaccountable to the voters because of skewed districting. Put differently, "rotten" legislators can render the right to vote quite as ineffective as "rotten" boroughs. One might even argue that "on its face" such a state policy is quite invidious and needs detailed and careful consideration before it can be upheld.[34] It seems that ten years in the political thicket have failed to provide us with any additional criteria for distinguishing between what is "rational" and what is "arbitrary" as concerns the nonquantitative aspects of representation.

V

Once the Supreme Court had rendered its decisions in *Wesberry* and *Reynolds*, and particularly after *Kirkpatrick*, the question was whether the Court in reviewing congressional and state reapportionment would emphasize the formal difference between the sources of reapportionment law (Article I on the one hand and the Fourteenth Amendment on the other) and develop different

---

[34] An "effective choice," it could be said with reason, is one which has the potential of removing a representative. The fact is that the nineteenth-century tradition of turnover has given way to a tradition of tenure which may have insulated the House from popular control. The percentage of freshmen in the Ninety-first Congress was 9.2—the lowest in American history. Mayhew, *Congressional Representation: Theory and Practice in Drawing Districts*, in POLSBY, note 5 *supra*, at 249, 259. I am not repeating this point in order to either endorse the desirability of high turnover or to engage in yet another comparison between the "golden age" of the early Republic and present conditions. High turnover can obviously prevent representatives from acquiring necessary expertise. Too much of it may have been undesirable even in the early years of the United States. Furthermore, we are apt to overlook the fact that nowadays opportunities for influencing one's representatives have increased enormously owing to improved communications between "the people" in its various manifestations and those who govern. This contrasts sharply with the conditions prevailing, for instance, during the Jeffersonian era in what Young has characterized as the "sylvan solitude" of "the Washington community": "Theirs was the lot of governing a society which they could neither see clearly nor know well except in the fragments of it that were their own home constituencies." Even as to the latter they governed "in uncertainty, if not ignorance," "save as they made their hazardous journey home once each year in spring thaws or summer heat." YOUNG, THE WASHINGTON COMMUNITY 1800–1828 33 (1966).

standards of review for the two categories of cases, or whether the Court would put the accent on the identity of the principle underlying its reapportionment decisions: "equal representation for equal numbers of people."

The next major case, *Swann v. Adams*,[35] did not address that question. A federal district court sustained the constitutionality of a Florida plan in which ratio between the largest and smallest districts was 1.30:1 for the state senate and 1.41:1 for the house. The Court said:[36]

> As this case comes to us we have no alternative but to reverse. The District Court made no attempt to explain or justify the many variations among the legislative districts. As for the State, all it suggested in either the lower court or here is that its plan comes as close as "practical" to complete population equality and that the State was attempting to follow congressional district lines. There was, however, no attempt to justify any particular deviations, even the larger ones, with respect to either of these considerations.

The Court, speaking through Mr. Justice White, reaffirmed the standard of review announced in *Reynolds*, that variations from a pure population standard might be justified by such state policies as regard for the integrity of political subdivisions, the maintenance of compactness and contiguity in legislative districts or the recognition of natural or historical boundary lines. The state, however, had failed to put forward any such consideration. With respect to its *de minimis* argument, the Court simply said the variations in *Swann* could hardly be deemed *de minimis*. *Swann* was decided two years before *Kirkpatrick*, over the dissent of Justices Harlan and Stewart. Two years after *Kirkpatrick*, in *Whitcomb v. Chavis*,[37] the Court again struck down district variations similar to those in *Swann*. Justices Burger and Blackmun, who had meanwhile replaced Warren and Fortas, joined the majority.

The same day that *Whitcomb* was decided, however, the Court ruled in a case involving local government to which, in 1968, the reapportionment mandate had been extended.[38] The maximum range in *Abate v. Mundt*[39] was 11.9 percent and was justified by

---

[35] 385 U.S. 440 (1967).

[36] *Id.* at 445.   [38] Avery v. Midland County, 390 U.S. 474 (1968).

[37] 403 U.S. 124 (1971).   [39] 403 U.S. 182 (1971).

a long-standing policy in Rockland County, New York, to preserve an exact correspondence between each town in the county and one of the county legislative districts so as to encourage town supervisors to serve on the county board. The Court, per Mr. Justice Marshall and over the dissents of Justices Brennan and Douglas, upheld the reapportionment. The Court invoked the *Reynolds* standard of review and emphasized "that our decision is based on the long tradition of overlapping functions and dual personnel in Rockland County government and on the fact that the plan before us does not contain a built-in bias tending to favor political interests or geographic areas. And nothing we say today should be taken to imply that even these factors could justify substantially greater deviations from population equality."[40] Justices Brennan and Douglas, on the other hand, thought that *Kirkpatrick* required reversal, stressing "equal representation for equal numbers of people."

If one views the Court's opinion in *Abate* as a rejection of the Brennan view, it is reasonable to conclude that by 1971 the Court had implicitly answered the question posed at the beginning of this section: different standards were applicable for state and national districting. This, in any event, was the way the case was read by some district courts;[41] others were more cautious or restricted *Abate* to its facts.[42]

The explicit answer to the question came in February of last year in the Virginia state legislative apportionment case of *Mahan v. Howell*.[43] Mr. Justice Rehnquist wrote the majority opinion, Mr. Justice Brennan, joined by Justices Douglas and Marshall, the dissent. Justices Rehnquist and Brennan did not altogether agree on what the facts of the case were.[44] Although the dispute is important, since it highlights difficulties associated with the methods of calculation, we shall postulate for our purposes that the majority was correct in its interpretation of the variations involved.

At stake was the apportionment of the Virginia House of Dele-

---

[40] *Id*. at 187.

[41] See, *e.g.*, Kelly v. Bumpers, 340 F. Supp. 568, 571 (E.D. Ark. 1972).

[42] See, *e.g.*, Hensley v. Wood, 329 F. Supp. 787, 791 (E.D. Ky. 1971); Grivetti v. Illinois State Electoral Board, 335 F. Supp. 779, 789 (N.D. Ill. 1972); Sims v. Amos, 336 F. 924, 935 (M.D. Ala. 1972).

[43] 410 U.S. 315 (1973).

[44] Cf. *id*. at 336–38 (Brennan, J., dissenting).

gates by the General Assembly in 1971. The maximum range between the largest and the smallest district was 16.4 percent. Generally, district lines followed the jurisdictional lines of counties and
cities. A consolidated District Court made up of four judges declared the reapportionment plan unconstitutional. Referring primarily to *Reynolds* and *Swann*, the court found the 16.4 percent
range sufficient to condemn the plan. "The state has proved no
governmental necessity for strictly adhering to political subdivision
lines."[45] The District Court thus applied the *Reynolds* standard,
"legitimate considerations incident to the effectuation of a rational
state policy."

This application points to a problem concerning the *Reynolds*
standard of review. The *Reynolds* standard on its face seems different from the District Court application. It refers to "effectuation
of a rational state policy." While this sounds like the traditional
equal protection standard of review, it is not quite that, because the
Supreme Court in *Reynolds* also made clear that only certain state
policies would be considered rational. The policy pursued by Virginia in this case—to insure some voice to political subdivisions qua
subdivisions—was among those mentioned as possible candidates. A
further *Reynolds* restriction was that even pursuit of a recognized
rational apportionment policy did not permit abandoning population as the "controlling consideration." "Governmental necessity"
for an otherwise recognized policy did not, however, seem to be
required by *Reynolds*.[46] Yet a "necessity" standard, which seems
akin to the "compelling state interest" test applied in some other
voting rights cases,[47] is used both by the District Court and the dissenters in *Mahan*.[48]

While this apparent striving for a uniform standard of review to
be applied in all cases where a restriction on the right to vote is
challenged is understandable, it strikes me as calling for further
justification in the apportionment context, since *Reynolds* made no
mention of "necessity" in carving out the "political subdivisions"
exception. Under *Reynolds* and *Abate* the major question to be

[45] Howell v. Mahan, 330 F. Supp. 1138, 1140 (E.D. Va. 1971).

[46] Cf. 410 U.S. at 326.

[47] See, *e.g.*, Williams v. Rhodes, 393 U.S. 23, 31 (1968).

[48] Mr. Justice Brennan referred to the "burden of presenting cogent reasons." 410
U.S. at 340.

answered by the Court had to be whether a 16.4 percent maximum range which resulted from the pursuit of a rational state policy made population less than the "controlling consideration" in the Virginia reapportionment plan. The answer depended on the position the Court would take on the relevance of *Kirkpatrick* to state legislative apportionment.

In adopting a restrictive view of *Kirkpatrick*, the Court could and did rely on *Reynolds* and *Abate*. In addition, Mr. Justice Rehnquist offered some functional considerations:[49]

> Application of the "absolute equality" test of *Kirkpatrick* and *Wells* to state legislative redistricting may impair the normal functioning of state and local governments. Such an effect is readily apparent from an analysis of the District Court's plan in this case. Under Art. VII §§ 2 and 3 of Virginia's Constitution, the General Assembly is given extensive power to enact special legislation regarding the organization of, and the exercise of governmental powers by, counties, cities, towns and other political subdivisions. The statute redistricting the House of Delegates has consistently sought to avoid the fragmentation of such subdivisions, assertedly to afford them a voice in Richmond to seek such local legislation.

This argument points to another element in the Court's standard of review. Attention will be paid to the particular context of a reapportionment plan, a "variation from the norm as approved in one State has little bearing on the validity of a similar variation in another State."[50]

The Court, in *Mahan*, has clearly confirmed a case-by-case approach to state reapportionment without taking up Mr. Justice Brennan's challenge to explain how the decision could be reconciled with the major premise of all reapportionment: the weight of a citizen's vote cannot be made to depend on where he lives.[51] Two restrictions on the sweep of the decision should, however, be recognized. (1) The District Court's "absolute equality" substitute for the General Assembly plan, in the Supreme Court's reckoning, still resulted in a maximum range of 10 percent. Thus the Court was called upon, as it were, to override a rational state policy in the

---

[49] *Id.* at 323.

[50] Swann v. Adams, 385 U.S. 440, 445 (1967). This standard also was first announced in *Reynolds:* "What is marginally permissible in one State may be unsatisfactory in another, depending on the particular circumstances of the case." 377 U.S. at 578.

[51] 410 U.S. at 339, n.7.

interest of 6 points, and at the price of crossing subdivision lines in twelve instances. (2) Mr. Justice Rehnquist stated that the 16 percent maximum range found to exist in *Mahan* "may well approach tolerable limits."[52] In spite of the Court's emphasis on a case-by-case approach, there is no indication that it will disturb what it refers to as "the most stringent mathematical standard heretofore imposed." the *Swann* disallowance of a 26 percent maximum range.

While it is my conviction that *Mahan* can easily be reconciled with the letter if not all of the spirit of the previous decisions, the Court was on shakier ground in the most radical reapportionment decision of the 1972 term which it handed down the same day as the Texas case, *White v. Weiser*, discussed in Part IV above.

VI

The 1965 Connecticut Constitution provides that decennial reapportionment must comply with federal constitutional standards, that Senate and House districts must be contiguous, and that in House districting no town may be divided, except for forming assembly districts wholly within a town. Reapportionment plans have to be adopted upon completion of the United States census by a two-thirds majority of each house. If that cannot be mustered, a bipartisan commission is to be established. In case the commission also fails, reapportionment becomes the responsibility of a three-member board composed of two Superior Court judges, one each to be chosen by the Speaker and the Minority Leader of the House, plus a third member to be agreed upon by the two Superior Court judges.

At stake in *Gaffney v. Cummings*[53] was a board plan adopted by a two-to-one vote. One member of the majority was Judge Saden, who had been selected for the board by the leader of the House Republican minority and who had formerly been General Counsel to the Republican party. The other majority member was Justice Thim of the Connecticut Supreme Court, also a Republican and former Speaker of the House. The Democratic board member was Judge Parskey. In drawing up a reapportionment plan, Judge Saden primarily made use of the assistance of a counsel to the Republican party named Collins. It was pointed out by the National Legislative Conference and the Council of State Governments that

---

[52] *Id.* at 329.   [53] 412 U.S. 735 (1973).

the unanimous United States District Court which held the plan unconstitutional consisted of three Democrats.[54]

The board plan was described by the District Court in the following way:[55]

> In developing the Plan, Mr. Collins, acting for the Board under the direction of Judge Saden, gave principal weight to two considerations in Senate and House districting, numerical equality and a partisan balancing of strength in each house, and in the House districting also the undesirability of splitting towns.
>
> The partisan balancing of strength in each house, termed by intervening defendants a "fair political balance" and by plaintiffs "political gerrymandering" was obtained by so adjusting the census areas utilized as building blocks into the structuring of Senate and House districts that, on the basis of the vote for all the Senate candidates of each party in the elections of 1966, 1968, and 1970, whichever party carried the state should carry a majority of Senate seats proportional to the statewide party majority, and likewise in the House, based on the party vote for all the House candidates of each party in the same three elections.
>
> In one or more House and one or more Senate districts some accommodation was also made in the interest of retaining in office a particular incumbent.
>
> The result apparently obtained by Mr. Collins made up a House of approximately 70 safe Democratic seats, 55 to 60 safe Republican seats, with the balance designed as probable Democratic, swing Democratic, probable Republican, swing Republican, or just plain swing.
>
> The Senate result was characterized as 16 solid Democratic, 2 probable Democratic, 12 solid Republican, 4 probable Republican and 2 swing.
>
> The method used resulted in creating some districts with highly irregular and bizarre outlines.

Since the United States Supreme Court had stayed the District Court decision, the 1972 elections were held under the board plan. Before the 1972 election, the Connecticut House was composed of 99 Democrats and 78 Republicans, the Senate of 19 Democrats and 17 Republicans. The 1972 election put the Republicans in solid control of both chambers: 93 Republicans against 58 Democrats in

---

[54] The National Legislative Conference and the Council of State Governments, Reapportionment in the States 42 (1972).

[55] Cummings v. Meskill, 341 F. Supp. 139, 147 (D. Conn. 1972).

the House (the size of the House had been cut as part of the reapportionment plan) and 23 Republicans against 13 Democrats in the Senate. In the House, the Republicans won 62 percent of the seats as compared with 53 percent of the popular vote. In the previous three elections (1966, 1968, 1970) the Republicans had won 46, 48, and 50 percent of the popular vote which gave them 34, 38, and 44 percent, respectively, of the seats. Projected outcomes of seat distribution for any of the various plans submitted by the plaintiffs suggest that the result for 1972 would not have been very different had any of their plans or the plan of the District Court–appointed master been adopted.[56]

The board plan had resulted in a maximum range of 7.83 percent for the house. In order to achieve the state policy of "political fairness," 55 of the 151 assembly districts involved the segmenting of towns. It was a particular twist of the Democratic complaint against the plan that the plaintiffs made the following argument to the District Court: "The Board erroneously applied the one man–one vote doctrine of the Fourteenth Amendment to the United States Constitution to achieve smaller deviations from population equality than was required by the Fourteenth Amendment to the United States Constitution in view of Article 3, Section 4 of the State Constitution and thereby was compelled to segment an excessive number of towns in forming assembly districts."[57] Though the plaintiffs in the United States Supreme Court repeated the argument based on the state constitutional prohibition against segmenting House districts, they abandoned reliance on the *Reynolds* exception for attacking deviations as *too small*.

Mr. Justice White, for the majority in *Gaffney*, held that appellees had failed to make out a prima facie violation of the Equal Protection Clause. With respect to the "equal numbers" aspect of the case, the Court could arrive at this result only if it concluded that a 7.83 maximum range did not amount to a prima facie case of invidious discrimination. This conclusion had to be based on the major premise that "making out a prima facie case" required a showing of "substantial dilution" of the right to vote. The standard of review announced in *Reynolds* as well as the Court's emphasis on "substantial equality" in that case were sufficiently ambiguous

---

[56] Reply Brief for Appellant, Appendix 3a.

[57] Gaffney v. Cummings, Appendix at 8.

to permit construction of such a major premise. On the other hand, it is equally possible to read *Reynolds* as requiring justification on the part of the state for any deviation. The reference to "substantial equality" in *Reynolds* is immediately followed by this language: "So long as the divergencies from a *strict* population standard are based on legitimate considerations incident to the effectuation of a rational state policy, *some* deviations . . . are permissible."[58]

Again, the answer to the quest for the proper standard of review turns on the significance of *Kirkpatrick*. The majority got rid of *Kirkpatrick* by referring to *Mahan*, *Weiser*, and the Article I origins of the strict congressional rule. I submit that *Mahan* was an easier case, since the *Reynolds* decision had explicitly recognized the political subdivisions exception. Moreover, part of the *Kirkpatrick* rationale for rejecting the *de minimis* contention is *clearly* applicable to state legislative districting: "There are other reasons for rejecting the *de minimis* approach. We can see no nonarbitrary way to pick a cutoff point at which population variances suddenly become *de minimis*. Moreover, to consider a certain range of variances *de minimis* would encourage legislators to strive for that range rather than for equality as nearly as practicable."[59] Indeed in *Gaffney* the Court seems to have felt that the ground on which it was moving was not all solid. It uses such circumlocutions as: "[i]t is now time to recognize, in the context of the eminently reasonable approach of *Reynolds v. Sims*, that minor deviations . . . are insufficient to make out a prima facie case," or "[w]e doubt that Reynolds would mandate any other result."[60]

It should be made clear that the Court does not once characterize its approach as adoption of a *de minimis* standard. If a *de minimis* exception implies no federal court jurisdiction at all, this is clearly correct, since plaintiffs remain free to show that the districting otherwise fails to satisfy equal protection requirements. The new rule is that "minimal" deviations do not require state justification and that in such cases the burden is upon the plaintiff to show that a plan is invidious. The companion case of *White v. Regester*[61] suggests that the "shifting point," *i.e.*, the point at which the burden of proving the case, as to both facts and law, is shifted back to the state, is somewhere around a 10 percent maximum range.

---

[58] 377 U.S. at 579. (Emphasis added.)

[59] 394 U.S. at 531.

[60] 412 U.S. at 745.

[61] 412 U.S. 755 (1973).

The Court justified adoption of its new standard by referring to the fact that census data to some extent are unreliable and that, in any event, the states are not bound to use total population figures since "census persons" are not voters.[62] Furthermore, "[f]air and effective representation may be destroyed by gross population variations among districts, but it is apparent that such representation does not depend solely on mathematical equality among district populations. . . . An unrealistic overemphasis on raw population figures, a mere nose count in the districts, may submerge these other considerations and itself furnish a ready tool for ignoring factors that in day-to-day operation are important to an acceptable representation and apportionment arrangement."[63] I shall presently return to the concept of "fair and effective" representation. Here, only the obvious will be noted: it is difficult to see how this statement of principle is reconcilable with *Weiser*, or how *Weiser* can be reconciled with *Gaffney*, at least on this level of abstraction.

Finally, the Court stressed that state reapportionment is the task of local legislatures or of those organs of state government selected to perform it. "That the Court was not deterred by the hazards of the political thicket when it undertook to adjudicate the reapportionment cases does not mean that it should become bogged down in a vast, intractable apportionment slough, particularly when there is little, if anything to be accomplished by doing so."[64]

Since, under the burden of "proof" distribution in *Gaffney*, the state was not called upon to justify its "political fairness" approach, plaintiffs had to satisfy the threshold requirement of proving a prima facie case of invidious discrimination in effect or by design. Labeling the board plan "a gigantic political gerrymander" was not considered sufficient. The Court apparently agreed with Professor Dixon's proposal (Dixon was counsel for Connecticut) that—though justiciable as matter of principle—partisan apportionment be subject to a stringent burden of proof.[65] What this burden of proof entails, what would amount to a prima facie case of invidious discrimination, the Court failed to indicate. Instead, we were treated to such "political question" truisms as, "[t]he reality is that districting in-

---

[62] See Burns v. Richardson, 384 U.S. 73, 91–92 (1966).

[63] 412 U.S. at 748–49.

[64] *Id.* at 749–50.

[65] DIXON, DEMOCRATIC REPRESENTATION 498 (1968).

evitably has and is intended to have substantial political consequences."[66] The failure of the Court in this respect, however, is not
too interesting, since it merely confirms the Court's well-established
reticence when partisan gerrymandering is alleged. More importantly, Mr. Justice White suggested strongly that appellants were
right in their insistence that the board plan was the very opposite of
a "political gerrymander," as traditionally understood:[67]

> The record abounds with evidence, and it is frankly admitted
> by those who prepared the plan, that virtually every Senate
> and House district line was drawn with the conscious intent to
> create a districting plan that would achieve a rough approxi-
> mation of the statewide political strengths of the Democratic
> and Republican parties, the only two parties in the State large
> enough to elect legislators from discernible geographic areas.
> Appellants insist that the spirit of "political fairness" under-
> lying this plan is not only permissible, but a desirable consid-
> eration in laying out districts that otherwise satisfy the popu-
> lation standard of the reapportionment cases.

In a way, this is an appealing manner of looking at the reapportionment problems, since it returns us to the basic question: what
is the nature of representation? "Equal representation for equal numbers of people" is essentially an empty slogan if the emphasis is
on equal numbers. Whether our concept of representation is descriptive representation ("an exact portrait, in miniature, of the
people at large") or whether it is a concept of "acting for," rather
than "standing for,"[68] it refers to looking after the interests of people. To the extent to which "territorial" representation (based on
the assumption that "relevant political cleavages run along territorial lines")[69] *and* majority rule have been among the major premises
of American political thought, the Supreme Court decisions since
Baker have made sense as seeking some reconciliation between the
two. Many critics, of course, have interpreted the cases since 1964
as losing sight of the "territorial representation" concept without
achieving majority rule. "Neutral," computer designed, mathematically equal districts—in particular if regularly redrawn—seemed to
accomplish only one goal: they gave access to a "representative"
to equal numbers of people.

---

[66] 412 U.S. at 753.   [67] *Id.* at 752.

[68] PITKIN, THE CONCEPT OF REPRESENTATION 60 *et passim* (1967).

[69] Rae, *Reapportionment and Political Democracy*, in POLSBY, note 5 *supra*, at 91, 108.

Territorial representation alone, however, is an equally barren notion, since, in actuality, political parties are the major vehicle of representation in present-day America. If greater heed were paid to the role of political parties in representation, "fair" representation would have to look for some measure of proportional representation (which could, of course, be combined with territorial representation).[70] The Connecticut plan was rationalized in terms of "fair" party representation. The Supreme Court accepted this self-understanding: "[N]either we nor the district courts have a constitutional warrant to invalidate a state plan, otherwise within tolerable population limits, because it undertakes, not to minimize or eliminate the political strength of any group or party, but to recognize it and, through districting, provide a rough sort of proportional representation in the legislative halls of the State."[71]

The Court had never before gone so far in supporting proportional representation as an ideal. To be sure, in legitimizing a state policy of "fair representation," it has not turned such a principle into a requirement of the Equal Protection Clause. But even the limited approval that the Court expressed raises a host of questions. For instance, when and if a state decides to adopt a policy of proportional representation, is a "rough sort" good enough under the Equal Protection Clause? The Court has in the past insisted that not every political group has a right to be represented in the legislature. Does that leave the two major parties free to make the world of proportional representation quite safe for themselves even where there are independent third forces, which apparently was not the case in Connecticut?[72] Is a state, under the Equal Protection Clause, really free to pursue a policy of "fair representation" if that policy conflicts with a state constitutional requirement of territorial representation, which was the case in Connecticut as far as the House was concerned?[73] Can the Court really expect to deal with these matters by combining a stringent burden of proof requirement with "political question" restrictions? The Court said in *Gaffney:* We

---

[70] For an example see Dixon, note 65 *supra*, at 95.

[71] 412 U.S. at 754.

[72] This would seem to raise problems under Williams v. Rhodes, 393 U.S. 23, 32 (1968). Cf. Casper, *Williams v. Rhodes and Public Financing of Political Parties under the American and German Constitutions*, 1968 SUPREME COURT REVIEW 271.

[73] See Neal, *Baker v. Carr: Politics in Search of Law*, 1962 SUPREME COURT REVIEW 252, 291.

have not "attempted the impossible task of extirpating politics from what are the essentially political processes of the sovereign States."[74] Is the apportionment slough any less justiciable than the reapportionment thicket? If so, what are principled ways of distinguishing the two?

VII

While the Court thus continued to shy away from what, in a somewhat belittling manner, is generally referred to as "partisan gerrymandering," it also continued to display sensitivity toward gerrymandering against classes of voters identifiable in social, ethnic, or racial terms. Indeed, the 1973 Term saw the first multimember districts declared unconstitutional by the Supreme Court.[75]

In addition, the Term provided us with a Supreme Court decision upholding a district court-ordered multimember district as an interim remedy for voting discrimination against military personnel. In *Gaffney*, the Supreme Court told us that census figures were not the only data base for achieving equal voter representation. In *Mahan v. Howell*, a unanimous Court showed that this argument can cut both ways. For census purposes, all naval personnel "homeported" in Norfolk are treated as if they lived aboard their vessels, the census tract for which is located in the Fifth Senatorial District of Virginia. In reality, about half, *i.e.*, approximately 18,000 Navy-associated people live outside the Fifth District. Virginia's reapportionment plan assigned all 37,000 to the Fifth District. Since voting discrimination against a class of individuals merely because of the nature of their employment is impermissible,[76] the Court agreed with the District Court finding of substantial malapportionment. Given severe time pressures, the District Court did not abuse its discretion when it remedied the situation by combining three single-member districts into one multimember district comprised of Norfolk and Virginia Beach.[77] In short, for certain purposes, the weight of a citizen's vote does depend on where he lives: territorial representation takes precedence over representation qua military personnel.

---

[74] 412 U.S. at 754.

[75] White v. Regester, 412 U.S. 755 (1973).

[76] Davis v. Mann, 377 U.S. 678, 691 (1964).

[77] 410 U.S. at 330–33.

Multimember districts have been a major headache for the Court. The question was squarely presented for the first time in *Fortson v. Dorsey*.[78] Rejecting the challenge there offered over the lone dissent of Mr. Justice Douglas, Mr. Justice Brennan, speaking for the Court, intimated the standard of review: "It might well be that, designedly or otherwise, a multimember constituency apportionment scheme, under the circumstances of a particular case, would operate to minimize or cancel out the voting strength of racial or political elements of the voting population. When this is demonstrated, it will be time enough to consider whether the system passes constitutional muster."[79]

After some intervening cases, the major challenge came in 1971 in *Whitcomb v. Chavis*.[80] The standard of review was summarized by stating that multimember districts were not per se illegal under the Fourteenth Amendment and that the challenger carries the burden of proving that multimember districts unconstitutionally operate to dilute or cancel the voting strength of racial or political elements. The charges made in *Whitcomb*, a case from Indiana, were not proved to the satisfaction of the Court, Justices Douglas, Brennan, and Marshall excepted. This is not the place to reexamine the complicated facts and claims put forward in that case. It must suffice to recite the way the problem generally was viewed by the Court. As distinguished from his opinions in *Gaffney*, Mr. Justice White's opinion for the Court displayed subtlety and unease:[81]

> We are not insensitive to the objections long voiced to multimember district plans. Although not as prevalent as they were in our early history, they have been with us since colonial times and were much in evidence both before and after the adoption of the Fourteenth Amendment. Criticism is rooted in their winner-take-all aspects, their tendency to submerge minorities and to overrepresent the winning party as compared with the party's statewide electoral position, a general preference for legislatures reflecting community interests as closely as possible and disenchantment with political parties and elections as devices to settle policy differences between contending interests. The chance of winning or significantly influencing intraparty fights and issue-oriented elections has seemed to some inadequate protection to minorities, political, racial, or economic; rather, their voice, it is said, should also be heard

---

[78] 379 U.S. 433 (1965).

[79] *Id.* at 439.

[80] 403 U.S. 124 (1971).

[81] *Id.* at 157–60.

in the legislative forum where public policy is finally fashioned. In our view, however, experience and insight have not
yet demonstrated that multi-member districts are inherently
invidious and violative of the Fourteenth Amendment. Surely
the findings of the District Court do not demonstrate it. Moreover, if the problems of multi-member districts are unbearable
or even unconstitutional it is not at all clear that the remedy is
a single-member district system with its lines carefully drawn
to ensure representation to sizable racial, ethnic, economic, or
religious groups and with its own capacity for overrepresent-
ing and underrepresenting parties and interests and even for
permitting a minority of the voters to control the legislature
and government of a State. The short of it is that we are un-
prepared to hold that district-based elections decided by plurality vote are unconstitutional in either single- or multi-member districts simply because the supporters of losing candidates
have no legislative seats assigned to them. As presently advised
we hold that the District Court misconceived the Equal Protection Clause in applying it to invalidate the Marion County
multi-member district.

As concerns the burden of proof and specifically with regard to
the charge that the Marion County multimember district minimized
the voting power of ghetto blacks, the Court discovered nothing
in the record indicating "that poor Negroes were not allowed to
register or vote, to choose the political party they desired to support, to participate in its affairs or to be equally represented on
those occasions when legislative candidates were chosen. Nor did
the evidence purport to show or the court find that inhabitants of
the ghetto were regularly excluded from the slates of both major
parties, thus denying them the chance of occupying legislative
seats."[82]

In 1973, the Court finally came across a record strong enough
to uphold a district court decision invalidating multimember districts in Dallas and Bexar counties, Texas, and ordered their recon-
stitution into single-member districts.[83] In *White v. Regester*,[84] a
unanimous Supreme Court agreed that multimember districts can
be unconstitutional in fact, not just in theory. Mr. Justice White's
opinion has a slight flavor of Supreme Court restraint vis-à-vis the
fact finder. The Court in *Regester* concluded its opinion with the

---

[82] *Id.* at 149–50.

[83] Graves v. Barnes, 343 F. Supp. 704, 724–34 (W.D. Tex. 1972).

[84] 412 U.S. 755 (1973).

following sentence: "On the record before us, we are not inclined to overturn these findings, representing as they do a blend of history and an intensely local appraisal of the design and impact of the Bexar County multi-member district in light of past and present reality, political and otherwise."[85]

The charge with respect to Dallas County concerned minimizing the voting strength of blacks. The Court's terse opinion is largely restricted to a recital of the District Court's findings among which were the following: since Reconstruction days, there have been only two blacks in the Dallas delegation to the Texas House; there was a history of official racial discrimination in Texas, touching voting rights of blacks; there was effective exclusion of blacks from participation in the Democratic primary selection process; there were racial campaign tactics on the part of Dallas Democrats; and there were invidious effects of certain Texas primary and election laws.

While the emphasis in the Dallas case was on past and present discrimination in connection with the electoral process proper,[86] the Bexar County portion of the opinion, though also referring to a history of voting discrimination (poll tax "and the most restrictive voter registration procedures in the nation"), stressed "the cultural and economic realities of the Mexican-American community in Bexar County."[87] The decision is reminiscent of *Katzenbach v. Morgan*[88] in the way in which it looks at the electoral process as a means of eliminating discrimination "in the fields of education, employment, economics, health, politics and others." The parallel with *Morgan* extends to language: "The typical Mexican-American suffers a cultural and language barrier that makes his participation in community processes extremely difficult."[89]

Both portions of the opinion talk in terms of barriers to "participation" in the political process. Indeed, the concept of "participation" is at the core of the Court's reformulation of the standards for evaluating evidence: "The plaintiff's burden is to produce evidence to support findings that the political processes leading to

---

[85] *Id.* at 769–70.

[86] On this approach generally, see Fiss, *Gaston County v. United States: Fruition of the Freezing Principle*, 1969 SUPREME COURT REVIEW 379.

[87] 412 U.S. at 768, 769.

[88] 384 U.S. 641 (1966).   [89] 412 U.S. at 768.

nomination and election were not equally open to participation by the group in question—that its members had less opportunity than did other residents in the district to participate in the political processes and to elect legislators of their choice."[90] Before it be concluded that the Court was adding the notion of "participatory democracy" to the confused debate about political representation, one should be aware that the concept of participation was used by the Court in order to prevent the conclusion that the right to vote entails a right to representation. The Court explicitly stated that the District Court paid due heed to *Whitcomb* by not holding that every racial or political group has a constitutional right to be represented in the state legislature.[91] Put differently, *Regester* is a kind of present-day version of the "white primary" cases. Multimember districts, it would seem, violate the Equal Protection Clause, not because they overrepresent or underrepresent pure and simple, but because they do that in a context where all stages of the electoral process have been effectively closed to identifiable classes of citizens, making the political establishment "insufficiently responsive" to (Mexican-American) interests.

The Court's decision in *Regester* strikes me as being at one and the same time limited and open-ended. If the comparison with the "white primary" cases holds, then the decision merely says that as long as the normal, established channels (parties) remain closed to minorities, the Court will see to it that they get some representation. On the other hand, in order to arrive at that judgment, the Court will not only look at "opportunities to participate" but also at opportunities to achieve representation.

Constitutional consideration of representation in terms of the underlying institutions and the interests they are serving responds to the general challenge that we reconsider the concept of representation: "to construct institutions and train individuals in such a way that they engage in the pursuit of the public interest, the genuine representation of the public; and, at the same time, to remain critical of those institutions and that training, so that they are always open to further interpretation and reform."[92]

The Court can do no more than lend a helping hand. In that regard, however, the reapportionment and voting rights decisions are

---

[90] *Id.* at 766.

[91] *Id.* at 769.   [92] PITKIN, note 68 *supra*, at 240.

no different from anything else the Court does. To move toward a reconsideration of our institutions and laws rather than to accept the status quo or to try to attain perfection may be the proper and realistic function of judicial review. The apportionment decisions of the Burger Court last Term indicate that by and large the Court remains aware of the challenge. Though the Court has contributed to the clarification of standards of review, it has mostly refrained from substituting its own easy formulas for those of the Warren Court in its later years. "Careful and meticulous" scrutiny, as demanded in *Reynolds*, may anyway be the most meaningful, because least deceptive, standard. It at least does not create the impression that complicated matters can be resolved through such slogans as "political question," "one man, one vote," or "compelling state interest."

VIII

Mr. Justice Marshall analyzed the standards applicable to voting rights in the 1972 case of *Dunn v. Blumstein*.[93] At stake was a Tennessee requirement making residence in the state for one year and in the county for three months a prerequisite for voter registration. According to Marshall, three major factors are, or should be, considered in deciding any case under the Equal Protection Clause: (1) the character of the classification; (2) the individual interests affected by it; and (3) the governmental interests asserted in support of it. As to the character of the classification: The Court treats, for instance, racial classifications as inherently suspect. Legislation using these classifications will be upheld only if justified by a "compelling state interest." Strict scrutiny of governmental interest is also set in motion if the individual interests affected have been recognized by the Court as "fundamental." For instance, a restriction of the "constitutionally protected right to participate in elections on an equal basis with other citizens in the jurisdiction" leads to Court determination whether exclusions are necessary to promote a compelling state interest. Not only must the interest be compelling, but the means chosen to serve it must be necessary.[94]

Of course, this way of looking at the problem provides guidance only once the Court has chosen to treat a classification as suspect; *e.g.*, the Court, last Term, refused to make sexual classifications a

---

[93] 405 U.S. 330, 335–37 (1972).   [94] But see text *supra*, at note 46.

"suspect" categorization,[95] or to treat educational equality as a fundamental" right.[96] Even then, the ambiguities associated with "compelling interest" or "necessary means" remain, since these are conclusionary rather than analytic categories which can be applied to cases only after some balancing of interests has been engaged in.[97] As Mr. Justice Marshall understated in *Dunn*, tests like "compelling interest" "do not have the precision of mathematical formulas." "The key words emphasize a matter of degree: that a heavy burden of justification is on the State, and that the statute will be closely scrutinized in light of its asserted purposes."[98] Since the operational part of this statement is "close scrutiny," it turns out that the "compelling interest" standard is really no more than "close scrutiny," which in turn may not be as many light years removed from the ordinary "rationality" test as we are sometimes led to believe. For instance, a majority of six Justices last Term upheld an Arizona fifty-day durational voter residency requirement and a fifty-day registration requirement. The District Court had applied *Dunn* and had found the requirements unconstitutional. Justices Marshall, Douglas, and Brennan agreed. The majority, in a per curiam opinion, apparently also applying *Dunn*, had this to say:[99]

> The Arizona scheme, however, stands in a different light. The durational residency requirement is only 50 days, not a year or even three months. Moreover, unlike Tennessee's, the Arizona requirement is tied to the closing of the State's registration process at 50 days prior to elections and reflects a state legislative judgment that the period is necessary to achieve the State's legitimate goals.
>   We accept that judgment, particularly in light of the realities of Arizona's registration and voting procedures.

To be sure, outcomes may depend upon emphasis and upon the distribution of the burden of making out one's case as to facts and law. Furthermore, strict standards of review warn both the parties

---

[95] Frontiero v. Richardson, 411 U.S. 677 (1973).

[96] On the dispute among the Justices about which interests are to be deemed "fundamental," see San Antonio Independent School District v. Rodriguez, 411 U.S. 1, 33 (Powell, J.), and 99 (Marshall J., dissenting) (1973).

[97] Cf. Comment, *Fundamental Personal Rights: Another Approach to Equal Protection*, 40 U. CHI. L. REV. 807, 825 (1973).

[98] 405 U.S. at 342–43.

[99] Marston v. Lewis, 410 U.S. 679, 680 (1973). See also Burns v. Fortson, 410 U.S. 686 (1973).

and the Court not to take a matter lightly. Finally, and perhaps most importantly, they provide the Court with a means to inform us as to which rights and principles it considers basic and indispensable.[100] Some symbolic ranking of the multitude of claims pressed in a democracy may be necessary in order to sustain the polity as a meaningful experience.[101]

Yet we must remain careful about falling victim to procrustean categorizations. Mr. Justice Marshall's dissent in *Rodriguez*, which bears very close reading, put it very well indeed:[102]

> The Court apparently seeks to establish today that equal protection cases fall into one of two neat categories which dictate the appropriate standard of review—strict scrutiny or mere rationality. But this Court's decisions in the field of equal protection defy such easy categorization. A principled reading of what this Court has done reveals that it has applied a spectrum of standards in reviewing discrimination allegedly violative of the Equal Protection Clause. This spectrum clearly comprehends variations in the degree of care with which the Court will scrutinize particular classifications, depending, I believe, on the constitutional and societal importance of the interest adversely affected and the recognized invidiousness of the basis upon which the particular classification is drawn. I find in fact that many of the Court's recent decisions embody the very sort of reasoned approach to equal protection analysis for which I previously argued—that is, an approach in which "con-

---

[100] This, if no other reason, makes some consistency desirable and justifies Mr. Justice Powell's sharp criticism of the majority in *Rosario v. Rockefeller*, a case involving restrictions on the right to vote in primaries. 410 U.S. 752, 767 (1973). The majority treated the question which standard of review was applicable rather cavalierly, *i.e.*, not at all. On the substantive issues raised by *Rosario*, see the thoughtful Comment, *The Right to Vote and Restrictions on Crossover Primaries*, 40 U. Chi. L. Rev. 636 (1973). The problem of consistency also came up in *Salyer Land Company v. Tulare Lake Basin Water Storage District*, 410 U.S. 719 (1973). Both the majority and the minority conceived of the case as a voting rights case, though they applied different standards of review. *Salyer* may not have been a voting rights case at all. The water district looked more like a private cooperative with limited governmental powers than a special purpose government. I admit that as long as we do not have a consensus on governmental functions and how they are affected by private property rights, the difference may exist in the eyes of the beholder only. Cf. Associated Enterprises Inc. v. Toltec Watershed Improvement District, 410 U.S. 743 (1973).

[101] On this use of the concept of symbols, cf. Jaeger & Selznick, *A Normative Theory of Culture*, 29 Am. Soc. Rev. 653, 662 (1964).

[102] 411 U.S. at 98–99. On equal protection and the Burger Court in general, see Gunther, *Foreword: In Search of Evolving Doctrine on a Changing Court: A Model for a Newer Equal Protection*, 86 Harv. L. Rev. 1 (1972).

centration [is] placed upon the character of the classification in question, the relative importance to the individuals in the class discriminated against of the governmental benefits that they do not receive, and the asserted state interests in support of the classification."

With regard to last Term's apportionment cases, it seems that the Court is moving from policing numbers to viewing representation as a concept which needs further clarification. It is doing so within the broad framework established by the Warren Court, while simultaneously turning away from syllogistic reasoning. This is accomplished by deemphasizing the catchwords in favor of a case-by-case strict scrutiny. In the apportionment area it will probably be a long time before the Court can restrict itself to a close analysis of "means"[103]—if that then is desired. Both, the substance of the link between voting and representation as well as the constitutional innocence of state apportionment goals, remain too uncertain. Indeed, the "fundamental" interest in representation is the first candidate for careful and meticulous scrutiny. The facets of a multifaceted notion of representation which became visible last Term are: equal size districts, representation of territories (political subdivisions), guaranteed representation of racial or ethnic interests where opportunities to participate in the political process do not exist, proportional representation of political parties, representation by incumbents so as to make a state delegation in the Congress more effective. I call this a "notion," rather than a "concept" or "theory," for the obvious reason that the list is neither exhaustive nor carefully considered in its details. The only conflict among its elements which has more or less been worked out is that between equal size districts and territorial representation, emphasis on the former comes first when the maximum range approaches 26 percent. However this may be, we are leaving the era of *re*apportionment and beginning the quest for representative apportionment.

---

[103] See Gunther, note 102 *supra*, at 17–20.

JUDITH AREEN and LEONARD ROSS

THE RODRIGUEZ CASE: JUDICIAL

OVERSIGHT OF SCHOOL FINANCE

School finance has been the subject of an extraordinary and instructive chapter in the history of judicial reform. It is a history that must still be written on loose-leaf pages, like the Great Soviet Encyclopedia, allowing for short-notice reversals between dogma and heresy. Through the early sixties, liberals brought court cases against the uneven distribution of public services in general,[1] and educational expenditures in particular,[2] with little success. The judiciary treated taxing and spending as quintessentially political matters into which it would not intrude. But by the late sixties the mood had changed. As Philip Kurland noted (and deplored) in 1968, the "activist" decisions of the Warren Court provided the straight edge and compass for the logical construction of an argument for court-ordered reform of school finance—in Kurland's words, "the easy case for equal educational opportunity."[3] And liberals, previously preoccupied with reapportionment and desegre-

Judith Areen is Associate Professor of Law, Georgetown University.

Leonard Ross is Assistant Professor of Law, Columbia University.

[1] See Hawkins v. Town of Shaw, 437 F.2d 1286 (5th Cir. 1971), *aff'd en banc* 461 F.2d 1171 (5th Cir. 1972), in which the court intervened to redress racial rather than economic discrimination. For a statement of the traditional doctrine of nonintervention, see McQuillan, Law of Municipal Corporations § 10.33 (3d ed. 1966).

[2] McInnis v. Shapiro, 293 F. Supp. 327 (N.D. Ill. 1968), *aff'd sub nom.* McInnis v. Ogilvie, 394 U.S. 322 (1969); Burruss v. Wilkerson, 310 F. Supp. 572 (W.D. Va. 1969), *aff'd* 397 U.S. 44 (1970).

[3] Kurland, *Equal Educational Opportunity: The Limits of Constitutional Jurisprudence Undefined*, 35 U. Chi. L. Rev. 583, 584 (1968).

gation, found new energies for an attack on unequal school expenditures. Urban education was in a notorious state of collapse, with parochial schools closing their doors and central city public schools seemingly the next to go.[4] The integration movement was succumbing to self-doubt and northern opposition.

In this atmosphere, economic reform proposals understandably were well received. As Stephen Goldstein noted, they involved "the movement of inanimate dollars, not live children."[5] Scholars developed the thesis that the overwhelming reliance on the local property tax for school finance was not merely inequitable and inefficient, but unconstitutional. The "quality of public education," read Proposition I in the Coons-Clune-Sugarman book, "may not be a function of wealth other than the wealth of the state as a whole."[6] Within a few months after the book was published, its message began to emerge as law in the California Supreme Court's opinion in *Serrano v. Priest*.[7]

Serrano came at a particularly propitious time. Inflation and the rising level of local government expenditures in the sixties produced something of a taxpayers' revolt.[8] Higher tax rates, and the painful and arbitrary process of reassessing property to keep pace with inflation, generated a new constituency for property tax reform.

---

[4] Silberman, Crisis in the Classroom (1970) is representative of the literature of alarm.

[5] Goldstein, *Interdistrict Inequalities in School Financing: A Critical Analysis of* Serrano v. Priest *and Its Progeny*, 120 U. Pa. L. Rev. 504, 506 (1972).

[6] Coons, Clune & Sugarman, Private Wealth and Public Education 304 (1970). See also Coons, Clune & Sugarman, *Educational Opportunity: A Workable Constitutional Test for State Financial Structures*, 57 Calif. L. Rev. 305 (1969); Wise, Rich Schools, Poor Schools: The Promies of Equal Educational Opportunity (1968); Horowitz & Neitring, *Equal Protection Aspects of Inequalities in Public Education and Public Assistance Programs from Place to Place within a State*, 15 U.C.L.A. L. Rev. 787 (1968).

[7] Serrano v. Priest, 5 Cal.3d 584 (1971). *Serrano* was decided on demurrer. It held a complaint, that the California educational financing system was unconstitutionally discriminatory, stated a cause of action. *Serrano* left for trial the questions of remedy and proof of the factual premise underlying its conclusion, that there was a systematic relationship between educational quality and educational expenditure. See Goldstein, note 5 *supra*, at 521. A case following *Serrano*, Van Dusartz v. Hatfield, 334 F. Supp. 870 (D. Minn. 1971), reformulated the Coons proposition and held flatly that school expenditures (as opposed to "the quality of education") cannot be made a function of district wealth.

[8] "In 1960, 23 per cent of the bonds for elementary and secondary education were defeated, whereas in 1971, 55.7 per cent were defeated." Levin, *Alternatives to the Present System of School Finance: Their Problems and Prospects*, 61 Geo. L.J. 879, 881 n.8 (1973).

Every major presidential candidate in 1972 pledged a federal program for "relieving the burden" of the property tax. A few states
scheduled referenda on proposals to abolish it completely. *Serrano*
gave this reform movement the imprimatur of constitutional right
and the practical sense of inevitability. With remarkably little resistance, dozens of state legislatures began work on what many
assumed to be an unavoidable overhaul of educational finance. State
or lower federal court decisions in seven states followed or strength-
ened *Serrano*.[9]

While all this was going on, however, some reformers were taking a new, statistical look at the Coons proposition.[10] Districts with
high property tax bases per pupil, it turned out, were not merely
the affluent suburbs but the big cities which, however indigent,
nonetheless retained their high-valued industrial and commercial
tax bases.[11] A shift from the local property tax to a uniform, state-
wide levy would, according to recent Urban Coalition figures, disadvantage schools in twenty-five out of thirty-four big cities.[12]
Other standard reform proposals, including the "district power
equalizing" plan advocated by Coons, discussed below, would hurt
most city schools just as much.[13] Abolishing the property tax entirely might simply substitute regressive sales taxes for what economists had come to believe was a mildly progressive (if scattershot)
levy on capital.[14]

By the early seventies, conservative enthusiasm for property tax
reform had also began to wane. The Nixon Administration in 1971
saw a chance to link property tax relief with the introduction of a
Value Added Tax, a kind of national sales tax that would allow an
unpublicized devaluation of the dollar. Congressional reaction was
chilly. The Administration abandoned the VAT before the 1972
elections, and property tax relief afterward. Voters in California

---

[9] See REISCHAUER & HARTMAN, REFORMING SCHOOL FINANCE 59 n.4 (1973).

[10] See LEVIN, MULLER, SCANLON & COHEN, PUBLIC SCHOOL FINANCE: PRESENT
DISPARITIES AND FISCAL ALTERNATIVES, PREPARED BY THE URBAN INSTITUTE FOR THE
PRESIDENT'S COMMISSION ON SCHOOL FINANCE (1972).

[11] "Per pupil wealth . . . is $48,837 in the central cities, exceeding the suburban average
by about 35 per cent" and rural areas' average by 77 per cent. *Id.* at 53.

[12] CALLAHAN, WILKEN & SILLERMAN, URBAN SCHOOLS AND SCHOOL FINANCE REFORM:
PROMISE AND REALITY (paper for the National Urban Coalition, July 1973) Table V.

[13] *Id.* at 6–12.

[14] See REISCHAUER & HARTMAN, note 9 *supra*, at 27–31.

and Oregon rejected proposals for abandoning the local property tax; even Orange County, California, preferred the devil it knew.

It was in this swiftly altered climate of opinion that the Court examined constitutional aspects of educational finance in the 1972 Term. In *San Antonio Independent School District v. Rodriguez*,[15] a five-to-four majority rejected a constitutional challenge to the (fairly typical) Texas system of school finance.[16] Four Justices thought the property tax unconstitutional. Four admitted some of the criticisms *arguendo* but found it constitutionally permissible. Mr. Justice Stewart shared the critical tone of the former group while joining in the decision and opinion of the latter. "The method of financing public schools in Texas, as in almost every other State," he wrote, "has resulted in a system of public finance that can fairly be described as chaotic and unjust."[17] But, he contended, "I cannot find that this system violates the Constitution of the United States."[18] The Court's decision thus seemed to put an end to the constitutional argument for massive judicial intervention in school finance.[19]

More broadly, *Rodriguez* can be read as a retreat from the looming egalitarianism of the late Warren Court, or as a generalized rejection of activist jurisprudence. The Court's language in *Rodriguez* suggested a narrowing of both the great boulevards of the

---

[15] 411 U.S. 1 (1973).

[16] Approximately half of total school expenditures in Texas are financed from the Minimum Foundation School Program, which in turn receives about 80 per cent of its funds from general state revenues and the remaining 20 per cent from school districts as a group. Each district's share of this obligation is determined according to a formula designed to reflect relative taxpaying ability. *Id.* at 9.

National figures for 1971–72 show that states supplied about 39 per cent of all school expenditures, and about 41 per cent of the nonfederal total. REISCHAUER & HARTMAN, note 9 *supra*, at 6–7. Seven-eighths of state funds are designed to provide a minimum, basic level of funding, or to compensate for interdistrict disparities in taxing power. The remainder is devoted to special service programs, which may also have some equalizing effect.

[17] 411 U.S. at 59.   [18] *Ibid.*

[19] Subsequent to *Rodriguez*, the New Jersey Supreme Court held that state's school finance system unlawful under a state constitutional clause obliging the state to provide public education. Robinson v. Cahill, 118 N.J. Super. 223 (1972), *aff'd* 62 N.J. 473 (1973). California's *Serrano* decision seemingly rested in part on state constitutional provisions held to parallel the federal Equal Protection Clause. See Goldstein, note 5 *supra*, at 504. Since most states have one or another (or both) of these provisions in their constitutions, state court intervention may survive *Rodriguez*.

"new" equal protection, "suspect classifications" and "fundamental interests." According to the Court, the class of families residing in low tax-base districts lacked the traditional indicia for suspicion: "the class is not saddled with such disabilities, or subjected to such a history of purposeful unequal treatment, or relegated to such a position of political powerlessness as to command extraordinary protection from the majoritarian political process."[20]

The category of "fundamental interests" was stated by the majority to be limited to those "explicitly or implicitly guaranteed by the Constitution."[21] Although the Court conceded some plausibility to the argument that education was fundamental because it was related to the right to vote, the argument was rejected on the ground that it proved too much. Decent food and shelter, which had already been excluded from the select company of "fundamental interests," could also be thought necessary to full political freedom.[22]

In addition, the Court suggested two new equal protection criteria. "[A]t least where wealth is involved, the Equal Protection Clause does not require absolute equality or precisely equal advantages," the Court observed.[23] The test, rather, is whether there has been an "absolute deprivation" of education. Moreover, the Court suggested that any injustices in the Texas system were mitigated by the fact that the system was improving over time, suggesting a kind of "good behavior" exemption for otherwise delinquent state institutions:[24]

> Of course, every reform that benefits some more than others may be criticized for what it fails to accomplish. But we think it plain, that in substance, the thrust of the Texas system is affirmative and reformatory, and therefore, should be scrutinized under judicial principles sensitive to the nature of the State's efforts and to the rights reserved to the States under the Constitution.

In our view, even this language does not warrant the gloomy conclusion of a general retreat from Warren Court egalitarianism. This interpretation would read too much into the language of *Rodriguez* and too little into its context. As momentum gathered

---

[20] 411 U.S. at 28.

[21] *Id*. at 33–34.

[22] *Id*. at 37.

[23] *Id*. at 24.

[24] *Id*. at 39. This argument, although used to justify judicial nonintervention, embodies the same sort of political criteria which others would use to support intervention.

in the state and lower federal courts, the school finance issue came to the Supreme Court in terms that invited a clear-cut decision: Either accept the Coons-*Serrano* proposition and replace the local property tax with an equalizing, "wealth-free" formula, or withhold judicial intervention altogether. Given these choices, a bare majority of the Court decided on nonintervention. But, at least in theory, a third course was possible: a decision involving judicial intervention but not judicial specification of the ultimate result. In what follows, we attempt to sketch the arguments for that course and some of its difficulties, as an exercise in exposition rather than advocacy.

The place to begin is with the first of the "new" equal protection cases, the original Warren Court reapportionment decision, *Baker v. Carr.*[25] The Court in *Baker* dealt with a Tennessee legislative apportionment that could fairly be described as "chaotic and unjust." The *Rodriguez* Court's arguments against judicial intervention virtually echo those of the *Baker* dissent a decade earlier: financial, like legislative, apportionment is a matter of political compromise, involving questions of social value, mathematical complexity, and raw power unsuited to the judiciary. Even granted that the instant case exemplified an irrational or unjust solution, closer cases arising later would force the Court itself to be arbitrary—either by ad hoc, case-by-case fiat or by pronouncing a simple mathematical rule which ignored legitimate distinctions. In *Baker*, critics foretold the future rule of "one man, one vote." In *Rodriguez*, the Court majority saw the danger of a Court-dictated financing scheme along equally simplified lines—one child, one budget, or one district, one tax base; to the Court a fearful symmetry.

Some contemporary defenders of *Baker v. Carr* had an answer to this vision: "The Supreme Court," wrote Nicholas Katzenbach, "has not attempted to define what are the inequities of representation or to prescribe possible remedies. It has issued merely a call for action."[26] The Court had simply announced to the state legislatures that they could not apportion seats free of constitutional scruple, but the remaining range of freedom could be considerable. Similarly, Alexander Bickel, though fearful of the inherent logic of *Baker*, applauded the decision as a potential exemplar of the passive

---

[25] 369 U.S. 186 (1962).

[26] Katzenbach, *Some Reflections on Baker v. Carr*, 15 VAND. L. REV. 829, 832 (1962).

virtues: a case which could serve state legislatures as a word to the wise, rather than a brusque about-face:[27]

> *Baker v. Carr* does not hold that the Court is a fit body to take over from the political institutions . . . , the pragmatic management of the complex and often curious adjustments that have made us a democracy and maintained us as such. . . . The point decided was not what function the Court is to perform in legislative apportionment, but whether it can play any role at all. . . . The Court here opened a colloquy, posing to the political institutions of Tennessee the question of apportionment, not answering it for them.

Most significantly, this was the view of *Baker* suggested by Mr. Justice Stewart in his concurrence there and in his dissents in subsequent one-man, one-vote cases.

In the reapportionment cases, then, there were three posible judicial strategies: inaction; resolution by formula; and what Bickel terms elsewhere a "remand."[28] If in *Baker* the Court claimed to be following the remand strategy, it soon proved its critics correct: "one man, one vote" was law within a few years. Yet it is conceivable that the Court could have adhered to the intermediate course on apportionment, brandishing the Constitution but holding the states on a looser rein.

Rodriguez offered basically the same set of alternatives. This time, the Court rejected the remand strategy at the outset. It saw the alternatives as abstention or dictation, and frankly preferred the former. The remand strategy has thus been twice rejected as a means of reforming political institutions under the Equal Protection Clause: first by "activists" anxious for a definitive standard, then by "passivists" afraid of such a standard. This rejection may reflect, not a general disinterest in the strategy, but simply the feeling of each Court majority that it knew for sure what the Constitution did or didn't require, and that nothing would be accomplished by ambiguity or delay. But another possibility is that in each case the Court was influenced by some characteristic weaknesses of the "remand." Arguably, it never does any good to let the states grope for years for ways to satisfy a delphic Court decision. This, indeed, may have been a lesson derived from *Brown v. Board of Education*.[29] The process can be ineffective and unedify-

---

[27] BICKEL, THE LEAST DANGEROUS BRANCH 195–96 (1962).

[28] *Id.* at 165.   [29] 347 U.S. 483 (1954).

ing: wrongs are not righted, feathers are not smoothed, and the Court is reduced to hiding behind certiorari or pronouncing "I know it when I see it" decisions that diminish its stature. To explore these objections, we set forth one theory of the "remand" strategy and its application to school finance.

Four conditions seem necessary for the Bickelian "remand." At the outset, of course, there must be a prima facie constitutional case against the challenged governmental practice, *i.e.*, it must seriously intrude upon constitutionally protected values. Otherwise the Court would have no need to remand. Dismissal would suffice. Conversely, the challenged practice must be one not susceptible to simple reversal, either because competing constitutional values would make an outright prohibition inappropriate or because some alternative formula would have to be substituted to allow government to function. Thus, in a reapportionment challenge, the Court could not simply disband the legislature without providing for its replacement. Third, it must be either inappropriate or impossible for the Court to proceed to a swift determination of the relevant constitutional standards. As Bickel saw the reapportionment cases, a one-man, one-vote rule was inadmissibly strict; even a rationality test would fail:[30]

> Alluding to Thayer's rule of the clear mistake, the Court [in *Baker*] indicated that its function might be to impose a requirement of rationality. But Thayer's rule can lead nowhere in this instance, for most apportionments can be deemed irrational only if the legislature is *a priori* foreclosed from pursuing certain purposes, such as over-representation of some or of all rural areas.

By this view, the Court could neither specify a single, constitutionally mandated formula for apportionment, nor even a range of acceptable formulas. Any such ruling would be possible only through judicial neglect of some of the relevant values, either jurisdictional values such as federalism or substantive values such as geographic balance. Thus in the field of apportionment, Bickel suggested, the Court's foreclosure from rule-making should be permanent, since the states' legitimate interests involved imponderable value choices. In other applications of the "remand" technique, however, the Court might simply be suspending judgment, awaiting experiments

---

[30] BICKEL, note 27 *supra*, at 196.

in the "fifty laboratories" before concocting a formula on its own.

Finally, an implicit condition for choosing the remand strategy is the belief that it will neither indefinitely delay reform nor intolerably confuse the law. For Bickel, a narrowly interpreted *Baker v. Carr* would have met this test:[31]

> The decision in *Baker v. Carr* may thus be read as holding no more than that, Tennessee having last been malapportioned sixty years ago, the situation there is the result, not of a deliberate if imperfect present judgment of the political institutions, but merely of inertia and oligarchic entrenchment. In the face of so faint an assertion, if any, by the political institutions of their own function, the principled goal of equal representation had enough vitality to enable the Court to prod the Tennessee political institutions into action. The judgment in *Baker v. Carr* is likely to generate effective pressure for legislative action, which may ameliorate the inequity somewhat. . . . Once a new apportionment statute has been passed, curing the situation in some degree, there will be little more that the judicial process can or should do.

An argument for a remand decision in the school finance cases can be sketched along very similar lines. The brief for prima facie unconstitutionality follows the Kurland schematic:[32] (1) From the reapportionment cases, we learn that "accidents of geography and the arbitrary boundary lines of local government can afford no basis for discrimination among the citizens of a state." (2) Using the local property tax to finance education imposes a disadvantage on students living in low tax-base districts. (3) This disadvantage constitutes a "suspect," wealth-based classification, as in *Douglas v. California*.[33] (4) In practical terms, the disadvantage can be severe (the court in *Serrano* noted that Beverly Hills could finance its schools from a property tax base of $50,885 in assessed valuation per pupil, while the comparable figure for neighboring Baldwin Hills was only $3,706). (5) Judged by the strict equal protection tests for "suspect" classifications and "fundamental" rights, school financing through the property tax offends important constitutional values.

Accepting this reasoning, one proceeds to the next criterion for a "remand." Is it inappropriate or impossible for the Court promptly

---

[31] *Id.* at 196–97.

[32] Kurland, note 3 *supra*, at 582, 584–89.   [33] 372 U.S. 353 (1963).

to set constitutional standards? On this question a considerable literature has developed. The findings need only be summarized here. The constitutional standard urged on the judiciary by reformers has been Coons's: that the quality of education (inferentially, per-pupil spending) cannot be related to district wealth. Several reform schemes might meet this injunction: (1) The state might simply assume the entire financial burden of education, as Hawaii did before *Serrano*.[34] (2) The state might adopt a "district power equalizing" plan, of the sort developed by Coons and his associates.[35] Under this model, each district could choose the amount it wanted to spend on education by selecting a tax rate. The state would provide a fixed amount of money per pupil for any given tax rate. In effect, it would subsidize districts whose tax base failed to produce the appropriate dollar total for the selected tax rate, with surplus funds from districts whose base produced an excess total. The plan is designed to allow district choice about levels of school expenditure, while eliminating disparities in the tax bases available to different districts. (3) The state might (as Mr. Justice Marshall suggested in his *Rodriguez* dissent) adopt a "wealth reapportionment" of school districts, changing their boundaries to accomplish a uniform distribution of per-pupil tax base.[36]

Critics have pointed out complications with each of these plans. Full state funding implies that parents in rich districts could no longer purchase more expensive public education for their children, no matter how much they were willing to pay.[37] This scheme, if ever adopted, might well result in raising educational expenditures close to the level desired by the more affluent districts. The venture could be costly. To take an extreme example, to raise all Texas dis-

---

[34] The Court's opinion in *Rodriguez* noted that in 1968 Hawaii "amended its educational finance statute to permit counties to collect additional funds locally and spend those amounts on its schools." 411 U.S. at 48 n.102. Local funding, however, contributes only a small fraction of total school expenditures in Hawaii: 4.8 percent of nonfederal spending in 1968–69, 2.9 percent in 1970–71. Levin, *et al.*, note 10 *supra*, at 217–18.

[35] Coons *et al.*, note 6 *supra*, at 201–42.

[36] 411 U.S. at 130 n.98.

[37] Editorial comment on *Serrano* in both the *New York Times* and the *Washington Post* urged the importance of allowing local supplementation. (Reform, said the *Times*, should take place "without discouraging additional investment by education-minded communities in the betterment of their schools.") N.Y. Times, 2 Sept. 1971, p. 32, col. 1; Wash. Post, 21 May 1972, p. A16, col. 2.

tricts to the current spending levels of the top tenth of one percent of districts would require an additional $2.4 billion.[38] It would also be wasteful if additional inputs into education had as little effect on output as much recent work indicates.[39] On the other hand, if state expenditure were set much lower than the current maximum, affluent parents might either send their children to private schools or attempt tax-supported local cultural enrichment programs that would substitute for fancy schools: swimming pools, ballet classes, etc. Courts might police against these subterfuges, but only at some expense of energy and goodwill.

District "power-equalizing" has similar problems. Again, the affluent would be tempted to flee the public schools or opt for low public expenditures and high private supplements.[40] A "power equalizing" formula based only on property tax valuation would ignore other indices of local need or ability to pay. Big cities, which show up as wealthier-than-average on a comparison of property tax bases, nonetheless have below-average median incomes, an exceptionally high number of handicapped or financially disadvantaged children, and a surplus of noneducational problems which drain their resources. To be sure, "power-equalizing" formulas can be designed to take into account any number of these special factors. For example, state aid could be increased according to a local cost-of-services index, or could be set higher for disadvantaged pupils.

---

[38] Brief for Appellants in *Rodriguez*, p. 40.

[39] See JENCKS, INEQUALITY (1972); U.S. OFFICE OF EDUCATION, EQUALITY OF EDUCATIONAL OPPORTUNITY (1966) (the Coleman report) and other sources cited by the Court in *Rodriguez*, 411 U.S. at 43 n.86.

In addition, the argument has been made that state finance would lead to an increase in input prices through collective bargaining or inelasticity in the supply of teaching services. See Simon, *The School Finance Decisions: Collective Bargaining and Future Finance Systems*, 82 YALE L.J. 409 (1973); Moynihan, *Equalizing Education: In Whose Benefit?* 29 PUB. INT. 69 (1972); Moynihan, *Can Courts and Money Do It?* N.Y. Times, 10 Jan. 1972, § E, p. 1, col. 3, at 24. "The effect of [judicial intervention], almost certainly, will be to raise educational expenditures. The only certain result that will come from this is that a particular cadre of middle-class persons in possession of certain licenses—that is to say teachers—will receive more public money in the future than they do now."

[40] For criticism of the "power-equalizing" formula, see Michelman, *The Supreme Court, 1968 Term, Foreword: On Protecting the Poor through the Fourteenth Amendment*, 83 HARV. L. REV. 7, 50–56 (1969); Wise, *School Finance Equalization Lawsuits: A Model Legislative Response*, 2 YALE REV. LAW & SOC. ACT. 123, 125 (1971): "If it is children who are entitled to equal protection, then it is difficult to understand how the quality of a child's education should be subjected to a vote of his neighbors." PRESIDENT'S COMMISSION ON SCHOOL FINANCE, SCHOOLS, PEOPLE, AND MONEY 33 (1972).

But such modifications involve value judgments of a kind which a simple judicial formula must seek to avoid. For a court to determine that each handicapped child is worth 2.3 times the allotment of the normal child demands the same cabalistic insight as giving rural Tennessee 2.3 times the voting power of urban Tennessee.

Wealth-based reapportionment is vulnerable to the same objections as district power-equalizing, and to one more. It sacrifices whatever community of interest exists in current school districts. If local control is so weak a value as to be subordinated to the need to frame districts of equal taxing power, perhaps the district should be removed from the process entirely. A "voucher" system could do just that, by letting families themselves decide how much to spend on their children's education. Under Coons's "power-equalizing" voucher scheme, families could choose among alternative tax rates keyed to different school spending levels.[41] Tax rates could be made strongly progressive, so that the cost to a poor family of sending its children to a high-expense school might be less than the cost to an affluent family of choosing a cheaper institution. Thus the cost of a child's education would no longer be shaped by the vote of its neighbors or the constraints of the local property tax. Critics have pointed out, however, that it would still be tied to the parents' tastes, perhaps an even more significant barrier to equal opportunity. Moreover, public schools under this voucher system might be constrained to operate at the lowest expense level, if (as seems likely) affluent parents sent their children to private schools. Public schools, in consequence, would be left with the most educationally disadvantaged students and the fewest resources, hardly an endearing prospect to the proponents of educational equality.[42]

The difficulty of finding an appropriate judicial standard for

[41] COONS et al., note 6 supra, at 256–68.

[42] Other voucher schemes have been considered in the last few years. See, e.g., FRIEDMAN, CAPITALISM AND FREEDOM 86–98 (1962). Friedman proposes a system which will allow families to supplement the voucher from their own resources, a plan which critics charged would lead to a system of schools segregated by price and therefore even more segregated by family income than the present system. The Office of Economic Opportunity (OEO) began a test in San Jose, California, of a more egalitarian model which limited all children of a given age to a single voucher amount and prohibited schools from charging extra tuition. See CENTER FOR THE STUDY OF PUBLIC POLICY, EDUCATION VOUCHERS: A PROPOSAL FOR FINANCING EDUCATION BY GRANTS TO PARENTS. A REPORT TO OEO (1970); A PROPOSED EXPERIMENT IN EDUCATION VOUCHERS (OEO NO. 3400 N-1, 1971).

school finance reflects much more than technical complexity. A fundamental clash of values is involved. The *Rodriguez* Court characterized this conflict as one between equality and local self-determination. Full state funding of schools, for example, might well inhibit local choice of curricula, and by definition would ignore local differences in the relative value placed on education.[43] But the most significant value counterpoised to equality is not localism; it is, quite simply, inequality. Mandating equal expenditures deprives affluent parents, as well as districts, of the ability to give their children special advantages through increased spending on education (except to the extent that equalization drives the affluent out of the public school system altogether). At the very least this contradicts a tacit promise made by a competitive, capitalist society, that money made by the parents can buy comfort, status, "the chance we never had" for the offspring. And if one assumes (as most reformers have) that extra money spent on schools actually results in a better education, the conflict becomes even more severe. In Kurland's words, it is a clash between quality and equality, a question whether there should be "some improvement of the worst at the expense of the best."[44] For the Supreme Court to decree that the suburbs can't have more elegant schools than the slums would in some ways be more startling than for it simply to rewrite the tax laws and redistribute income. It would be to let the affluent keep their money but to deny them their most selfless plans for spending it. The Coons-*Serrano* formula that "quality cannot be a function of wealth" brings out, as no other social reform could, the basic contradiction between competition and equality.[45]

It is not surprising, then, that the Supreme Court should have been reluctant to leap to any form of the equal-expenditure rule. But rejecting the pure egalitarian challenge does not necessarily im-

---

[43] 411 U.S. at 49–53.

[44] Kurland, note 3 *supra*, at 590.

[45] The reformers' proposition can be criticized for being too narrow as well as too broad. JENCKS, note 39 *supra*, at 26, notes that there are major inequalities in public spending on students' education over a lifetime. These disparities largely reflect the varying number of years that students spend in school. Even "ignoring expenditure differences between one school and another," he "estimated that the most extensively educated fifth of the population received about 75 percent more than their share of the nation's educational resources, while the least extensively educated fifth received about half their share."

ply complete judicial abstention. Other solutions are possible. Two
are of special interest.

Most simply, reformers could argue for a "minimal protection"
rule. The system (everywhere or in some states only) is unconstitutional because it deprives the poorest districts of the means to provide
a minimum, basic educational budget. By the Michelman reading
of the "new" equal protection, education—like justice and suffrage—
cannot be rationed solely by the marketplace: subminimal expenditures on the poor are unconstitutional.[46] But this approach
presents difficulties as severe as true egalitarianism. As Michelman
recognizes, education even more than other goods and services is
valued largely in comparative terms.[47] "Minimal protection," then,
has no empirical referent and resolves into a kind of half-hearted
equal protection. It lacks the precision and ideological appeal of a
simple egalitarian norm, while representing little less of a value
judgment.

A very different line of attack would aim, not at the exact results
of the school finance system, but at the way in which the choice is
made. By this argument, financing schools through the local property tax does not represent a contemporaneous, avowed choice for
unequal expenditures. Rather, inequality is a by-product of a system which exists for historical reasons and persists through inertia,
or vested interest. The property tax for generations has proved a
most difficult institution to change. No doubt, the difficulty is in
part that shared by all reforms: as Machiavelli said, they have "enemies in all those who profit by the old system, and only lukewarm
defenders in all those who would profit by the new order, [for like
all mankind] they do not truly believe in anything new until they
have had actual experience of it."[48] But more distinctively, the property tax has the characteristic of creating equities that make any
reform seem as arbitrary as the abuse itself. A family moves to the
suburbs, lured by low property taxes or good schools. The price it
must pay for a home reflects these expectations. Is it fair suddenly
to "equalize" the state's tax base, so that suburban taxes go up while
school expenditures decline? Legislatures tend to avoid tough questions such as these. In a minor way, reforming school finance re-
sembles reapportionment, an unpleasant task easily postponed. To

---

[46] Michelman, note 40 *supra*, at 57.   [47] *Id*. at 58.

[48] MACHIAVELLI, THE PRINCE 24 (World Classics ed. 1957).

be sure, legislators have a direct, personal stake in perpetuating malapportionment. But the constituent interests that vest in a continuing system of property tax finance can be similarly compelling.

Needless to say, it requires some effort to transform this argument from armchair political science to constitutional doctrine. To begin with, one should separate two alternative claims. First, that the property tax is not merely specially entrenched but also inherently biased against educational equality. Second, that although not consistently biased for or against equality, it is nonetheless capricious in its choice of competing values.

In one sense, the "bias" argument is obviously true. Financing the public schools through a local property tax leads to inequality. But this is simply a restatement of the pure egalitarian case already considered. To show any stronger form of bias, one must establish that the system is more heavily weighted against equality than would be one which reflected merely the influences of income and taste. Put another way, would abolition of the local property tax lead to increased equality, if states were free to substitute a system which still allowed for local choice of expenditures?

Here one can merely conjecture. Under the property tax system, there is enormous dispersion in the amount of locally raised funds to support education. In the sample of Texas school districts cited in *Rodriguez*, local revenues per pupil ranged from a $610 average in the highest base districts to an average of $63 in the lowest base districts; with state funds added, the range was $815–$306.[49] The highest group had a tax base at least ten times greater than the lowest group. Studies of other jurisdictions show that the range in median income, median total personal wealth, or other comprehensive measures of ability to pay is considerably narrower than the range in per-pupil property values or per-pupil local educational revenues.[50] One can speculate, therefore, that a shift to some other system of finance—even one which allowed local communities full freedom to spend lavishly on schools—would narrow the range of school expenditures in states which rely heavily on the local property tax.

---

[49] 411 U.S. at 134.

[50] "[Using per pupil tax base as a measure,] some districts in a state have 10,000 times the fiscal capacity of others, and even within narrow confines of a metropolitan area there are variations of ten or fifteen to one." REISCHAUER & HARTMAN, note 9 *supra*, at 67.

For states like Texas, however, which have substantial state "foundation" or equalization systems, the inference is less clear. And in any case, the range of educational expenditures is but one possible statistical measurement of the degree of inequality in spending. A more commonly used gauge of inequality takes account of dispersion in the center of a distribution, as well as between its extremes.[51] By this standard, there is little basis for saying whether current systems offer more or less equality than those which might take their place.

Although the range between extremes does not establish the bias of the local property tax system, it may be some evidence of caprice. Without much elaboration, Mr. Justice White's dissenting opinion in *Rodriguez* makes this second charge against the Texas school finance system: that it is "irrational," because Texas denies parents living in property-poor school districts, whether the parents themselves are rich or poor, the "practical and legal" ability to provide a high level of spending for their children's education:[52]

> If the State aims at maximizing local initiative and local choice, by permitting school districts to resort to the real property tax if they choose to do so, it utterly fails in achieving its purpose in districts with property tax bases so low that there is little if any opportunity for interested parents, rich or poor, to augment school district revenues.

Mr. Justice White's observation about the legal unavailability of the property tax was based on a state-set ceiling, of $1.50 per $100 valuation, on the maximum maintenance tax rate any district could impose.[53] For property-poor districts, such as Edgewood, to reach the same level of per-pupil spending as in some of the richer districts, they would have to raise taxes far above the state maximum. But, as the majority pointed out, Edgewood's tax rate at the time of the litigation was $0.55 per $100—hardly bumping up against the ceiling.[54] Plaintiffs didn't claim that the ceiling presently barred tax increases in Edgewood or elsewhere. The case against "legal" unavailability was thus premature. What remains is the contention

---

[51] One commonly used index of inequality is the Gini coefficient, which measures the relative deviation of the cumulative distribution curve (Lorenz curve) from the diagonal (representing complete equality).

[52] 411 U.S. at 68.

[53] *Id.* at 67.   [54] *Id.* at 50, n.107.

that property tax increases are "practically" unavailable in low-base districts.

Some obvious arguments can be marshaled to make this case, although the most obvious argument must be put aside. It is not enough to observe that districts with low tax bases are likely to be inhabited by taxpayers with below-average incomes. For to deny the permissibility of a link between income and school spending is simply to make the pure egalitarian case again. It seems apparent, however, that a district with a high tax base can raise money with less "effort" than one with a low base; and that a low-base district risks the loss of local business and industry (and even the more mobile homeowners) if it charges the extraordinary rates necessary to equal the revenues raised by high-base districts. While these disadvantages may reflect in part differences in income among districts, they may also be significantly a result simply of the use of property as the standard for ability to pay. In addition to these inherent characteristics of the property tax, one might cite its administrative inequities as a reason why low-base districts find it "impractical" to raise high revenues through the tax. A tax that involves such evident interpersonal inequity,[55] such a haphazard relationship to short-term changes in ability to pay,[56] and such widespread unpopularity[57] may place the service which it finances at a peculiar disadvantage.

However obvious, many of these complaints against the property tax have recently been challenged as untrue. Economists have argued, for example, that a district's tax base will be reflected in the cost of buying land. To enjoy the advantages of the Beverly Hills high base (and low tax rate) you must first buy a lot there. The price of the lot will incorporate anticipated tax benefits.[58] Similarly,

[55] ". . . a study of Boston showed that in 1962 the ratio of assessed to market value of single family homes ranged from 0.28 in East Boston to 0.54 in predominantly black Roxbury, while assessment ratios on commercial property ranged from 0.59 in Hyde Park to 1.11 in South Boston." REISCHAUER & HARTMAN, note 9 supra, at 27, citing Oldman & Aaron, Assessment-Sales Ratios under the Boston Property Tax, 4 ASSESSORS J. 13, 18–19 (April 1969).

[56] See REISCHAUER & HARTMAN, note 9 supra, at 40.

[57] "A recent survey found that Americans consider the local property tax to be the least fair form of taxation. This view is shared 'regardless of age, income, area of residence, type of employment, race and other such factors.' " Levin, note 8 supra, at 911 n.146.

[58] These arguments are outlined in REISCHAUER & HARTMAN, note 9 supra, at 32–34.

just because Beverly Hills has a low tax rate it doesn't necessarily have an innate advantage in luring industry. Businesses scared off by Baldwin Park's high taxes may also run from Beverly Hills's real estate prices. Moreover, one could argue, if the property tax were so unpopular it wouldn't have survived so long. Its very inelasticity—its built-in resistance to rapid expansion—may have endeared it to a tax-weary electorate.

The economic argument about the reflection of tax rates in land values remains a speculative one., The real estate market is imperfect and ill-understood, and if it adjusts to tax-rate changes it may do so over a time period longer than that relevant to the voters in school bond elections. Moreover, voters may behave as if a high rate in District A is more onerous than a low rate in District B, disregarding what economists may think they know about the compensating variance in land prices.

The data now being collected about school finance allow one rough empirical test of these arguments. If a district's property tax base is, and is perceived to be, irrelevant to the expenditure decision, then there ought to be no correlation between tax base and expenditures. If tax base is related to expenditures only because there is some correlation between tax base and personal income, then one can control for income and see whether any relationship remains. Indications are that one does. A study of Connecticut school finance showed a correlation of .49 between per-pupil expenditures and per-pupil tax base, with median income held constant. By comparison, the correlation between expenditures and median income, holding per-pupil tax base constant, was only slightly higher (.51).[59] By this standard, tax base was almost as powerful an independent explanation of expenditures as was median income. Other studies have shown that income has twice or three times the influence of tax base, but that the latter remains significant. Unpublished work by Grubb and Michelson, for example, suggests that a 30 percent increase in a district's tax base is associated with a 10 percent in-

---

[59] Note, *A Statistical Analysis of the School Finance Decisions: On Winning Battles and Losing Wars*, 81 YALE L.J. 1303, 1333 (1972). Using mean income instead of median income, the correlation between expenditures and base (income constant) falls to .39, and that between income and expenditures (base constant) rises to .57; this would suggest that, as in the studies cited in note 60 *infra*, income is "more important" than base in explaining school expenditures, but that base has significant independent explanatory power.

crease in its per-pupil expenditures, with per pupil income held constant.[60]

Three studies are hardly proof of anything. High-base districts may share some other characteristics—young families with a taste for expensive education—that explain high educational expenditures. Nonetheless, these studies might reconcile one to the common-sense view that the property tax exercises an influence on educational spending, quite apart from the influence of income and taste.

Is it therefore unconstitutional? If so, what can be done about it? In our view these questions are legitimately related. Though one can believe that judicial intervention would be pragmatically beneficial, but improper, the reverse set of beliefs seems untenable. Utility is a postulate of the "remand." So we will first discuss the remedy, and then the right.

The remedy might well depend on the language the courts would use to strike down the property tax system. The White and Marshall dissents in *Rodriguez* suggest two different equal protection tests. Mr. Justice White invokes the classic "rational relationship" standard, while Mr. Justice Marshall would require a showing of "compelling state interest" to justify suspect classifications trenching on fundamental rights. At first glance, these alternative standards would seem neatly paired with the two alternative claims of capriciousness or bias in the existing system. If the system is loaded against the poor, it seems natural to demand a "compelling state interest" for its continuance. An objection that the system is arbitrary seems well tailored to the "rationality" standard.

Each of these approaches, however, invites difficulty. The "compelling state interest" test is well adapted to invalidating a substantive result that the Court deems unnecessarily restrictive of a constitutionally protected interest. It has not been used, and might not be easily adapted, to accomplish a purely structural remedy: in this case, removing a system thought to bias the choice against educational equality, without imposing any substantive choice of the court's own. Trouble would arise in a case of a state using a new system—*e.g.*, general state revenues supplemented by a local income

---

[60] Telephone conversation with W. Norton Grubb, September 1973, based on statistical work underlying Grubb & Michelson, *Public School Finance in a Post-Serrano World*, 8 HARV. CIV. RT.–CIV. LIB. L. REV. 550 (1973). See also, FELDSTEIN, WEALTH, NEUTRALITY, AND LOCAL CHOICE IN PUBLIC EDUCATION (Harvard Institute of Economic Research paper #293, 1973).

or sales tax—to reach inegalitarian results. A court that had just finished demanding a "compelling state interest" to justify one type of inequality might feel impelled to thwart the same result reached through different means.

The difficulty critics find with the rationality test is of a different sort. The test itself, if construed literally, is meaningless.[61] Virtually any legislative decision is rational if the end sought by the legislature is described with sufficient specificity and imagination. Even the hereditary law-review instances of irrationality—e.g., the law prohibiting red-heads from becoming river-boat pilots—can be justified on theories of statistical correlation no more whimsical than those on which most human decisions are made. To use a recently adjudicated example, it is hardly irrational to say that men make better executors than women—or vice versa.[62] Half-baked empirical judgments such as these are the very stuff of legislation. If they are objectionable, it is because they involve suspect classifications or protected interests. By this reasoning the rationality test, if ever used to reverse state action, is merely a camouflaged version of the new equal protection.[63]

This argument, persuasive as far as it goes, nonetheless leaves out one conceivable specialized function of the rationality test. A demand that the legislature be "rational" can be construed as a demand

---

[61] This argument is presented forcefully in Note, *Legislative Purpose, Rationality, and Equal Protection*, 82 YALE L.J. 123 (1972).

[62] Compare Reed v. Reed, 404 U.S. 71 (1971), in which a unanimous Court invalidated as irrational a state statute giving men a mandatory preference over women as administrators of a decedent's estate.

[63] Gunther, *The Supreme Court 1971 Term, Foreword: In Search of Evolving Doctrine on a Changing Court: A Model for a Newer Equal Protection*, 86 HARV. L. REV. 1 (1972), suggests that the rationality test has been used as a technique for avoiding a difficult definition of substantive constitutional rights. Last year's Supreme Court decisions reveal no consistent pattern in the use of "rationality." *Compare* United States v. Kras, 409 U.S. 434 (1973) (upholding requirement of $50 fee to file in bankruptcy), and McGinnis v. Royster, 410 U.S. 263 (1973) (upholding New York correctional law giving no "good behavior" credit for pretrial county jail detention), *with* U.S. Dep't of Agric. v. Murry, 93 S. Ct. 2832 (1973) (invalidating denial of food stamps to households with members over eighteen previously claimed as dependents), and United States Dep't of Agric. v. Moreno, 93 S. Ct. 2821 (1973) (invalidating denial of food stamps to households with unrelated members). In *McGinnis*, the Court stressed that it would uphold a challenged statute if the means selected were rationally related to *any* valid purpose the legislature might have had in mind. *Murry*, on the other hand, closely fits Gunther's paradigm: a substantive equal protection claim, made dubious by Dandridge v. Williams, 397 U.S. 471 (1970), finds vindication through the "rationality" test.

that, in the particular case or class of cases, it be explicit about its choice of ends. The test thus functions as a kind of "remand"—demanding of the legislature not necessarily that it abandon its values but that it make them clear. So construed, a finding of "irrationality" is precisely the appropriate form of judicial intervention against a school finance system thought to be unconstitutionally inexplicit and random in its resolution of competing values. On this strategy, the Court would simply hold that a school finance system based primarily on the local property tax could not stand. Any alternative system which responded to any of the relevant values—parental choice, municipal overburden, special educational problems of the disadvantaged—would be acceptable, whether or not it resulted in any formula that could meaningfully be called "equalizing."

How would such a remand work, and what would it accomplish? One can only conjecture. Our guess is that it would be widely accepted by the states. It might result in new systems of educational finance that would reduce the extreme dispersion in per-pupil spending, but would not significantly accomplish a progressive redistribution of taxes or expenditures (and might even do the reverse). The courts, even under a permissive "rationality" test, would become involved at least temporarily in arbitrary value choices. They would have to decide when a system was "primarily" based on the property tax. And they might have to dictate an interim system of school finance to a few recalcitrant legislatures. The end results would not likely be pleasing to most judicial "activists," and the process would hardly be described by any literal notion of passivity. Thus, the "remand" would seem merely to offer something to offend everybody.

Before concluding on this note, we would recall Bickel's projection of a "remand" strategy for reapportionment:[64]

> Yet we will, apparently, witness not a little constitutional experimentation by lower federal and state courts; and even the Supreme Court may enter the "political thicket" in states where no branch of government, not even the executive, rests on the majoritarian principle.

Bickel foresaw, and was not appalled by, the prospect that the judicially induced reform of an arbitrary, entrenched system would

[64] BICKEL, note 27 supra, at 197.

itself necessitate some arbitrariness. If objectionable, this is a characteristic of the "remand," not merely of the "remand" as applied to school finance.

Nor is it a decisive objection that the reforms of any new system might embody value choices displeasing to the original enemies of the old, any more than one could argue against *Baker v. Carr* that it was meant to help cities but has in fact aided the suburbs. If what was constitutionally objectionable about the old system was not its inegalitarian results but its capricious and unexamined method, a New Look and not a New Deal is all that can be asked for.

Thus far we have eluded the question whether the "entrenchment" or "arbitrariness" of the property tax is, indeed, constitutionally objectionable. All political systems are to a large degree inertial. Every law on the statute books creates "vested" interests. And if there is to be a constitutional Rule against Perpetuities, it is not clear which of them must fail. Similarly, all taxes are to a large degree arbitrary. If our evidence on the effects of the local property tax on school expenditure is still thin, how much thinner is our conjecture about the effects of whatever tax would be substituted for it?

These queries raise two different objections to the "remand" argument. First, an objection to anyone concluding, as a matter of prediction, that a "remand" would lead to a wholesome, constructive reopening of the political process and to a finance system more explicit and less haphazard in its choice of values than the current one. Second, to the propriety of resting this decision in the judiciary. For it is clearly a "political" decision, a conclusion that the political system is in a rut and is capable of being jolted out of it. Is the decision a correct one? And who should have the power to make it?

In our view, school finance through the local property tax is one of those established institutions that can profit from forced reexamination. It is, of course, inaccurate to call the system "unexamined." Texas, like most states, was constantly changing (and, as the *Rodriguez* Court pointed out, making modestly more equal) its school finance system.[65] Yet the system was based upon a structure—school districts which could raise funds only through real estate taxes—that was not itself subject to change. One can certainly

---

[65] 411 U.S. at 11.

argue that it was not changed because it was satisfactory. Our view is that it is possible for a system to be unsatisfactory, even by the values of the majority of its participants, yet to be practically immutable because of the uncertainties of change. Recent theoretical work has suggested that democratic decisions do not necessarily represent an optimum result even for the group that voted for them.[66] School finance may be an illustration.

Accepting this view does not, of course, establish the crucial proposition that the judiciary should take over from a hidebound legislature. For the courts to order a "remand" is, as the name implies, to treat the legislature as an errant administrative agency. The court would be saying, as the Court of Appeals for the District of Columbia has often said to federal regulatory commissions: "We can't make your decision for you. But we can force you to have another try and come up with better reasons." Is this avuncular, tutelary role vis-à-vis the legislature itself an appropriate one for courts in a democracy?

We submit that the answer depends on which courts one is referring to. State courts historically have occupied a different role with respect to their legislatures from that of the Supreme Court with respect to Congress or the state legislatures. State court judges are often elected. In some states they customarily issue advisory opinions. They have in many jurisdictions managed to keep alive the coals of economic due process without burning down the house. The constitutions they enforce are amendable with far greater ease and regularity than the Constitution of the United States. Moreover there are fifty of them and they can learn from each other's mishaps. *Serrano* was a bold and, so far as can be told, singularly successful undertaking, if success is defined in the precise sense of forcing a reexamination and encouraging a transition to a less random system. It largely accomplished the legitimate function of a "remand," both in California and elsewhere. A Supreme Court decision along the same lines might have been unnecessary as well as far more hazardous and antidemocratic, precisely because it would be the Supreme Court's and not a state court's decision. We see no contradiction in viewing both *Serrano* and *Rodriguez* as correctly decided.

---

[66] See ARROW, SOCIAL CHOICE AND INDIVIDUAL VALUES (2d ed. 1963).

RICHARD E. MORGAN

THE ESTABLISHMENT CLAUSE AND SECTARIAN SCHOOLS: A FINAL INSTALLMENT?

Writing in the 1971 *Supreme Court Review*, Professor Donald Giannella predicted that the decision of the Supreme Court in *Lemon v. Kurtzman* (*Lemon I*)[1] would make another "round of controversy" over public aid to church-related schools inevitable.[2] His prediction has been borne out, and the purpose of this article is to describe what happened in that predicted "round," and suggest where, if anywhere, the controversy may go from here.

In three decisions announced on the last decision day of June 1973, *Levitt v. Committee*,[3] *Committee v. Nyquist*,[4] and *Sloan v. Lemon*,[5] the Supreme Court seems to have gone a long way toward settling the matter. It is much clearer now than it was after *Lemon I* that public funds may not be used in any major amount to relieve the economic distress of church-related schools. It is also much clearer why they may not. A few nagging questions, however, do remain.

Richard E. Morgan is Associate Professor and Chairman of the Department of Government and Legal Studies, Bowdoin College.

[1] 403 U.S. 602 (1971).

[2] Giannella, *Lemon and Tilton: The Bitter and the Sweet of Church-State Entanglement*, 1971 SUPREME COURT REVIEW 147.

[3] 413 U.S. 472 (1973).

[4] 93 S. Ct. 2955 (1973).   [5] 93 S. Ct. 2982 (1973).

The history of the Supreme Court's exegesis of the Establishment Clause limitations on aid to church-related schools is brief but tangled. In the late nineteenth and early twentieth centuries there had been eruptions of hard politics and high feelings over the issue in various state contexts.[6] But, while the Court came close to decision in a few instances,[7] the Justices managed to avoid addressing the issue directly. In the years immediately following World War II, however, a new set of pressures and interest groups and arguments grew up around "public monies for church schools," and in 1947 the Court engaged the question in *Everson v. Board of Education*.[8] This decision was the beginning of a fascinating chapter in our constitutional politics of which *Levitt*, *Nyquist*, and *Sloan* may prove to be the end.

I. A DARK AND BLOODY BACKGROUND

While lacking the politically destructive potential of racial cases, and the extreme emotional turbulance associated with the school prayer cases, the cases concerned with the Establishment Clause limitations on public aid to private, church-related schools have been among the more controversial issues handled by the Court since World War II. Church-related schools are overwhelmingly Roman Catholic parochial schools. These are characteristically based on individual parishes, in the case of elementary schools, and on dioceses and archdioceses, in the case of secondary schools. Again, characteristically, the elementary and secondary schools in a given diocese are presided over by a superintendent appointed by the bishop. By the early 1960s nonpublic schools enrolled about 5,600,000 children, or roughly 11 percent of the national elementary and secondary school population. Almost 90 percent of these children attended Catholic parochial schools; another 5 percent at-

---

[6] For the best of the literature on nineteenth- and early twentieth-century church-school reactions, see BILLINGTON, THE PROTESTANT CRUSADE, 1800–1860 (1938); HIGHAM, STRANGERS IN THE LAND (rev. ed. 1963); and PRATT, RELIGION, POLITICS AND DIVERSITY: THE CHURCH-STATE THEME IN NEW YORK HISTORY (1967).

[7] Notably, Bradfield v. Roberts, 175 U.S. 291 (1899); Quick Bear v. Leupp, 210 U.S. 50 (1908); and Cochran v. Board of Education, 281 U.S. 370 (1930).

[8] 330 U.S. 1 (1947). For a brief account of the politics of aid to sectarian schools in the immediate postwar period, see MORGAN, THE POLITICS OF RELIGIOUS CONFLICT 19–47 (1968) (hereinafter POLITICS); and MORGAN, THE SUPREME COURT AND RELIGION 81–95 (1972) (hereinafter RELIGION).

tended Protestant and Jewish schools; and 5 percent were in secular, private, or "prep" schools.[9]

Progressively, since 1945 the cost squeeze has tightened on private, and especially church-related schools. For Catholic educators, gaining substantial forms of public aid, first a matter of righting an ancient wrong, came to be perceived as a matter of ensuring future growth and finally as a matter of raw survival.[10] Over the past half-dozen years parochial school enrollments have declined steadily, and parochial school closings are now commonplace.

During the 1960s, however, Catholic educators acquired some valuable allies as the Jewish Day School movement flourished and as certain Protestant bodies, such as the Episcopalians and the Missouri Synod Lutherans, ventured further into the school business. Throughout the period 1945 to the present, it is possible to identify fairly stable battle lines of interest groups on either side of the issue. The U.S. Catholic Conference (through its Education Division), Citizens for Educational Freedom, Agudath Israel and the National Association of Hebrew Day Schools, the National Catholic Educational Association, the Catholic League for Religious and Civil Rights, the Knights of Columbus, and the National Jewish Commission on Law and Public Affairs have all been found at one time or another to be lobbying or litigating for aid to church-related schools. This list includes only the larger, formal groups; in addition there are such individual "accommodationist" protagonists as Porter Chandler, who has so often appeared to defend the position of the

---

[9] The most reliable figures are the estimates published periodically by the U.S. Office of Education. For detailed discussion of the economics of parochial schools see BARTELL, COSTS AND BENEFITS OF CATHOLIC ELEMENTARY SCHOOLS (1969); and KOOB & SHAW, S.O.S. FOR CATHOLIC SCHOOLS: A STRATEGY FOR FUTURE SERVICE TO CHURCH AND NATION (1970). On the sociology of Catholic education, see GREELEY & ROSSI, THE EDUCATION OF CATHOLIC AMERICANS (1966).

[10] Some opponents of aid to church schools argue that there is no reason for Catholic parochial schools to fail without public aid. The Catholic community has sufficient resources to sustain its schools, it is suggested. Catholics simply do not want to pay the growing bills and would be pleased to transfer some of these to the tax base. Catholic school partisans respond that while Catholics could probably keep their school system going without mass starvation, this misses the point. In order to be a real option for pious parents, parochial school education must be priced substantially below actual cost. Theoretical ability to sustain the system and actual ability must be seen to differ greatly. The level of sacrifice which can reasonably be expected of a pious parent has been reached. And so the battle runs on. See N.Y. Times, 20 May 1973, p. 42, col. 1. for a recent skirmish.

Archdiocese of New York, and William Ball, who has worked long and closely with the U.S. Catholic Conference.

Ranged on the no-aid, or "separationist," side of the issue have been secular liberals (the American Civil Liberties Union, the NAACP, the American Association of Humanists), liberal Protestants (the National Council of Churches, the Unitarians), conservative Protestants (Americans United, the Baptist Joint Committee on Public Affairs, the Seventh-Day Adventist Religious Liberty Association), and liberal Jews (the American Jewish Congress, the Anti-Defamation League, and the American Jewish Committee). And, here, too, there are prominent individual separationists: Leo Pfeffer (long associated with the Commission on Law and Social Action of the American Jewish Congress), Kenneth Greenawalt (from the Church-State Committee of the ACLU), and nonlawyer Dean Kelley (of the National Council of Churches). In addition, there are coalitions which have formed in particular localities, the most important being the Committee for Public Education and Religious Liberty (PEARL) in the New York area. The principal partners in PEARL are the American Jewish Congress and the New York Civil Liberties Union, and its chief spokesman and legal tactician has been Leo Pfeffer. Two of the three cases decided last spring were brought by PEARL, the third also saw Leo Pfeffer on an amicus brief.

While there are obviously differences of orientation between the groups making up the two camps, it is fair to speak of accommodationist and separationist forces which have fought one another (in courts, legislatures, and for public opinion) for a quarter-century, over stakes that are not trivial either economically or psychologically.[11]

As suggested, in the beginning was *Everson*,[12] and the reading given to the Establishment Clause in that case by Justice Black set the parameters for discussion for a decade. Justice Black enunciated a sweeping theory of the Establishment Clause with swashbuckling borrowings from Madison and Jefferson: "No tax in any amount, large or small, can be levied to support any religious activities of institutions, whatever they may be called, . . ." This, followed by the declaration that "the clause against the establishment

---

[11] For PEARL's activities prior to 1970, see POLITICS at 115–16.

[12] Everson v. Board of Education, 330 U.S. 1 (1947).

of religion by law was intended to erect 'a wall of separation between church and State' "[13] sent accommodationist hearts plummet-
ing. But, as every student knows, Black found a way to save the
particular program before the Court that day. (New Jersey had
authorized its towns to reimburse parents for the cost of transport-
ing their children, on regular bus lines, to nonpublic schools.) The
beneficiaries, Black argued, were not the church schools, which he
asserted could not be aided, but the children. To keep all children
off dangerous streets was a legitimate public safety measure, and
while the bus plan "approache[d] the verge"[14] of an impermissible
benefit to religious institutions, it was saved by the fact that the
immediate and obvious beneficiaries were individuals.

Here was a wisp of doctrine at which accommodationists could
grasp, and the "individual benefit theory" soon burgeoned.[15] All
manner of public aids to religious schools were advanced as bene-
fiting individuals and not institutions. Throughout the 1950's the
key question in the debate was the extent to which the Supreme
Court might eventually come to approve various sorts of programs
on some variant of the individual-benefit theory. Accommodationists stressed Black's justification of the transportation allowances;
separationists stressed the "wall of separation" and the "verge"
which had been said to be so close.

The next Supreme Court utterance of major significance for the
controversy came in 1963 in Justice Clark's opinion for the Court
in *Abington School District v. Schempp*.[16] Clark wrote that the
crucial question for the constitutionality of any governmental program challenged on establishment grounds was: "[W]hat are the
purpose and primary effect of the enactment? If either is the ad-
vancement or the inhibition of religion then the enactment exceeds
the scope of the legislative powers."[17] As the occasion for this
formulation was the invalidation of Bible readings and recitations
of the Lord's Prayer in public schools, an outcome that was clearly
separationist, it was at least possible to see in "purpose and primary
effect" a constitutional lifeline for programs of aid to church-related schools. Perhaps this language could support even more public

---

[13] *Id.* at 16.   [14] *Ibid.*

[15] For a review and critique of the agreement, see La Noue, *The Child Benefit Theory
Revisited*, 13 J. Pub. Law 76 (1964).

[16] 374 U.S. 203 (1963).   [17] *Id.* at 222.

aid than could be justified under any version of the individual-benefit theory, which had to be based on, and was thus potentially constrained by, Black's *Everson* opinion.

Accommodationist optimism received another boost in 1968.[18] The decision that year in *Board of Education v. Allen*[19] established the high water mark of accommodationist success. Involved here was a program much more closely related to the educational enterprise than transportation. New York was providing textbooks (technically on loan) to nonpublic, including parochial, schoolchildren. Mr. Justice White wrote the opinion for the Court. While making some use of the individual-benefit theory,[20] his principal reliance in upholding the New York practice was on Clark's "purpose and primary effect" language.

While it was less than clear in 1963[21] that this *Schempp* "test" represented any advance beyond or alteration of what Justice Black and successive majorities had been saying in establishment cases (both religious practice and institutional aid cases)[22] before *Schempp*, the use Mr. Justice White made of Clark's words in 1968 did seem to indicate some alteration in the posture of the Court on the matter of public aid to religious institutions. All that Mr. Justice White asked of a governmental aid program was that there be a valid, secular legislative purpose and that neither the purpose nor the primary intent of the enactment be to aid religious activities.[23]

Five other members of the Court, including Chief Justice Warren, associated themselves in the majority opinion. Justice Harlan concurred with three paragraphs that would have allowed governmental aid to church-related institutions provided there was a pub-

---

[18] See Katz & Southerland, *Religious Pluralism and the Supreme Court*, 96 DAEDALUS 180 (1970).

[19] 392 U.S. 236 (1968).

[20] This argument was still being vigorously advanced in the period between *Shempp* and *Allen*. See Taylor, *Federal Aid for Children and Teachers in All Schools*, 12 CATHOLIC LAW 193, 195 (1966).

[21] See, for instance, Brown, *Quis Custodiet Ipsos Custodes?—The School-Prayer Cases*, 1963 SUPREME COURT REVIEW 1, 5–6.

[22] Notably McCollum v. Board of Education, 333 U.S. 203 (1948); Engel v. Vitale, 370 U.S. 421 (1962).

[23] 392 U.S. 236, 243–44 (1968). For a critique of *Allen* see Freund, *Public Aid to Parochial Schools*, 82 HARV. L. REV. 1680 (1969). For a response to Freund, see Valente & Stanmeyer, *Public Aid to Parochial Schools—A Reply to Professor Freund*, 59 GEO. L.J. 59 (1970).

lic purpose and no potential divisiveness or denial of free exercise.[24] Justice Black, whose *Everson* opinion was supposedly being followed, thought it was not, and that the New York arrangement represented precisely the sort of danger he had warned against in 1947.[25] Mr. Justice Douglas agreed in a lengthy dissent which argued the centrality of books to education and asserted the essentially sectarian nature of the parochial school enterprise.[26]

Clearly Justice Black was right. The decision in *Allen* went a step beyond *Everson* toward accommodation between church and state. And yet there was an opacity to Mr. Justice White's opinion that could allow for a quick, unembarrassing turn back in the separationist direction. In *Allen*, the Court did nothing to indicate how far it was prepared to go with White's fusion of "individual benefit" and "purpose and primary effect."

Nevertheless, accommodationists could hope that this was the break in constitutional law for which they labored so long. If the gravamen of constitutionality under the Establishment Clause was to be "purpose and primary effect," and if textbooks were an acceptable sort of "good" to be distributed among children in church-related schools, then why not instruction in chemistry and foreign language? The deepest bite into parochial school treasuries was the cost of instruction. With religious vocations declining, there were fewer and fewer nuns and brothers available to teach for token salaries. Increasingly, lay teachers had to be hired. Properly and inevitably these "nonreligious" looked longingly toward parity with their public school counterparts, and they unionized. The instruction bills went up and up. If these could be met in some substantial part by public funds, it could mean a new lease on life for parochial schools. In response to this asserted need and a perceived constitutional opportunity, several state legislatures moved to provide support for the instructional budgets of nonpublic schools.[27]

Before these laws could be tested in the Supreme Court, however, Earl Warren stepped down, and the new Chief Justice, Warren

---

[24] 392 U.S. 249.   [25] *Id.* at 252.   [26] *Id.* at 256–58.

[27] A common response was to support teacher salaries, either through "purchase of service plans or direct grants." See CONN. GEN. STAT. ANN. §§ 10-281 (1971 Supp.); LA. REV. STAT. ANN. §§ 17:1322–17:1325 (1971 Supp.); MICH. STAT. ANN. §§ 15.1919 (105–16) (1971 Supp.); N.J. STAT. ANN. §§ 18A:58-38–18A:58-58 (1971 Supp.); 24 PA. STAT. §§ 5601–5608 (1971 Supp.); and R.I. GEN. LAWS §§ 16-51-1–16-51-9 (1971 Supp.). Other approaches were tuition grants, state income tax credits, and "educational voucher schemes." The respective fates of these will be dealt with presently.

Burger, took the opportunity of writing for the Court in the next major Establishment Clause case to come before it. This did not involve aid to religious institutions but rather the worrisome old question of the constitutionality of tax exemptions for churches. For decades the matter of tax exemptions had vexed theoreticians of the law of church and state.[28] If it were unconstitutional to aid religious activity by positive grants, was it any less advantageous to the churches to have the contributions required of other social institutions forgiven them? The community, it was argued, was supporting religious activity either way, through tax contributions in the case of direct grants, or through paying higher taxes in the case of exemptions. Thus, brutally, the argument for the separationist plaintiff, Walz, was that it was impossible to distinguish between a tax exemption and a grant, and that as a grant was clearly unconstitutional, it must follow that tax exemptions must fall as well.[29] The question had the potential for becoming a sort of ultimate Establishment Clause teaser, and it was mildly interesting that the new Chief Justice chose to grasp the nettle of *Walz v. Tax Commission* himself.[30]

In a somewhat apologetic tone, the Chief Justice explained that while property tax exemptions undoubtedly carried indirect economic benefits for religious institutions, and thus involved government with religious institutions, the governmental involvement in the life of the church would be far greater (amounting to impermissible "entanglement") if church properties were valued and taxed. Furthermore, the Chief Justice argued, a tax exemption was not the same as a direct grant, even though it conferred some economic benefit:[31]

> The grant of a tax exemption is not sponsorship since the government does not transfer part of its revenue to churches but simply abstains from demanding that the church support the state. No one has ever suggested that tax exemption has converted libraries, art galleries, or hospitals into arms of the state or put employees "on the public payroll."

---

[28] For a recent comment see Bittker, *Churches, Taxes, and the Constitution*, 78 YALE L.J. 1285 (1969). See also Van Alstyne, *Tax Exemption of Church Property*, 20 OHIO ST. L.J. 461 (1959).

[29] For the somewhat shabby origins of the *Walz* case see *Brief of the United States Catholic Conference, Amicus Curiae*, in Walz v. New York, 397 U.S. 664 (1970), p. 22.

[30] 397 U.S. 664 (1970).   [31] *Id.* at 675.

The underlying value of the Establishment Clause for Chief Justice Burger seemed to be the avoidance of religio-political strife, and the tax exemption safeguarded rather than imperiled that value. For government to tax was for government to become entangled, and this would breed the strife the framers had sought to avoid.[32]

Presumably, although the Court did not say so, the same reasoning would hold for federal exemptions for church incomes as well as local exemption from real property taxes. To require disclosure necessary to payment would result in governmental "entanglement" in the affairs of religious institutions. It was the idea of "impermissible entanglement," of course, that became the focus of speculation among Court watchers.

In the spring of 1970, it was difficult to assess the importance of *Walz* for the development of the Establishment Clause. The easy conclusion, to which a few jumped,[33] was that the Chief Justice's opinion moved the Court still further away from *Everson* (with its sweeping separationist language and narrow margins for aid), and in the direction indicated by *Allen*. In other words, *Walz* was treated as a harbinger of still more accommodationist decisions to come in the Burger era. Ultimately, this proved to be right, but this was far from obvious from the Court's language. On reflection, it is hard to see how tax exemptions could have lost. In their suppor-

---

[32] *Id.* at 676. It is possible to argue that a parallel underlying value of "no-entanglement" is the avoidance of subtle governmental control over the internal affairs of religious institutions. In *Walz*, Burger can be read as suggesting that this is a danger and an evil independent of any strife which the entanglement might generate. But this is a formal, logical independence. As a practical matter, the two "values" are so close to congruent that I have chosen here to treat strife-avoidance as central. It strains the imagination to conceive of a real-world situation where government would begin, by design or accident, to exercise control within a religious institution which would not quickly result in religio-political strife.

[33] See, for instance, Katz, *Radiations from Church Tax Exemption*, 1970 SUPREME COURT REVIEW 93. Professor Katz sees *Walz* as a retreat from *Everson*, but overlooks a number of awkward facts. *Inter alia*, that Justice Black went along with the majority in *Walz* without a murmur. That this was not Black's habit when he thought he was being overruled is well known. Recall his reaction in *Allen* where *Everson* was, in fact, being diluted. Justice Black may just have been fooled or lazy, of course, but his silence should have put one on one's guard against overreading Chief Justice Burger's opinion. That those who saw accommodation in the Burger notion of entanglement eventually were proved right must, however, be regarded as mitigation. For another detailed analysis of the *Walz* opinions which guessed wrong as to the way Chief Justice Burger would apply entanglement state support of the secular activities of religious institutions see Kauper, *The Walz Decision: More on the Religion Clauses of the First Amendment*, 69 MICH. L.REV. 179, 208 (1970).

tive effect they may be economically indistinguishable from grants, but psychologically, historically, and politically, there is a great deal of difference. Few prestigious scholars or interest groups were urging the Justices to find against tax exemptions.[34] Furthermore, tax exemptions were an ongoing, low-visibility governmental practice, lacking the divisive potential of new grant programs that must be openly legislated. It did not require much of an accommodationist to sustain them. What the Burger position really meant would have to await several sessions to determine. It was June of 1971 before the Court was ready to speak to the constitutionality of the sort of teacher support programs that had been so quickly legislated after *Allen.*[35]

The other opinions in *Walz* did not shed much more light on the disposition of the Justices toward aid to sectarian schools. Mr. Justice Douglas alone dissented. The author of the famous "religious people" dictum[36] pointed out that New York City provided no property tax exemption for property used for "anti-theological purposes," "atheistic purposes," or "agnostic purposes."[37] As the believer and the unbeliever were not on the same tax footing, the exemption suffered from the fatal fault of underinclusion. For Mr. Justice Douglas, a favored tax category, restricted to the conventionally religious, was a discrimination forbidden by the Establishment Clause. Mr. Justice Brennan, in his concurring opinion, dwelt on the long history of tax exemption of church property in America,[38] and underlined the Chief Justice's distinction between direct grants and exemptions.[39] Justice Harlan found that the particular exemption afforded by New York neither encouraged nor discouraged participation in religious activity, but left open the possibility that some sorts of exemptions might involve government so deeply in the activities of religious institutions as to contravene the Establishment Clause.[40] Almost in passing, Justice Harlan also suggested that perhaps the Establishment Clause should be read to apply with

---

[34] The usual constellation of separationist groups was not present in *Walz*, only the hard line secularists. Madalyn Murray O'Hair was there as amicus, as was the ACLU, and the Society of Separationists, Inc.

[35] See note 27, *supra.*

[36] Zorach v. Clauson, 343 U.S. 306, 313 (1952).

[37] 397 U.S. 700.

[38] *Id.* at 681.

[39] *Id.* at 690.

[40] *Id.* at 698.

differential force to the states and to the federal government.[41] His suggestion was to fare no better in the religion cases than it had in the speech cases.[42]

II. BURGER RAMPANT: LEMON I AND II

Lemon v. Kurtzman[43] (*Lemon I*) actually stands for three cases, joined for decision by the Court during the 1970 Term.[44] *Lemon I* was a challenge to the constitutionality of a Pennsylvania statute that provided for the "purchase" of certain specified educational services (instruction in secular subjects) for private, including church-related, schools. *Earley v. DiCenso* and *Robinson v. DiCenso* tested a Rhode Island statute that made available direct payments to teachers in nonpublic schools in amounts up to 15 percent of their regular salaries.[45] Although there were some potentially important differences between the Rhode Island and Pennsylvania cases,[46] the Chief Justice disposed of both in the same opinion.[47]

The requirements he propounded were threefold: there must be an adequate secular legislative purpose;[48] the program's purpose and primary effect must neither advance nor inhibit religion; and government must not be excessively "entangled" (administratively or politically) with religious institutions in the mounting of the program.[49] Against this standard both the Pennsylvania and Rhode Island schemes (despite certain differences in their architecture and even despite the absence of a record in the Pennsylvania case) failed. They failed on the third element of the test—excessive entanglement.

---

[41] *Id*. at 699.

[42] See Roth v. United States, 354 U.S. 476, 496 (1957).

[43] See 310 F. Supp. 35 (E.D. Pa. 1969).

[44] 403 U.S. 602 (1971).

[45] See 316 F. Supp. 112 (D. R. I. 1970).

[46] The most important of which was that *Lemon v. Kurtzman* was before the Court on pleadings alone. There was no trial record to indicate how the program was actually working.

[47] 403 U.S. 606 (1971).

[48] This is the one element of an Establishment Clause test on which *everyone* is agreed. For an extended judicial essay on the subject see Chief Justice Warren's opinion in McGowen v. Maryland, 366 U.S. 420 (1961). For a scholarly treatment, see Choper, *The Establishment Clause and Aid to Parochial Schools*, 56 CALIF. L. REV. 260 (1968).

[49] 403 U.S. at 612–13.

Only Mr. Justice White (the author of *Allen*) dissented. He would have sustained the Rhode Island statute on his 1968 textbook rationale, and sent the Pennsylvania case back for trial. While associating himself with Chief Justice Burger's opinion, Mr. Justice Douglas, joined by Justices Black and Marshall, again expanded in a concurrence upon the dangers of religiously committed teachers larding their presentations with doctrine while being supported by public funds.[50] Mr. Justice Brennan did not join the opinion of the Court but concurred separately in the result. For him, the fatal flaws in the Pennsylvania and Rhode Island statutes were not simply those of "entanglement" or, as he put it, "too close proximity" of government and religious institutions, but rather that their effect was to aid substantially the sectarian school enterprise as a whole. The Brennan position was that even if the secular educational components could easily be separated from the religious activities of church-related schools, they still could not constitutionally be aided.[51] This reluctance of Justices Brennan, Douglas, and Marshall to commit themselves to the "entanglement" approach proved consequential two years later.

What precisely did the Chief Justice mean by "excessive entanglement"? He had used the phrase in both *Walz* and *Lemon I*. Did it refer to actual administrative involvements or to the likely generation of political tensions? While a great deal of effort can be spent attempting to separate these, it seems clear that for the Chief Justice the two were inextricable. The potential political divisiveness was seen as a function of administrative penetration.[52] Because it would require close and continuing oversight to ascertain that the subsidized private school teachers were not teaching religion, the entanglement was "excessive" and thus impermissible. In the public and political reaction to *Lemon I* there were distinct echoes of the reaction, almost a quarter-century before, to *Everson*. Sepa-

---

[50] "One can imagine," he remarked, "what a religious zealot, as contrasted to a civil libertarian, can do with the Reformation or with the Inquisition." 403 U.S. at 635–36. There is no hint of humor in this argument as Mr. Justice Douglas develops it.

[51] 403 U.S. 652, 655.

[52] The question arises whether an indirect government program involving no administrative entanglement could be struck down solely because of likely political entanglement in the legislative or electoral processes. The question is important, but not one with which Chief Justice Burger grappled in *Lemon I*. In his opinion in *Nyquist* he seems to answer in the negative, but this gets ahead of the story.

rationists trumpeted the decision, and the leaders of the Catholic community gathered themselves for counterattack.

On the evening of 17 August 1971, three weeks after *Lemon 1* came down, President Nixon addressed a meeting of the Supreme Council of the Knights of Columbus in New York. On the same platform, and speaking before the President, was Cardinal Spellman's successor to the Archbishopric of New York, Terrence Cardinal Cooke. The Cardinal attacked the recent decision: "As Catholic citizens of these United States we call upon our fellow Americans for justice."[53] The President, in his turn, spoke sympathetically, if unspecifically, of the Cardinal's complaint.[54] The next morning the President breakfasted at the Waldorf with Governor Rockefeller and Attorney General Mitchell, and one of the topics on the agenda was the Governor's experience, in New York, in attempting to aid church-related schools in the face of stiff opposition.[55] Ten days later the President's Panel on Non-Public Education announced to the press it was favorably disposed toward federal tax-credit schemes to relieve parochial school parents.[56] And in the next few months a number of state legislatures moved to enact various sorts of "post *Lemon*" programs.[57]

These initiatives were of three basic sorts: tax credits, tuition grants to parents, and educational voucher arrangements. The first two provided the principal bases for the Establishment Clause

---

[53] N.Y. Times, 18 Aug. 1971, p. 1, col. 3.

[54] *Id.* at p. 23, col. 1.

[55] N.Y. Times 19 Aug. 1971, p. 22, col. 8.

[56] N.Y. Times, 26 Aug. 1971, p. 1, col. 7; and 21 April 1972, p. 45, col. 1. For final report, see *Nonpublic Education and the Public Good*, the President's Panel on Nonpublic Education of the President's Commission on School Finance, 14 April 1972.

[57] Tax credits were tried first in Minnesota before *Lemon I*. Ohio and New York followed suit. Ohio's program was declared unconstitutional in Kosgdar v. Wolman, 353 F. Supp. 744 (S.D. Ohio 1972). New York's was sustained in Committee v. Nyquist, 350 F. Supp. 655 (S.D. N.Y. 1972), but undone, as we shall see, by the Supreme Court. A federal proposal was also considered. See H.R. 16141, 92d Cong., 2d sess., the Public and Private Education Assistance Act of 1972. Tuition grants were tried in Ohio, New York, and Pennsylvania, and other states were gearing up before district courts mowed the leaders down. Wolman v. Essex, 342 F. Supp. 399 (S.D. Ohio 1972); Committee v. Nyquist, 350 F. Supp. (S.D. N.Y. 1972); Lemon v. Sloan, 340 F. Supp. 1356 (E.D. Pa. 1972). True educational voucher plans (including public schools) have not yet been attempted, but both the federal OEO and the California legislature have toyed with the idea. See Arons, *Equity, Option, and Vouchers*, 72 TEACHER'S COLL. REC. 337 (1971).

events of the spring of 1973. The third, educational vouchers, poses the last important unanswered question in the area of aid to sectarian schools. These were advertised as avoiding the excessive entanglement against which the Chief Justice had set his face.

The church-state season of 1973 opened with Chief Justice Burger still Court spokesman on Establishment Clause matters, but he was seeking to control a fractious team. *Lemon v. Kurtzman*[58] (*Lemon II*) was back before the Court on the question whether Pennsylvania sectarian schools could receive payments, under the now defunct purchase-of-service plan, for services performed before *Lemon I* was decided. It is with his opinion in *Lemon II* that solicitude toward church schools really became apparent in the Chief Justice's writing. The schools, he said, could indeed receive what was legally owed them on the night before *Lemon I*. For, while the Pennsylvania statute had involved impermissible entanglement, an unconstitutional statute is not absolutely void, but is a practical reality "on which people must rely in making decisions and in shaping their conduct."[59] Courts, he concluded, should recognize such realities.

This opinion brought a sharp dissent from Mr. Justice Douglas, with which Justices Brennan and Stewart associated themselves. "There is as much a violation of the Establishment Clause . . . whether the payment from public funds to sectarian schools involves last year, the current year, or next year."[60] Because Mr. Justice Marshall took no part, the Court was divided five to three. The three were strict separationists from the *Lemon I* majority. Thus, the Chief Justice's majority depended on the concurrence of Mr. Justice White, the most consistently accommodationist of the Justices. The veterans of the Warren era, Mr. Justice White excepted, manifested variously strong separationist tendencies where money to church schools was concerned.[61] The Chief Justice had

---

[58] 93 S. Ct. 1463 (1973).   [59] *Id.* at 1468.   [60] *Id.* at 1473.

[61] The separationism of Mr. Justice Stewart is not altogether easy to make out. In the area of governmentally sponsored religious exercises (school prayers) he is quite accommodationist. See *Schempp* 374 U.S. at 308 (dissenting opinion). And in *Sherbert v. Verner* he chided the majority Justices for creating a tension between the Free Exercise Clause—which was read, in that case, to require exemption of an individual from an otherwise valid secular regulation because of religious scruple—and the strict separationism of the school prayer cases—which allowed no governmental bending toward religion. 374 U.S. at 413–18 (concurring opinion). It was certainly no surprise to find

to carry all three other Nixon appointees with him if he were to have any hope of using the entanglement notion to move toward accommodation. Justices Douglas, Brennan, and Stewart had served notice in *Lemon I*, and Mr. Justice Marshall had previously given indication, that they were of a strict separationist bent.[62]

III. BURGER UNDONE: NYQUIST AND SLOAN

The suspicion flickering after *Lemon I* (and stronger after *Lemon II*) that the Chief Justice had left a doctrinal door open to some sort of significant relief for church-related schools was confirmed by the decisions and opinions of last Term. He had left a door open, but his brethren refused to allow him to go through it.

In the first of the cases, *Levitt v. Committee*,[63] the legislature of New York had moved in 1970, in the wake of *Allen* and before *Lemon I*, to provide for payments to private schools to compensate them for performing certain state mandated services.[64] PEARL moved to challenge the program, and in 1972, after *Lemon I*, a divided three-judge federal district court held the statute unconstitutional and granted the requested injunction.[65] It should be noted that the mandated services involved, principally, the administration of compulsory attendance laws, the compilation of health records, and the proctoring and grading of Regents' examinations and other pupil evaluation tests. The district court considered it unclear whether private-school-teacher-designed tests could qualify for compensation.[66] Nonetheless, the majority found, following *Lemon*,

---

him going along with Mr. Justice White in *Allen*, and Chief Justice Burger in *Walz*. But with *Lemon I* he voted silently with the majority against the aid programs. He has continued to do so in the elementary and secondary school aid cases. In the higher education cases, he has, as we shall see, followed the leads of Justices Burger and Powell in distinguishing such support from the elementary and secondary school aid programs.

[62] See Mr. Justice Marshall's dissent in Tilton v. Richardson, 403 U.S. 672 (1971), which will be treated below.

[63] 413 U.S. 472 (1973).

[64] Mandated Services Act of 1970, ch. 138, N.Y. Laws 863.

[65] Committee for Public Education and Religious Liberty v. Levitt, 342 F. Supp. 439 (S.D. N.Y. 1972).

[66] The majority opinion of the district court implied that teacher-devised testing could be compensated but then proceeded to deal exclusively with Regents' examinations and standardized tests on the theory that if these are impermissible under *Lemon* (and this, of course, was the conclusion toward which the majority was steaming) then teacher-designed tests were also clearly out. This neatly removed the need to resolve the ques-

an impermissible administrative entanglement of government and sectarian institution.

Immediately the district court's application of *Lemon* to *Levitt* was criticized as "mechanical" and uncomprehending of the spirit of Burger's 1971 effort. It was pointed out that there was a great difference between policing what and how teachers teach (the entanglement contemplated by *Lemon*) and the fairly simple administrative task of overseeing the distribution of compensation for giving standardized tests. There was little opportunity for the most zealous sectarian teacher, so the criticism went, to slip in any religious messages into what New York was paying for in *Levitt*.[67]

In the outcome (if not the reasoning) the *Levitt* district court got the best of this argument. In an opinion for the Court, Chief Justice Burger himself approved the reading given his *Lemon* opinion below, but he gave himself a somewhat easier job of it than had the district court. Rather than exclude the possibility of teacher-prepared exams from statutory concept, the Chief Justice concluded from the arguments that these were to be compensated under the statute and buttressed his conclusion with reference to both appellees' and appellants' briefs.[68] In fact, according to this version, teacher-generated testing accounted for the bulk of the testing which could, under the 1970 law, be compensated by New York. Rather than writing as if the compensation were for standardized tests, the Chief Justice wrote as if the compensation was for teacher-designed tests. Testing, he observed, was simply one medium of teaching, and the policing of teaching would lead precisely to the sort of administrative-and-then-political entanglement that *Lemon I* proscribed.[69] As the New York legislature had intertwined compensation for services that would result in entanglement with services that might not, the whole package was necessarily disallowed. It was not the task of the Court to untangle the forbidden from the possibly allowable for New York.[70]

In *Levitt* the implications of Chief Justice Burger's approach, one

---

tions: (1) whether the statute contemplated such payments (supposedly unclear from its language and legislative history) and (2) whether those in the New York Department of Education charged with the administering of the act entertained the assumption that such payments were authorized (supposedly unclear from the trial record).

[67] Note, *Nonestablishment of Religion*, 86 HARV. L. REV. 1068 (1973).

[68] 413 U.S. at 475, n.3.

[69] *Id.* at 480.   [70] *Id.* at 482.

might even say his strategy, on the question of aid to sectarian schools became much clearer. There was something more to it (or, perhaps, less to it) than the threefold test of *Lemon I*. For him, the primary evil to be avoided emerged as direct aid to religious activity. The intent of the legislature must be other than to advance such activity. And when support is furnished directly to church-related institutions the state must exercise itself to see that none of its monies are used for religious activity.[71] If accomplishing this requirement would be too complicated, or would require great administrative penetration of church school by state, then the secondary, but also fatal, evil of entanglement emerges. This administrative entanglement is socially undesirable and constitutionally forbidden because it leads to the sorts of political entanglements and strife against which the framers of the First Amendment warned. Put this way, the open doctrinal door to accommodation of church schools is obvious. If the aid were to be indirect, the *Lemon I* rules need not be applied. It is the direct nature of the confrontation between church and state that necessitates separating the aided secular sanction from the unaided religious activity and creates the occasion for "entanglement." Alter the nature of the governmental program, eliminate the interface, and the need to separate secular and religious activity vanishes, and with it the potential for administrative and finally political entanglements. The hint of accommodation which some had thought they heard in *Walz*, and even in *Lemon I*,[72] was heavy in *Levitt*. The constitutional theory that would allow for

[71] *Id.* at 481. It is pertinent to ask why, if the "direct-indirect" distinction is beginning to emerge in Chief Justice Burger's *Levitt* opinion, three Justices, Stewart, Blackmun, and Powell, associated themselves with Burger's *Levitt* opinion when in *Nyquist* and *Sloan*, decided the same day, they deserted him. Mr. Justice Powell firmly rejected that distinction. It might be suggested either that the distinction was not readily apparent in *Levitt*, or that the three Justices were very dull fellows to take contradictory positions on the same day. A possible explanation is that in *Levitt* the outcome was right for Justices Stewart, Blackmun, and Powell, and, that being so, they were prepared to stay with the Chief Justice's short opinion and not write separately. It is also certainly true that the expression of the direct-indirect distinction is drawn much less sharply by the Chief Justice in his *Levitt* majority opinion than in his *Nyquist* dissent.

[72] I should have been pleased had I taken those hints more seriously. In fact, I saw the "direct-indirect" possibility after *Lemon I*, saw that certain state legislatures were acting on it, and declared that they were reading Burger incorrectly. They were right about Burger but wrong about the eventual outcome. I was right about the likely outcome, but wrong about what the Chief Justice was up to with "entanglement." RELIGION 114. There is not much satisfaction in being right for the wrong reason.

governmental relief of the church schools, for which the President had hoped, was at hand.

But there was no Court majority to support it. Decided on the same day as *Levitt* were *Nyquist v. Committee* and *Sloan v. Lemon* and they tested the Burger thesis. *Nyquist* involved still another New York statute,[73] this one passed after *Lemon I*, which had three major provisions. First, it made available direct grants for "maintenance and repair" of facilities and equipment to nonpublic schools serving high concentrations of pupils from low-income families. Second, it offered tuition grants ($50 for elementary school, $100 for high school, up to 50 percent of actual tuition to parents of nonpublic school children with incomes of $5,000 per year or less). Third, for parents above the $5,000 income line, a sliding scale of state income tax deductions was established.[74]

On the first program, Chief Justice Burger had no trouble finding unconstitutionality under the Establishment Clause, "because it is a direct aid to religion."[75] It was "direct" in the literal sense that the money flowed directly from the treasury to the school. No provision was made for separation of secular and religious uses, and the Chief Justice thought *Lemon I* and *Levitt* covered the situation. On the grants and the tax credits, however, he would have sustained the New York law.

These programs were not direct and that was crucial:[76]

> While there is no straight line running through our decisions interpreting the Establishment and Free Exercise clauses of the First Amendment, our cases do, it seems to me, lay down one solid, basic principle: that the Establishment Clause does not forbid governments, state or federal, from enacting a program of general welfare under which benefits are distributed to private individuals, even though many of these individuals may elect to use those benefits in ways that "aid" religious instruction or worship.

In support of this, the Chief Justice proceeded to produce that oldest chestnut of the accommodationists argument, the "G. I. Bill"

---

[73] Health and Safety Grants for Nonpublic School Children, N.Y. Laws 1972, c. 414, § 1, amending N.Y. Educ. Law, Art. 12, §§ 549–53 (Supp. 1972).

[74] "Estimated Net Benefit" to a one-nonpublic-pupil family earning $9,000 or less was $50. At $24,999 it was $12, and cut-off came at $25,000.

[75] 93 S. Ct. at 2989.   [76] *Ibid.*

aid which eligible veterans could use where they chose.[77] To sum
up the matter, he observed:[78]

> government aid to individuals generally stands on an entirely
> different footing from direct aid to religious institutions. I say
> "generally" because it is obviously possible to conjure hypo-
> thetical statutes that constitute either a subterfuge for direct
> aid to religious institutions or a discriminatory enactment fa-
> voring religious activities over nonreligious activities. Thus, a
> State could not enact a statute providing for a $10 gratuity to
> everyone who attended religious services weekly. Such a law
> would plainly be governmental sponsorship of religious activi-
> ties; no statutory preamble expressing purely secular legislative
> motives would be persuasive. But at least where the state law
> is genuinely directed at enhancing the freedom of individ-
> uals to exercise a recognized right, even one involving both
> secular and religious consequences as is true of the right of
> parents to send their children to private schools, see *Pierce* v.
> *Society of Sisters*, 268 U.S. 510 (1925), then the Establish-
> ment Clause no longer has a prohibitive effect.

This was the sort of theory of the Establishment Clause which accommodationists had thought to be heralded by *Allen*. Where *Allen*
had been a breakthrough, this would have been a victory. But in
Nyquist the theory had been tumbled into dissent. The Chief Justice carried only Justices White[79] and Rehnquist[80] with him.

This six-to-three alignment hardened further in the third school

---

[77] The separationist response to this has been the lame one that the G.I. Bill funds
were actually a part of the soldier's pay—saved for him, presumably, by a benevolent
and forward-looking government.

[78] 93 S. Ct. at 2990–91.

[79] Mr. Justice White associated himself, in part, with the Chief Justice's dissent. He
would have sustained not only the New York and Pennsylvania tuition grants and the
New York tax credit but the New York repair and maintenance grants as well. "I am
quite unreconciled," he wrote, "to the Court's decision in *Lemon* v. *Kurtzman*." *Id.*
at 2996.

[80] Mr. Justice Rehnquist joined the Chief Justice's opinion and also wrote for himself.
He scored the opinion of the Court heavily, and especially its failure to distinguish the
New York tax credit program from *Walz*. He pointed out that Brennan, who had aligned
himself with Powell's majority opinion, had himself enthusiastically endorsed the distinction between tax relief and granted funds in a concurring opinion in *Walz*. "While it is
true," Rehnquist remarked, "that the Court reached its result in *Walz* in part by examining the unbroken history of property tax exemptions for religious organizations in this
country, there is no suggestion in the opinion that only those particular tax exemption
schemes that have roots in pre-Revolutionary days are sustainable against an Establishment
Clause challenge." *Id.* at 2979. The decision in *Nyquist* also accomplished the scuttling
of the federal tax credit proposal.

case decided that day, *Sloan v. Lemon.*[81] In the wake of *Lemon I*, the Pennsylvania legislature enacted a new law, the "Parent Reimbursement Act for Non-Public Education,"[82] and the litigious Mr. Lemon (with interest group support ranging from the Pennsylvania CLU to Americans United) sued to enjoin its effectuation. As with New York's scheme of grants and tax credits, the Pennsylvania statute was prefaced by a legislative finding of fact that sought to establish a public purpose for the program. In addition, in an elaborate attempt to skirt the entanglement language of *Lemon I*, a "Pennsylvania Parent Assistance Authority" was created to disburse the funds while commanded to avoid all involvement with any nonpublic schools. The dissenting trio in *Nyquist* would have sustained the Pennsylvania program. But Mr. Justice Powell saw no distinguishing difference between the Pennsylvania and New York laws, nor did Justices Brennan, Stewart, Marshall, and Blackmun.

What can one make of Chief Justice Burger's performance in the *Lemon I* to *Nyquist-Sloan* sequence? In discussing *Lemon I* in his 1971 article, Giannella argued:[83]

> In the *Allen* case in 1967, the Court went over the verge and sanctioned the free loan of textbooks. In *Lemon* the Court sought to scramble back, reaching out for any support it could find on the constitutional landscape. The nearest at hand was the "excessive entanglement" notion recently enunciated in the *Walz* case and the Court seized on it.

It now seems that this assessment was wrong—at least as far as Chief Justice Burger, the author of "entanglement," is concerned. Far from being a branch clutched in panic, *Walz* appears a carefully planted post which was to allow the Court to negotiate the "slippery slope" of aid to church schools by disallowing any program which brought government into direct contact with church schools (*Lemon I* and *Levitt*) but allowing certain forms of aid such as the tax credits and parental tuition grants as in *Nyquist* and *Sloan*.

Those accommodationists who saw *Walz* as encouraging were right in 1970 and wrong, after *Lemon I*, in 1971 to suppose that the

---

[81] 93 S. Ct. 2982 (1973).

[82] Laws of Pa., 1971, Act 92, 24 PA. STAT. ANN. §§ 5701–09 (Supp. 1972). The program provided $75 for each dependent in nonpublic elementary school and $150 for each dependent in nonpublic high school—providing the amount of the grant not exceed the actual tuition paid in each case.

[83] Giannella, note 2 *supra*, at 148.

threefold test used there, which included "entanglement" as its final element, meant disaster for their cause. It now seems that Chief Justice Burger had only been waiting to drop the second shoe or, to alter the figure, to reveal the accommodationist edge of the "entanglement" notion. His necessary allies, Justices Blackmun and Powell, however, could not be persuaded. Mr. Justice Powell plucked the issue from him just as the Chief Justice was about to complete a design perhaps three years in the making.[84]

IV. POWELL EMERGENT: THE "EFFECT-OF-ADVANCING" APPROACH

The conclusion is irresistible that the four separationist veterans of the Warren Court (Justices Douglas, Brennan, Marshall, and, on money matters, Stewart) never felt themselves committed to the Chief Justice's approach to the meaning of the Establishment Clause.[85] They went along with him in *Walz* and *Lemon I* because the outcomes were right, not the reasoning. When the true accommodationist drift in the Chief Justice's thinking revealed itself, they abandoned him. That they are for the moment arrayed behind Mr. Justice Powell's opinions in *Nyquist* and *Sloan* may mean little more than did their alliance with Chief Justice Burger. Nonetheless, Mr. Justice Powell's would seem to be the "approach of the hour," and his separationism seems to accord roughly with the dominant disposition of the Constitution.

It must be realized that Justices Powell and Burger are agreed on

---

[84] It is possible to argue, of course, that the Chief Justice simply switched sides between 1971 and 1973—that Giannella and Morgan were right in seeing *Lemon I* simply as a scramble back toward *Everson*, and that the public reaction to *Lemon I*, and the repeated desire of his friend and President, Richard Nixon, to find some way of aiding church-related schools, persuaded the Chief Justice to come about by tacking onto the "primary effect" notion a direct-indirect distinction which had not previously been part of his thinking on the subject. Looking back over *Walz* and *Lemon I* from the perspective of *Levitt* and *Nyquist*, I think the internal evidence is against the crude "switch-and-quick-to-please-Dick" theory. The Chief Justice had been looking forward to accommodation since *Walz*. He saw *Lemon I* as a step toward his goal.

[85] Mr. Justice Brennan never formally associated himself with the "excessive entanglement" approach. He concurred in the result in *Walz* and in *Lemon I*. Mr. Justice Douglas dissented in *Walz*, but, while adding an opinion of his own, was associated with the majority opinion in *Lemon I*. Justices Stewart and Marshall went along with Burger's work both in *Walz* and *Lemon I*. Of the Nixon appointees, Mr. Justice Blackmun did not arrive in time for *Walz* but went along in *Lemon I*. For Justices Powell and Rehnquist the 1973 cases were first efforts at interpreting the Establishment Clause.

the form (that is, the words) of the test to be applied. It is the familiar threefold test of *Lemon I:* secular purpose, no primary effect of advancing or inhibiting religion, no excessive entanglement. Mr. Justice Powell claimed to be applying it in *Nyquist* and *Sloan,* and carefully repeated it in *Hunt v. McNair.*[86] To this extent that test can be said to be settled doctrine. The heart of the difference between Justices Powell and Burger has to do with the way they read "primary effect," the second element in the test.

As Chief Justice Burger's position finally emerged in his *Nyquist* opinion, primary effect is determined principally by who is the immediate, direct beneficiary. If the direct beneficiary is a religious institution, then the support can be used only for secular purposes and this apportioning must be policed. If the policing significantly involves government in the affairs of the religious institution, there is excessive entanglement that requires a finding of unconstitutionality.

For Mr. Justice Powell, it matters little who gets the money directly. Nor does it matter that there is some substantial benefit of a nonreligious sort accruing to the direct grantee. If there is a substantial benefit to a religious institution, albeit at some remove from government, this is still the "primary effect." An effect is "primary" if it substantially "advances" religious activity, and it is not the less primary by virtue of standing second in a chronological sequence of effects from the same grant.

To the church-state *aficionado* it was clear from the beginning of Mr. Justice Powell's opinion that he was heading in a strict separationist direction. Madison and Jefferson are invoked by the second paragraph. Praise is lavished on the *Memorial and Remonstrance,* and Virginia's experience is urged as "one of the greatest chapters in the history of this Country's adoption of the essentially revolutionary notion of separation between Church and State."[87]

New York's maintenance and repair grants were disposed of with measured sternness. These, after all, were direct grants, with no attempt made to apportion them strictly to the secular dimensions of sectarian school activity. Here, of course, the Chief Justice and Mr. Justice Rehnquist agreed. Only Mr. Justice White voted to sustain these grants. Turning to New York's tuition reimbursement, Mr. Justice Powell posited that such unapportioned grants, if made

---

[86] 93 S. Ct. 2868.   [87] *Id.* at 2958–59, 2964.

directly to the schools, would surely be unconstitutional. "The controlling question here," he observed, "is whether the fact that the grants are delivered to parents rather than schools is of such significance as to compel a contrary result."[88] This framed the issue concisely. The answer was equally crisp.

In holding that the indirect quality of the benefit did not render it constitutional, Mr. Justice Powell showed himself a worthy separationist successor to Justice Black. Indeed, Black's angry dissent from *Allen* was invoked to underline the point. Justice Black had warned of a variety of schemes the Court would find itself approving if it took what he regarded as the fatal first step of approving the New York textbook law. Mr. Justice Powell pridefully responded that Black's gloomy prediction was proved wrong. The important separationist lines were being held:[89]

> His [Black's] fears regarding religious buildings and religious teachers have not come to pass, . . . and insofar as tuition grants constitute a means of "pick[ing] up . . . the bills for the religious schools," neither has his greatest fear materialized. But the ingenious plans for channelling state aid to sectarian schools that periodically reach this Court abundantly support the wisdom of Justice Black's prophesy.

Clearly, Mr. Justice Powell saw the New York program as "offering to pick up the bills," and the parents as mere channels employed to that end. That New York's tuition grants program did other things as well was beside the point. It had the "impermissible effect" of substantially "advancing" religious institutions. This was the primary effect regardless of any others that might occur before it or simultaneously with it.

In the matter of New York's tax credit scheme (the third program embodied in the statute attacked by PEARL in *Nyquist*) Mr. Justice Powell had a somewhat harder time, and wrote less forcefully. The trouble lay in distinguishing *Walz*. Mr. Justic Powell was unembarrassed by participation in *Walz*. He concluded that the credits advanced religion just as surely as tuition grants (although more indirectly). But what of the briskly urged argument that *Walz* stood for the principle that an exemption did *not* have the same constitutional significance as a grant? Mr. Justice Powell's first appeal was to the antiquity of tax exemptions of church prop-

---

[88] *Id.* at 2969.   [89] *Id.* at 2972.

erty. But recognizing the vulnerability of this defense, he rushed on to argue that the result in *Walz* was dictated by the necessity of accommodating the requirements of the Establishment Clause to those of the Free Exercise Clause:[90]

> Thus, if taxation was regarded as a form of "hostility" toward religion, "exemption constitut[ed] a reasonable and balanced attempt to guard against those dangers." . . . Special tax benefits, however, cannot be squared with the principle of neutrality established by the decisions of this Court. To the contrary, insofar as such benefits render assistance to parents who send their children to sectarian schools, their purpose and inevitable effect are to aid and advance religious institutions.

There were difficulties with this position. Why was a tax on all real property, some of which may be devoted to religious purposes, "hostile" to religion (thus *requiring* exemption), and a tax on incomes, portions of which may be devoted to advancing religion, not hostile to religion? Furthermore, income tax deduction of contributions to religious institutions has been a constant feature of American internal revenue arrangements. It is more than a little hard to understand why a pious Roman Catholic may be allowed to reduce his income tax liability at one point on his return by deducting his donations to his parish, but constitutionally forbidden a credit on another point in his return, for part of the tuition of his children at parochial school. As if in recognition of such problems, Mr. Justice Powell remarked, finally, that *Walz* "is a product of the same dilemma and inherent tension found in most government-aid-to-religion controversies."[91]

Mr. Justice Powell fared much better, when after escaping the problems of distinguishing *Walz*, he settled down to explain why his reading of "primary effect" was the correct one.[92] Just as with the formal "test," the primary value in the case of Establishment Clause limitations on governmental aid to religious institutions was the same for Mr. Justice Powell as for Chief Justice Burger: the avoidance of religio-political strife. But for the Chief Justice that strife was seen as a likely function either of unapportioned direct

---

[90] *Id.* at 2975–76.

[91] *Id.* at 2976.

[92] The question of possible entanglements in the New York programs need not be dealt with, Mr. Justice Powell concluded, because they were unconstitutional in any case on the "primary effect" test. *Ibid.*

aid to religious activity or direct aid apportioned to the secular activities of religious institutions which involves such continuing and intrusive governmental policing as excessive entanglement. Mr. Justice Powell does not see that the fact that aid to church institutions is indirect makes it any less likely to result in creedal strife: "competition among religious sects for political and religious supremacy has occasioned considerable civil strife."[93]

For Chief Justice Burger the direct-indirect distinction is legally crucial because he sees it as behaviorally significant. Indirect aids need not be constitutionally excluded because they do not run the same risks of social disturbance as direct aids. For Mr. Justice Powell, governmental programs which make life significantly easier for religious institutions are as likely to cause political trouble whether they are direct or indirect, whatever other social purposes they serve, or however scrupulously they may be administered. Political campaigns may be mounted to raise or lower the amounts of tuition grants and tax credits just as easily as they could be to raise or lower direct payments to sectarian schools for teachers or maintenance costs.

Put another way, what is involved between the two Justices are varying perceptions of where troublesome tensions develop in the American political order. The Chief Justice focuses on actual administrative involvements as the triggers of discord. If administrative confrontations are absent and there is no direct subsidizing of religious activities, there is less cause to worry about religio-political strife. Mr. Justice Powell focuses on the legislative process. For him the creedal strife, against which (almost everyone agrees) the framers were seeking to hedge in the First Amendment, arises as easily in legislative corridors as in principals' offices and state education departments. There will be struggling over funding levels whether the aid is direct or indirect. Chief Justice Burger is not insensitive to the danger of sectarian warfare in the legislative-allocative process; he simply considers it unlikely if the form of the aid is indirect. Ultimately, Chief Justice Burger's accommodationist "direct-indirect" version of the *Lemon I* test and Mr. Justice Powell's separationist "effect of advancing" version rest on these differing assertions about what causes people to behave in particular ways, and the brief opinions in *Sloan* confirm this contrast.

---

[93] *Id.* at 2977.

V. The Higher Education Distinction

What are now the limits of the permissible? What sorts of supportive arrangement between government and church schools may still pass muster? The marginal pupil benefits (bus transportation, hot lunches, textbooks,[94] and the like) are still acceptable. There seems little enthusiasm on the Court to reverse *Everson* or *Allen*.[95] But perhaps the most significant bend in the "church-state wall in education" involves aid to religiously affiliated colleges and universities. Decided on the same day as *Lemon I* was *Tilton v. Richardson*,[96] in which the Court engaged the question of the implications of the Establishment Clause for higher education, and distinguished church-related colleges and universities from elementary and secondary schools. Decided the same day as *Nyquist* was *Hunt v. McNair*[97] which confirmed that distinction.

In the early 1960s several states (notably New York) began experimenting with programs of aid to private institutions of higher learning within their borders in the form of tuition grants. After the passage of the federal Higher Education Facilities Act of 1963,[98] several states (notably Maryland) followed this federal model and began providing "brick and mortar" support to their private colleges and universities. In 1966 the Maryland Court of Appeals took a tough separationist line in response to arguments of First Amendment unconstitutionality by the Horace Mann League.[99] For the Maryland Court, there could be no support to sectarian (meaning identifiably religious) institutions. Considering such factors as the stated purpose of the institution, the composition of the faculty, and the financial relationships with denominational bodies, the Maryland Court found that of the four institutions involved, only Hood College, with its nominal attachment to the United Church of

---

[94] Cf. Norwood v. Harrison, 93 S. Ct. 2804 (1973), where the Court was concerned with textbooks for private racially segregated schools.

[95] There may be some. See the discussion of Mr. Justice Marshall's views in the text *infra*, at notes 114–15.

[96] 403 U.S. 603 (1971).

[97] 93 S. Ct. 2868 (1973).

[98] 77 Stat. 364, repealed, 86 Stat. 303 (1972), as amended, 20 U.S.C. §§ 711–21 (1964 ed. and Supp. V). For an excellent summary of the law as of mid-1970, see Gellhorn & Greenawalt, The Sectarian College and the Public Purse (1970).

[99] Horace Mann League v. Board of Public Works, 242 Md. 645 (1966).

Christ, was "non-sectarian" and eligible. The United States Supreme Court declined to consider the case,[100] and so the matter of grants to colleges and universities rested until 1971.

Tilton was the culmination of a separationist challenge to the 1963 Federal Act as implemented in Connecticut. The arguments made concerning the federal grants to four Connecticut colleges (all with Catholic affiliations) were substantially the same as those made earlier concerning the Maryland grants. This time, however, the Supreme Court was faced with a decision of a three-judge Federal District Court disallowing all the grants as violative of the Establishment Clause, and the Justices did not duck.

Chief Justice Burger, speaking for a plurality of the Court including Justices Harlan, Stewart, and Blackmun, sustained the grants. Rather than proceeding as had the Court of Appeals of Maryland, by examining each institution involved for signs of fatal sectarianism, the crucial point for the Chief Justice was the distinction between institutions of higher learning and elementary and secondary schools. College students were less impressionable than younger persons, and institutions of higher learning (even though they might have ties to religious organizations) were not characteristically so devoted as parochial primary and secondary schools to propagating the faith. Furthermore, the Chief Justice argued, the sort of aid given (buildings) was not likely to involve governmental agents in close and continued monitoring of the work of the recipient institutions. The degree of entanglement was not sufficient to require invalidation under the Establishment Clause.

Chief Justice Burger did concede that it might be possible for a particular college or university to be so extensively engaged in the propagation of religious doctrine as to disqualify it from participation altogether. The record, however, did not indicate that this was the case with any of the Connecticut institutions at bar. Chief Justice Burger's idea of what was "too sectarian to take" seemed narrower than that of the Maryland Court of Appeals in the 1966 case. It was hard to become "entangled" with colleges, especially when government was buying only bricks and mortar and not contributing directly to anyone's salary or the support of any particular program, which could require continuing review. Certainly some policing would be necessary to make sure that the federally granted

[100] 385 U.S. 97 (1966).

buildings were not used for specifically religious activities, but this was a tolerable level of involvement.[101]

There were four dissenters in *Tilton*. Mr. Justice Douglas, joined by Justices Black and Marshall, found the distinction between elementary and secondary education and higher education unpersuasive. The grants conferred a substantial benefit on church-affiliated institutions (the four Connecticut campuses) and that was the end of the matter. To twist the knife, Mr. Justice Douglas went on to speak of the entanglement that would result from the governmental "surveillance" of federally assisted facilities necessary to insure that they were not converted to religious purposes. That the surveillance might be any easier when the issue was college buildings rather than primary school teachers' salaries was labeled "sophistry." Writing separately,[102] Mr. Justice Brennan also refused to accept the distinction between higher and "lower" education, and argued further that the suggestion that policing the program would not involve entanglement was fatuous.

The swing vote between Chief Justice Burger's four-vote plurality opinion and the four dissenters was that of Mr. Justice White. Once assured by the record that the federally assisted facilities of the Connecticut institutions were not used for actual religious exercises, he would have sustained the act on his *Allen* grounds, a combination of "individual benefit" and "purpose and primary effect."

The significant point about *Tilton* is the fragility of the higher education distinction. There were only four votes to support it. *Hunt* is, therefore, rather remarkable. For on the same day that Mr. Justice Powell was giving a separationist reading to *Lemon I* he was also shoring up the shaky higher education of *Tilton*. Over the dissent of Mr. Justice Brennan (with Justices Douglas and Marshall joining), Mr. Justice Powell sustained an arrangement under the South Carolina Educational Facilities Authority Act[103] by which

---

[101] Although Chief Justice Burger wrote only for a plurality, all the Justices were agreed that the provision of the act that lifted the ban on religious activities in federally supported buildings twenty years after their completion (and the loans were amortized) was unconstitutional. Once federal dollars had been used, if only to defray the costs to the institutions of borrowing money commercially, the "period of federal interest" was the life of the facility. 403 U.S. at 683.

[102] In a single opinion for all three cases, he explained his concurrence in *Lemon I* and his dissent in *Tilton*. 93 S. Ct. at 2879.

[103] S. C. CODE ANN. §§ 22–41 *et seq.* (cum. supp. 1971).

revenue bonds were issued to provide for construction of facilities at the Baptist College at Charleston.

Mr. Justice Powell faithfully recited the threefold *Lemon I* test.[104] The purpose of the South Carolina statute was "manifestly" secular. Here there was no difficulty. But on the issue of "primary purpose," did the program not advance religion? Mr. Justice Powell said no, because the institution involved was not itself very seriously involved in advancing religion:[105]

> Aid normally may be thought to have a primary effect of advancing religion when it flows to an institution in which religion is so pervasive that a substantial portion of its functions are subsumed in the religious mission or when it funds a specifically religious activity in an otherwise substantially secular setting.

Passing on to the final element in the test—the possibility of excessive entanglement—Mr. Justice Powell invoked Chief Justice Burger's *Tilton* arguments to the effect that since "religious indoctrination is not a substantial purpose or activity of these church-related colleges and universities,"[106] and since the form of aid (buildings) is not one that lends itself to abuse, only modest policing is needed, and excessive entanglement is not likely.

Mr. Justice Brennan followed the lines of his *Tilton* dissent. In addition, he suggested that South Carolina's program would entail even more continuing involvement of government in the life of the church-related institutions than did the Federal Act sustained in 1971. He did not accept the higher education distinction and he did not see how *Lemon I* kind of entanglement would be avoided (although it should be remembered he had never accepted the proposition that the secular activities of religious institutions could be aided at all).

VI. Brennan-Douglas-Marshall Recalcitrant: The Super-Separationist Alternative

Thus far I have concentrated on Warren Burger and Lewis Powell as the Establishment Clause protagonists. In fact, Mr. Justice Brennan has blazed a lonely path in aid-to-school cases, and has lately shown that he can attract the support of Justices Douglas

---

[104] Hunt v. McNair, 93 S. Ct. 2868, 2873 (1973).

[105] *Id.* at 2874.   [106] 403 U.S. at 687, quoted 93 S. Ct. at 2876.

and Marshall.[107] The difficulty with Mr. Justice Brennan's position is not with the consistency of his words but with their meaning. In several Establishment Clause cases since *Schempp* in which Mr. Justice Brennan has written separately, he has urged the same test for constitutionality:[108]

> What the Framers meant to foreclose, and what our decisions under the Establishment Clause have forbidden, are those involvements of religious with secular institutions which (a) serve the essentially religious activities of religious institutions; (b) employ organs of government for essentially religious means to serve governmental ends, where secular means would suffice.

The best indication as to the intention of this language, is the *Lemon I* concurrence (*cum Tilton* dissent) in which, as noted above, Mr. Justice Brennan denies that secular activities of sectarian schools can be supported at all, even if they could be cleanly separated (for purposes of administration) from religious activity. "I do not read *Pierce* or *Allen*," he wrote, "as supporting the proposition that public subsidy of a sectarian institution's secular training is permissible state involvement."[109]

For Mr. Justice Brennan, to subsidize a chemistry teacher in a parochial school is, apparently, to employ an essentially religious means to serve governmental ends when a secular means (presumably an expanded public school system) could do the job. To provide tuition grants and tax credits for parents whose children attend church-related schools is, apparently, to serve the essentially religious activities of religious institutions. Mr. Justice Brennan opposes governmental "policing" of the activities of religious institutions, but this is a secondary concern. There is little question that Mr. Justice Brennan's separationism is stronger than Mr. Justice Powell's. Despite this the fit between the views of Justices Powell and Brennan is much tighter than that between Justices Brennan and Burger. If, however, Mr. Justice Powell should be tempted in the future to distinguish any significant form of aid to church-related elementary and secondary schools, one can look for Mr. Jus-

---

[107] They joined Mr. Justice Brennan's opinion in *Hunt*. 93 S. Ct. at 2877.

[108] See 374 U.S. at 294–95; 397 U.S. at 680–81; 403 U.S. at 643; 93 S. Ct. at 2877. It may be presumed that by "secular institutions" Mr. Justice Brennan means government at its various levels.

[109] 403 U.S. at 655.

tice Brennan in dissent (as in *Hunt*) or, should the composition of the Court change, Mr. Justice Brennan might emerge the spokesman for a super-separationist majority.

Mr. Justice Douglas has also written extensively on Establishment Clause cases, and while his work does not include the persistent urging of a particular form of words, he rejects the higher education distinction and clearly shares the view that it is impermissible for government to finance the secular components of a sectarian school's program, even if this could be done without administrative entanglement.[110] Mr. Justice Douglas did join the Court's opinion in *Lemon I*, an association of which, among the super-separationists, only Brennan is innocent. But Mr. Justice Douglas has over the years demonstrated a separationism stricter than Mr. Justice Brennan's.[111]

Mr. Justice Douglas dissented in *Allen*, while Mr. Justice Brennan was silent in an accommodating majority spoken for by Mr. Justice White. And in *Walz*, Mr. Justice Douglas also dissented forcefully, while Mr. Justice Brennan concurred in the result. While it is not clear how seriously we are still meant to take the suggestion made in his concurrence in *Engel v. Vitale*,[112] that there might be something suspect about the national motto, Mr. Justice Douglas has a clear claim to being the strictest separationist now sitting.[113]

It is not possible to discuss Mr. Justice Marshall's separationism with precision. He has neither voted sufficiently nor written at all on this question. But a guess would place him closer to Mr. Justice Douglas than to Mr. Justice Brennan. Mr. Justice Marshall associated himself with Mr. Justice Douglas's concurrence on the Rhode Island programs that were dealt with under the *Lemon I* rubric,[114]

---

[110] *Id.* at 641.

[111] In discussing Mr. Justice Douglas's separationism, the problem of what to make of his *Zorach* opinion arises (see note 36 *supra*). For a suggestion in this regard see Religion at 133. The proximity of the *Zorach* decision day to the 1952 Democratic presidential convention might also be remarked.

[112] 370 U.S. at 438.

[113] Of former Justices, Black would come closest, of course, but he did join the *Walz* majority. It should also be remembered that Mr. Justice Douglas was the lone dissenter when Warren upheld Sunday closing laws against Establishment Clause attack in McGowan v. Maryland, 366 U.S. 420, 561 (1961). Frankfurter's separatism seemed roughly to match Black's, and it is useless to speculate as to how Jackson and Rutledge, the *Everson* dissenters, would have behaved in later cases.

[114] Mr. Justice Marshall took no part in *Lemon II* itself, but he associated himself with Mr. Justice Douglas's concurrence in *Farley* and *Robinson*.

but also with the Chief Justice's opinion in that case. Although he has yet to set forth his views on the Establishment Clause and education, he dropped a fascinating hint in *Lemon I*, concurring with Mr. Justice Douglas's opinion "while intimating no view as to the continuing vitality of *Everson v. Board of Education*, 330 U.S. 1 (1947)."[115] If this bespeaks a disposition to question even the marginal pupil benefits (such as bus transportation), then Mr. Justice Douglas may have to share his separationist mantle.

At the moment, then, the disposition of the Court is three to three to three. An accommodationist bloc (with Justices White [the most fervent], Burger, and Rehnquist), a super separationist bloc (Justices Brennan, Douglas, and Marshall), and a moderately separationist bloc (Justices Stewart, Blackmun, and Powell). It is the moderately separationist three who account for the difference in result between *Nyquist* and *Hunt*. Theirs are the "swing votes" and, therefore, the targets at which advocates in any future cases will be aiming.

VII. THE UNPROMISING FUTURE OF VOUCHER PLANS

The last interesting policy question, and the lingering hope for public support of those who manage the church-related schools, is whether the Court (that is, the middle three) can be moved to find a way of distinguishing some form of educational voucher plan from the forms of aid struck down in *Nyquist* and *Sloan*. Can a voucher plan be devised that will satisfy Mr. Justice Powell, or which can credibly be said to be distinguishable from *Nyquist?*

In discussing voucher plans one must take special pains to be clear what one is talking about. True voucher plans are alternatives to traditional educational financing. Instead of the public schools being funded completely and directly by government and private schools' being supported by gifts and tuitions, all children in a voucher district would be isued a chit, redeemable by any participating school from the public treasury either at face value or for the actual cost of the educational services rendered as determined by some set of formulas. The child would take his chit to the school of his (or his parents') choice. It would not matter whether a school was public or private, only whether it qualified to participate in the program. Suggested criteria for participation would require that a

---

[115] 403 U.S. at 642.

school meet minimum standards for facilities, teacher training, and curricula; that the chit be accepted as full payment of tuition and fees; and that there be no racial discrimination in admissions. It is suggested that a free market in educational services would be created. There is no such plan operating now. All the "voucher programs" attempted thus far have been private school tuition grant schemes in disguise. [116] Many commentators, in fact, have come to use "grants" and "vouchers" interchangeably, as if "voucher" referred only to the mechanism by which grants are made. But the basic voucher idea[117] is still alive and may gain momentum from last Term's decisions. Given the way in which the word "voucher" was used and misused in the state legislative reaction to *Lemon I*,[118] it is important to try to determine just what constitutional life, if any, is left to voucher plans.

---

[116] Thus far, both the federal (OEO) experiments, and the proposals entertained by most state legislatures have been severely treated. The legislatures of California, Indiana, Illinois, Iowa, Minnesota, Missouri, and Texas have all had plans before them which have been called "voucher plans," but except for California's, all have been tuition-grant plans. OEO has sponsored one pilot program in San Jose, California, which excluded private schools entirely, and was simply a "freedom of choice" program among a few public schools. Another OEO pilot program is proposed for New Hampshire. For a review of voucher proposals, see La Noue, *The Politics of Education*, 73 TEACHERS COLL. REC. 304 (1971).

[117] Simply to call a tuition grant a voucher does not remove it from the reach of *Nyquist*. As envisioned by voucher-plan theoreticians, there is just the possibility of a distinction. It is on that possibility that attention needs be centered. See CENTER FOR THE STUDY OF PUBLIC POLICY, EDUCATION VOUCHERS 1–6 (1970); FRIEDMAN, CAPITALISM AND FREEDOM 91–94 (1962). The Center for Public Policy Study is principally the work of Christopher Jencks. For more explicit statements of Jencks's position, see Jencks, *The Public Schools Are Failing*, SAT. REV. 23 April 1966; and Jencks, *Is the Public School Obsolete?* 2 PUBLIC INTEREST 18 (1966). On the merits and difficulties of voucher plans see LA NOUE, ed., EDUCATIONAL VOUCHERS: CONCEPTS AND CONTROVERSIES (1972).

[118] For a recent, but pre-*Nyquist*, review of the discussion of voucher plans see Golden, *Education Vouchers: The Fruit of the Lemon Tree*, 24 STAN. L. REV. 687 (1972). Unhappily, there is some confusion of voucher plans and tuition grants in this piece. Again, what makes a "plan" a "voucher plan" is not whether the payment comes by check or coupon, or whether it comes before or after the educational services are rendered by whatever institution renders them. What defines a voucher plan is that everybody participates. The present public schools must be included as well as the private schools or it is simply a grant program and naked to the scythe of *Nyquist*. Vivid indication of the staying power of continued interest in voucher plans is the article by Milton Friedman, *The Voucher Idea*, N.Y. TIMES MAG. 23 Sept. 1973. Friedman noted the difficulties posed by *Nyquist* and *Sloan* and suggested an argument, similar to that outlined below, for sustaining the constitutionality of a true voucher plan. He probably dismissed the constitutional difficulties too lightly.

There is, of course, one major anatomical difference between the New York tax credits and the New York and Pennsylvania tuition grants, on the one hand, and a true educational voucher arrangement on the other. In the former programs only private school children participated; life went on in public schools as usual. In the latter kind of program, participation would be universal, or at least include some present public schools so that parents could choose a "vouchered" private school, a "vouchered" public school, or conventional public school. It is this universality which, just possibly, might be developed by some future Court into a distinction between *Nyquist* grants and voucher plans.

There are several handles in Mr. Justice Powell's *Nyquist* opinion for such an argument. In attempting to distinguish the *Nyquist* programs from those the Court had approved in *Everson* and *Allen*, he wrote:[119]

> In *Everson*, the Court, in a five to four decision, approved a program of reimbursements to parents of public as well as parochial school children for bus fares paid in connection with transportation to and from school. . . . In *Allen*, decided some 20 years later, the Court upheld a New York law authorizing the provision of *secular* textbooks for *all children* in grades seven through 12 attending *public and non-public schools.* . . . Finally, in *Tilton*, the Court upheld federal grants for the construction of facilities to be used for clearly *secular* purposes by public and non-public institutions of higher learning.

He went on to remark that only the nonpublic school population participated in the programs at bar.

In addition, remembering Mr. Justice Powell's underlying fears as mentioned in *Nyquist*, it might be argued that voucher programs, in which all parents participate on a chit-for-child basis, avoid the dangers of creedal warfare in the legislature over the allocation of resources. Under grant and even tax credit arrangements it is possible to conceive, as Mr. Justice Powell does so vividly, of endless efforts by partisans of sectarian schools to raise the amounts, and by opponents of those schools to hold the amounts or reduce them. In a vouchered educational universe the sectarian school partisans would simply be one part of the educational lobby that would be continually pushing to raise the face amount of the chit. As there

---

[119] 93 S. Ct. at 2966. (Emphasis added.)

is no administrative confrontation there is no danger of strife caused by entanglement, and if the sectarian schools are not set apart with any special interest of their own to advance, the strife that Mr. Justice Powell feared becomes remote.

The closer one examines these distinctions, however, the more precarious they appear. Could the universality of participation in a true voucher scheme alter, for Mr. Justice Powell or any moderately separationist successor, the fact that substantial benefit would result for the church-related schools? Furthermore, the specter of sectarian school lobbying is not eliminated, only altered. The church-school partisans would still be there, albeit arrayed with spokesmen for the rest of the educational community in constantly urging that the vouchered sums be increased. And they would also be ready to split off to defend schools of their faith on a broad range of regulatory issues—ranging from the sorts of religious exercises permitted in participating schools, to the terms on which pupils might be expelled,[120] and the limits of clientele control over curriculum.[121] Mr. Justice Powell might have concluded that the chances of "politicizing religion" are just as great with a universal tuition grant arrangement as with one limited to private schools.

It also makes a great deal of difference whether the plan puts a face value on the chits, or whether the schools can apply for actual costs. If the former, it may be asked how is this different from the tuition grant program disallowed in *Nyquist*, except that parents who elect public schools are put through the senseless formality of handing in vouchers? If, however, it is actual per pupil cost that is vouched for by the chit, how is this to be determined? Does this not raise again the specter of the sectarian school lobbyist in the state house corridor urging the particular cost-assessing scheme that favors his clients? (Can the Roman Catholic school count, as part of the cost of instruction, the expense of maintaining the residence for teaching nuns; or can only the token salaries paid the nuns be counted?) If this is the case, and the government must get into the business of inquiring into private school operation to find out what is actually spent, are we not back to an impermissible entanglement? This is especially apparent when it is remembered that the sectarian schools would, in any accounting of their "actual costs," be required

---

[120] See Comment, *Public Control of Private Sectarian Institutions Receiving Public Funds*, 63 MICH. L. REV. 142 (1964).

[121] Cf. Epperson v. Arkansas, 393 U.S. 97 (1968).

to separate the costs of religious instruction from the "bill" they were submitting, and that this exclusion would have to be policed! Thus, there are arguments for voucher plans including sectarian schools, but they are weak-looking reeds.

One argument, which had been thought by church school supporters to hold promise of constitutional accommodation, relied on the Equal Protection Clause of the Fourteenth Amendment. If it were a legitimate secular purpose for the legislature to aid private schools generally, could private schools with a religious affiliation be excluded simply on the grounds of the affiliation? The Equal Protection Clause has enjoyed great vogue in recent years,[122] and the hope was not altogether without foundation.

Sustaining this hope was what seemed to some observers[123] the puzzling action by the Court in *Lemon I* in striking down the whole Pennsylvania scheme. About 20 percent of the participating schools in the Pennsylvania arrangement were non-Catholic and secular private schools. The legislature had written a clear separability clause into the statute.[124] The Court, however, observed almost in passing that most of the pupils in the Pennsylvania arrangement were in Catholic parochial schools (the district court had taken judicial notice of the extent of religious activity characteristic of Catholic schools),[125] and the whole program was declared unconstitutional. One possible explanation was the anticipation by the Justices of Equal Protection Clause embarrassment if the program remained in effect with lower courts making a school-by-school determination of eligibility based on the extent of religious infusion in each.[126]

This theory perished in *Sloan*. Speaking to the question of the separability of the Pennsylvania statute, Mr. Justice Powell found

---

[122] See Gunther, *In Search of Evolving Doctrine on a Changing Court: A Model for a Newer Equal Protection*, 86 HARV. L. REV. 1 (1972).

[123] See Giannella, note 2 *supra*, at 185.

[124] 24 PA. STAT. § 5608 (1971 Supp.): "If a part of this act is invalid, all valid parts that are severable from the invalid part remain in effect."

[125] 403 U.S. at 610.

[126] A simpler, more plausible explanation of the refusal of the Court to consider severance in *Lemon I*, and *Sloan* is that the majority Justices appreciated, and correctly so, that the underlying purpose of both statutes was to aid parochial schools, and that if this were impermissible, there was no parallel legislative purpose of aiding secular private schools. In fact, there had been no purpose of aiding private schools generally. It was the parochial system which had been Pennsylvania's concern.

no reason to question the district court's conclusion that the participation of non-Catholic private schools could not survive the excision of the parochial schools from the program. He went on, however, to deal with the hypothetical question. If the act could be separated, would the aiding of the secular schools and the exclusion of others solely on the grounds of religious affiliation and school practices, constitute a denial of equal protection?[127]

> Even if the Act were clearly severable, valid aid to non-public, non-sectarian schools would provide no lever for aid to their sectarian counterparts. The Equal Protection Clause has never been regarded as a bludgeon with which to compel a State to violate other provisions of the Constitution. Having held that tuition reimbursements for the benefit of sectarian schools violate the Establishment Clause, nothing in the Equal Protection Clause will suffice to revive that program.

The meaning of all this for voucher plans is clear. There is nothing faulty on equal protection grounds about a true voucher scheme that excludes church-related schools.

Given the massive political difficulties of setting up a true voucher plan,[128] the *Nyquist*-based arguments for keeping sectarian schools out, and the demise of the equal protection argument that they must be included, the possibilities of substantial public support to church-related schools now appear truly remote. Nonetheless, there is still a simmering of political activity. John Deedy, managing editor of *Commonweal*, reported in August 1973 that a Federation of Catholic School Parents had been formed in New York to advance the cause of aid to church-related schools, and that no extensive school closings are expected immediately.[129] One must be careful about writing off a constitutional issue with which a large and politically skillful group continues to be concerned. The door now seems to have been shut, but the future may bring arguments of an ingenuity yet undreamed of, and the shadows of personnel changes fall across all doctrinal sureties.

---

[127] 93 S. Ct. at 2988.

[128] The public education establishment is solidly opposed to the basic voucher idea. The National Education Association and the American Federation of Teachers are joined on this issue by the American Association of School Administrators, the National Association of Elementary School Principals, the Council of Chief State School Officers, the Horace Mann League, and so on.

[129] N.Y. Times, 12 Aug. 1973, § 4, at p. 9, col. 1.

VIII. CONCLUSION

The church educators have lost. If the decision sticks, it remains for future historians to answer whether society should thank the Court for this outcome. Quite possibly society will. It is also possible that another generation of Americans will wish that Chief Justice Burger's attempt at accommodation had succeeded, and that the Court will find itself pressed to undo Mr. Justice Powell's *Nyquist* work. What can be done now (no matter what one's reaction to the policy outcome) is to consider the quality of the Court's constitutional craftsmanship in dealing with the matter.

That craftsmanship is important need not be labored here. The settlements of major issues of constitutional politics must be acceptable to major interest groupings over the long haul or they will not hold up. If sufficiently powerful groups perceive a constitutional outcome as altogether outrageous, there are ways to continue the battle—through the amending process, through guerrilla warfare in the appointing process, through threats to the Court's appellate jurisdiction, and through campaigns of persuasion in the legal, academic, and media subcultures.[130] Inadequate craftsmanship marginally encourages such continuing hostilities and the attendant perceptions of instability in constitutional law. It arms dissatisfied groups to sustain a protracted guerrilla war in Congress and in the law reviews and in the "journals of opinion." And there is a further consequence of confusing and fragmentary explanations from the Supreme Court. This is the familiar observation that the sloppy craftsmanship erodes the prestige of the Court and thus its capacity to resolve future conflicts. While this relationship between craftsmanship and perceived legitimacy and institutional power has not yet been demonstrated to the satisfaction of the more behaviorally

---

[130] An excellent recent example of an unstable constitutional outcome involves First Amendment protection for sexually explicit materials. Mr. Justice Brennan essayed a "solution" in Roth v. United States, 354 U.S. 476 (1957), and glossed it in Ginzburg v. United States, 383 U.S. 463 (1966). His efforts were subjected to scathing attack from both pro- and anti-censorship quarters, and the Court has seemed, since 1966, to be wandering aimlessly through obscenity cases, turning one way for a few years, Ginsberg v. New York, 390 U.S. 629 (1968), and then another way for a few years, United States v. Reidel, 402 U.S. 351 (1971). And only last Term, the Court tried still another approach. See Miller v. California, 93 S. Ct. 2607 (1973); Paris Adult Theater I v. Slator, 93 S. Ct. 2628 (1973); Kaplan v. California, 93 S. Ct. 2680 (1973); United States v. 12 200-ft. Reels, 93 S . Ct. 2665 (1973); Heller v. New York, 93 S. Ct. 2789 (1973); Roaden v. Kentucky, 93 S. Ct. 2796 (1973).

oriented social scientists,[131] it is powerfully suggested by the historical literature,[132] and it is so well accepted among professional students of the Court[133] that it is a necessary preface to criticism of arguments advanced by the Justices to explain results. Three observations suggest themselves. First, Mr. Justice Powell deserves modestly high marks for craftsmanship in *Nyquist* and *Sloan*. Second, his elaboration of the higher education distinction in *Hunt* is less impressive. And, third, the present configuration of Establishment Clause doctrine alongside the configuration of Free Exercise Clause doctrine reveals some painfully apparent tensions that the opinions of last Term did nothing to reduce.

Whatever one thinks of the outcome in *Nyquist* (and I think it unfortunate), Mr. Justice Powell's reading of the primary-effect element in the *Lemon 1* test is more persuasive than Chief Justice Burger's. If the underlying value secured by Establishment Clause limitations on governmental involvement with religious enterprises is the avoidance of religio-political strife,[134] then it is clear that the

---

[131] A major difficulty that behavioralists encounter in discussing the relationship between judicial craftsmanship and the power of the Court is that their available instruments of research are crude. While it is quite possible accurately to sample mass attitudes toward the Court, it is the delicate, unmapped relationship between elite criticisms and secular changes in mass attitudes that is critical to the continuing prestige of the institution. This is much harder to get at than simple mass attitudes. For an interesting attempt see Murphy & Tanenhaus, *Public Opinion and the United States Supreme Court*, in GROSSMAN & TANENHAUS, FRONTIERS OF JUDICIAL RESEARCH (1969).

[132] A particularly insightful essay bearing on craftsmanship is MILLER, THE SUPREME COURT AND THE USES OF HISTORY (1969).

[133] For an excellent critical review of the various definitions of, and arguments about, judicial craftsmanship, see Deutsch, *Neutrality, Legitimacy, and the Supreme Court*, 20 STAN. L. REV. 169 (1968).

[134] It is sometimes suggested that "neutrality" is the underlying value of the Establishment Clause. But neutrality is not a value. To say so is to confuse means with ends. One attempts to behave in a neutral fashion in order to forestall developments that are regarded as undesirable to an extent outweighing any benefits which are foregone by neutrality. It is also occasionally suggested that the underlying value of Establishment Clause limitations on public aid to the educational and social service activities of sectarian institutions is to avoid offending the conscience of taxpayers who are "forced to contribute" to programs that have the effect of sustaining religious institutions they deplore. Their free exercise of religion is held infringed. Given the amounts involved for particular individuals, however, only a conscience of prodigious preciosity could be seriously offended. On reflection, it is hard to see how a problem of constitutional dimensions could be said to be created. When closely scrutinized, most arguments for Establishment Clause limitations are based on strife avoidance, and this is true of those of Justices Powell and Burger.

Chief Justice's direct-indirect approach sacrifices substance to form. There is little reason to suppose that strife is triggered only, or even principally, by direct administrative interfaces between government and religious institutions. Mr. Justice Powell's argument, that allocations will be fought over no matter the route they take to the sectarian institutions, is surely sound.[135] The outstanding problem with all this is that the premise is almost universally unexamined.[136] If the involvement of fighting religious groups in the political process is the danger to be avoided, does it obviously follow that the least risky strategy is to deny aid and avoid entanglements? Is it not at least possible that the obdurate exclusion of church-related institutions from governmental programs which utilize other nongovernmental entities will produce higher levels of strife than would be created through hard bargaining for shares if the religious institutions were included in the program?

On the matter of the higher education distinction it is difficult to see that *Hunt* added anything to *Tilton*. Colleges and universities, it is said, are different. The ways in which they are different have to do with the maturity of the students and the observation/conviction that the church-related institutions of higher learning are not, by and large, engaged in advancing the faith in the manner of church-related elementary and secondary schools. One wonders. What would Justices Powell and Burger make of Oral Roberts University? It might be answered that in *Tilton* and *Hunt* the Justices had recognized that there might be institutions so thoroughly infused with religion that they could not be allowed to participate in governmental programs, and that O.R.U. is one such. But how are the institutions thus far approved to be distinguished from O.R.U.? The Baptist College at Charlestown, at issue in *Hunt*, was operated by the South Carolina Convention. Had Mr. Justice Powell followed the Maryland Court of Appeals and held that only the most nominal sort of church attachment could be tolerated, the constitutional law of the matter would be a good deal clearer—but it is unlikely then that all the *Tilton* and *Hunt* institutions could have qualified.

---

[135] It is interesting to note that in attempting to distinguish *Walz* from the New York tax credit program, Mr. Justice Powell overlooked the argument that property tax exemptions do not need to be periodically reenacted, with built-in invitations to struggle over amounts.

[136] There is nothing novel about this point. For an extended discussion see Schwartz, *No Imposition of Religion: The Establishment Clause Value* 77 YALE L.J. 692 (1968).

Finally, there is the embarrassing problem of the Free Exercise cases, most notably *Sherbert v. Verner*.[137] In that instance, the Court (with only Mr. Justice Harlan dissenting) exempted an unemployed Seventh-Day Adventist, who had declined jobs requiring Saturday work, from the requirement of South Carolina's unemployment compensation statute. The South Carolina scheme provided that to be eligible for compensation an individual be available for work, that is, to accept jobs to which he is referred by the State Employment Service. The constitutional ground for Mrs. Sherbert's exemption was held, by strict separationist Mr. Justice Brennan, to be the Free Exercise Clause. Yet how can this be?[138] If the Establishment Clause is read as commanding that all but the most marginal benefits of government spending be denied religious institutions, how can very important and desirable exemptions from government regulatory arrangements be bestowed in the name of free exercise? It should not suffice to answer, "Ah, that is the pretty paradox, the marvelous mystery of the religion clauses." Nor can it be answered that monetary support engenders strife, but exemption for otherwise valid secular requirements does not.[139] Government in the business of defining the limits of various religious exemptions will truly be government besieged by the faithful. Now that the meaning of the Establishment Clause for aid to sectarian schools has been stated with firmness, it is to be hoped (if not expected) that the Court will proceed to rationalize its strictness as to establishment with its permissiveness as to free exercise.

---

[137] 374 U.S. 398 (1963). A significant state court decision in the same vein is People v. Woody, 40 Cal. Rep. 69 (1964). Another troubling Supreme Court decision is Yoder v. Wisconsin, 406 U.S. 205 (1972). See Kurland, *The Supreme Court, Compulsory Education and the First Amendment's Religion Clauses*, 75 W. VA. L. REV. 213 (1973).

[138] In dissent, Mr. Justice Harlan put this question with devastating precision. 374 U.S. at 419–23.

[139] For an extended treatment of the anomalous position into which the Court has worked itself with decisions such as *Sherbert* and *Yoder*, see RELIGION at 144–62.

G. E. HALE and ROSEMARY D. HALE

THE OTTER TAIL POWER CASE: REGULATION BY COMMISSION OR ANTITRUST LAWS

Over a decade ago we surveyed a number of regulated industries to determine whether it was unnecessary and undesirable that the industries be subject to the antitrust laws.[1] Our conclusion, in a nutshell, was that a "pervasively" regulated industry should be exempt from antitrust regulation.

There have been important developments in the intervening years. Courts have handed down scores of decisions. Technological changes have taken place, increasing the possibility of competition in what was once regarded as the public utility sector of the economy.[2] A microwave system operating between St. Louis and Chicago opens the door to competition in the telephone industry. CATV systems are growing despite FCC opposition. Another important development is the concept of Total Energy that envisions

G. E. Hale is a member of the Illinois Bar. Rosemary D. Hale is Professor of Economics, Lake Forest College.

[1] Hale & Hale, *Competition or Control VI: Application of Antitrust Laws to Regulated Industries*, 111 U. Pa. L. Rev. 46 (1962); Hale & Hale, *Mergers in Regulated Industries*, 59 Nw. U. L. Rev. 49 (1964).

[2] Gies, *The Need for New Concepts in Public Utility Regulation*, in Shepherd & Gies, eds., Utility Regulation: New Directions in Theory and Policy 88–111 (1966); Kestenbaum, *Competition in Communications*, 16 Antitrust Bull. 679, 773 (1971); Trebing, *Common Carrier Regulation—the Silent Crisis*, 34 Law & Contemp. Prob. 299 (1969); Rosan, *Comment*, in Trebing, ed., Performance under Regulation 128–30 (1968).

an arrangement whereby the proprietors of a shopping plaza or an office building generate their own electricity and use the exhaust for heating and cooling. Obviously such a system competes with regulated electric utilities.

With such developments in mind we propose, first, to ascertain from the new decisions the degree to which regulated industries are exempt from the antitrust laws, and, second, whether there are conflicts between regulation by commission and by the antitrust laws and how they might be reconciled.

I. Cases Applying Antitrust Principles to Utilities

It would be easy to make a case that the antitrust laws are now fully applicable to all public utilities and that commission regulation is no impediment thereto. A vivid illustration of that trend is found in the very recent decision of the United States Supreme Court in *Otter Tail Power Co. v. United States*.[3] Otter Tail is an electric utility regulated by both state and federal authorities. Under federal statutes the Federal Power Commission was expressly authorized to require Otter Tail to supply wholesale power to municipally owned distribution systems.[4] The FPC did not act and suit was brought under the antitrust laws against Otter Tail by the United States for refusing to sell at wholesale to the municipal distribution system. The United States Supreme Court, in a four-to-three decision, approved a decree requiring such an interstate connection. The opinion for the majority by Mr. Justice Douglas brushed aside the possibility of conflict with the jurisdiction of the Federal Power Commission, saying:[5]

> [The decree] . . . contemplates that future disputes over inter-connections . . . will be subject to Federal Power Commission perusal. It will be time enough to consider whether the anti-trust remedy may override the power of the Commission . . . as, if and when the Commission denies the interconnection and the District Court nevertheless undertakes to direct it.

In the concurring and dissenting opinion by Mr. Justice Stewart a more complex view was taken of the conflict between the two forms of regulation:[6]

---

[3] 410 U.S. 366 (1973).

[4] *Id.* at 373.

[5] *Id.* at 376–77.

[6] *Id.* at 394–95.

The Court goes on vaguely to suggest that there will be time to cope with the problem of a Commission refusal to order interconnection which conflicts with this antitrust decree when such a conflict arises.

But the basic conflict between the Commission's authority and the decree entered in the District Court cannot be so easily wished away. . . . The Court's decree plainly ignores the Commission's authority to decide *whether* the involuntary interconnection is warranted. . . . Unless the decree is modified, its future implementation will starkly conflict with the explicit statutory mandate of the Federal Power Commission.

Otter Tail is far from the only decision of its kind. Another devastating blow was dealt to regulation in *Cascade Natural Gas Corp. v. El Paso Gas Co.*[7] That prolonged litigation involved the acquisition by El Paso Natural Gas Company of another corporation also operating a gas pipeline. The two pipelines were not in competition since they did not traverse the same territory. They did, however, form a connection on an end-to-end basis. Here again, the jurisdiction of the state and federal regulatory agencies was ignored and the Supreme Court ruled that full divestiture of the acquired pipeline must be accomplished despite a lower court settlement of the matter to the contrary.

Numerous other cases can be cited to the same effect. Stockyards subject to the powers of the Secretary of Agriculture have also been subjected to the antitrust laws.[8] The New York Stock Exchange, regulated in detail by the SEC, was held liable in damages under antitrust principles.[9] The jurisdiction of the Federal Maritime Commission was not sufficient to prevent antitrust applications to the corporations it regulated.[10]

This trend is not new. For decades the antitrust laws have been

---

[7] 386 U.S. 129 (1967).

[8] Denver Union Stockyard Co. v. Denver Live Stock Commission Company, 404 F.2d 1055 (10th Cir. 1968).

[9] Silver v. New York Stock Exchange, 373 U.S. 341 (1963).

[10] Federal Maritime Comm'n v. Seatrain Lines, Inc., 411 U.S. 726, 732–33 (1973): "The Commission vigorously argues that such agreements can be interpreted as falling within the third category—which concerns agreements 'controlling, regulating, preventing, or destroying competition.' Without more, we might be inclined to agree that many merger agreements probably fit within this category. But a broad reading of the third category would conflict with our frequently expressed view that exemptions from antitrust laws are strictly construed, . . ." See also Deaktor v. L. D. Schreiber & Co., 479 F.2d 529 (7th Cir. 1973).

applied to the railroads despite the regulatory powers of the Interstate Commerce Commission.[11] And in some instances the regulatory commissions have themselves been directed by the courts to consider alleged antitrust issues in proceedings before them. Thus in *Gulf States Utilities Co. v. F.P.C.*,[12] it was said:

> This power clearly carries with it the responsibility to consider, in appropriate circumstances, the anticompetitive effects of regulated aspects of interstate utility operations pursuant to §§ 202 and 203, and under like directives contained in §§ 205, 206, and 207. The Act did not render antitrust policy irrelevant to the Commission's regulation of the electric power industry. Indeed, within the confines of a basic natural monopoly structure, limited competition of the sort protected by the antitrust laws seems to have been anticipated. . . .
>
> Nothing in the Act suggests that the "public interest" standard of § 204 contains any less broad directive than that contained in the other similarly worded and adjacent sections. Under the express language of § 204 the public interest is stressed as a governing factor. There is nothing that indicates that the meaning of that term is to be restricted to financial considerations, with every other aspect of the public interest ignored. Further, there is the section's requirement that the object of the issue be lawful. The Commission is directed to inquire into and to evaluate the purpose of the issue and the use to which its proceeds will be put. Without a more definite indication of contrary legislative purpose, we shall not read out of § 204 the requirement that the Commission consider matters relating to both the broad purposes of the Act and the fundamental national economic policy expressed in the antitrust laws. . . .

This direction, of course, is at variance with the decision in the natural gas pipeline cases where the implication was that the commission had no role whatsoever in such matters.

II. On the Other Hand

Despite the authorities just cited, a good many cases have gone in the other direction. Hence it is far from clear that the fact of regulation will not provide at least some degree of shelter from the application of the antitrust laws.

---

[11] See United States v. Trans-Missouri Freight Ass'n, 166 U.S. 290 (1897).

[12] 411 U.S. 747, 758–59 (1973); cf. Utility Users League v. F.P.C., 394 F.2d 16 (7th Cir. 1968).

First there is the doctrine of primary jurisdiction that requires submission of an antitrust issue to the regulatory commission in advance of court determination. The basic theory is that the regulatory body with its vast expertise will guide the court in the resolution of the antitrust issue. One might think in the light of cases such as *Otter Tail Power*, that no role was left for the application of that doctrine. To the contrary, the United States Supreme Court, in the 1972 Term, also handed down its opinion in *Ricci v. Chicago Mercantile Exchange*,[13] applying the doctrine of primary jurisdiction.

In that case the plaintiff had challenged the membership rules of the Chicago Mercantile Exchange. The Court coolly announced that the Commodities Exchange Act contemplated that the exchange and its members could engage in restraints of trade which might otherwise be held unreasonable.[14] Accordingly, the membership rules of the exchange fell under the jurisdiction of the Commodities Exchange Commission, and the case was referred to the commission to resolve issues with respect to the facts and to evaluate them. After such evaluation, the Court announced in a five-to-four decision, it would then be time to decide whether the antitrust suit would be barred.[15]

Other decisions invoking the doctrine of primary jurisdiction in recent years have involved REA Express,[16] Executive Airlines,[17] Monsanto Company,[18] and Macom Products Co.[19] The dissent in the *Otter Tail* case expressly referred to these matters and pointed out the seeming contradiction among them.[20]

The courts, however, have gone farther than to apply the doctrine of primary jurisdiction. In several important decisions they have found that the regulated industry was wholly exempt from the operation of the antitrust law. Perhaps the most startling decision was that in *Hughes Tool Co. v. T.W.A.*[21] After years of litigation in the lower courts, Trans World Airlines secured an enor-

---

[13] 409 U.S. 289 (1973).

[14] *Id.* at 303–04.   [15] *Id.* at 307–08.

[16] REA Express, Inc. v. Alabama Great Southern Railroad, 412 U.S. 934 (1973).

[17] Executive Airlines v. Air New England, 357 F. Supp. 345 (D. Mass. 1973).

[18] Monsanto Co. v. United Gas Pipe Line Co., 360 F. Supp. 1054 (D.D.C. 1973).

[19] Macom Products Corp. v. A.T.&T., 359 F. Supp. 973 (C.D. Cal. 1973). See also Price v. T.W.A., 481 F.2d 844 (9th Cir. 1973).

[20] 410 U.S. at 391.   [21] 409 U.S. 363 (1973).

mous judgment against Hughes Tool. That judgment was upset by
the United States Supreme Court on the ground that transactions
authorized by the Civil Aeronautics Board could not be the subject
of antitrust attacks. Competition was also given short shrift in approving the merger of the New York Central and Pennsylvania
railroads.[22] Other cases to the same effect can be found in recent
years.[23]

In the lower courts several decisions have involved clashes between gas and electric utilities. Typically, the gas companies have
attacked rates offered by the electric utilities. Here again, the courts
have found an exemption from the antitrust laws in the existence
of state regulatory approval. Even inaction by the regulatory commission has been held sufficient to confer an exemption from antitrust liability.[24]

Thus despite the vigorous language of the *Otter Tail* decision it
is far from clear that regulated utility companies are fully subject
to the antitrust laws. The resulting confusion has no doubt led in
some measure to disillusionment of the bar and the public utility
enterprises.[25]

III. FAILURE OF REGULATION

One factor bearing upon this problem is the tidal wave of
adverse comment that has descended upon the regulatory agencies
in recent years. Disillusionment with regulation is rampant. Professor George J. Stigler, characteristically more vigorous than other
economists, has asserted:[26]

> Regulation may be actively sought by an industry, or it may
> be thrust upon it. A central thesis of this paper is that, as

---

[22] Penn Central Merger Cases, 389 U.S. 486, 499–500 (1968).

[23] See Northern Natural Gas Co. v. F.P.C., 399 F.2d 953 (D.C. Cir. 1968). In *Pan
American Airways, Inc. v. United States*, 371 U.S. 296 (1963), the exemption from the
antitrust laws was expressly founded on the existence of regulation.

[24] Gas Light Co. of Columbus v. Georgia Power Co., 440 F.2d 1135, 1137–38, 1140
(5th Cir. 1971); Washington Gas Light Co. v. Virginia Electric Co., 438 F.2d 248, 252
(4th Cir. 1971); cf. Business Aides, Inc. v. Chesapeake & Potomac Tel. Co., 480 F.2d
754 (4th Cir. 1973); Utility Users League, note 12 *supra*; Mathews v. Jersey Central
Power & Light Co., CCH ¶ 50,176 (21 June 1973), see also Allstate Insurance Co.
v. Lanier, 361 F.2d 870 (4th Cir. 1966).

[25] Kauper, *The "Warren Court" and the Antitrust Laws*, 67 MICH. L. REV. 325 (1968).

[26] Stigler, *The Theory of Economic Regulation*, 2 BELL J. ECON. & MANAG. 3, 5 (1971).

a rule, regulation is acquired by the industry and is designed
and operated primarily for its benefit.

. . . .

The second major public resource commonly sought by an
industry is control over entry by new rivals. There is considerable, not to say excessive, discussion in economic literature
of the rise of peculiar price policies (limit prices), vertical
integration, and similar devices to retard the rate of entry
of new firms into oligopolistic industries. Such devices are
vastly less efficacious (economical) than the certificate of convenience and necessity (which includes, of course, the import and production quotas of the oil and tobacco industries).

Professor Stigler went on to suggest that regulated industry does
not try to extract money directly from government. Instead, it
seeks to bar new entrance into competition through governmental
machinery.[27]

We propose the general hypothesis: every industry or oc-
cupation that has enough political power to utilize the state will
seek to control entry. In addition, the regulatory policy will
often be so fashioned as to retard the rate of growth of new
firms.

After an industry has achieved entry control it will often, according
to Professor Stigler, want price controls administered by a body
with coercive power. This control is desired in order to obtain more
than a competitive rate of return. It will also, by statute or otherwise, seek to control or eliminate the production of substitutes.[28]

An important factor for consideration is the cost of administrative
proceedings. One student found that the price of gas sold in interstate commerce was 5 to 6 percent higher than that sold in intrastate
commerce because of the expense of proceedings before the Federal
Power Commission.[29] This is a not insignificant matter when one

---

[27] *Id.* at 5.   [28] *Id.* at 6.

[29] *Id.* at 7. Professor Stigler further noted: "The idealistic view of public regulation is
deeply imbedded in professional economic thought. So many economists, for example,
have denounced the ICC for its pro-railroad policies that this has become a cliché of the
literature. This criticism seems to me exactly as appropriate as a criticism of the Great
Atlantic and Pacific Tea Company for selling groceries, or as a criticism of a politician
for currying popular support. The fundamental vice of such criticism is that it misdirects
attention: it suggests that the way to get an ICC which is not subservient to the carriers
is to preach to the commissioners or to the people who appoint the commissioners. The
only way to get a different commission would be to change the political support for the

considers that assets of public utilities may constitute almost a fifth of total industrial capacity.[30]

Another student who takes a dim view of regulatory commissions is Professor Ronald Coase:[31]

> What I have in mind is a feature which, with the best will in the world, it seems to me very difficult to eliminate. However fluid an organization may be in its beginning, it must inevitably adopt certain policies and organizational forms which condition its thinking and limit the range of its policies. . . . It is difficult to operate closely with an industry without coming to look at its problems in industry terms. The result is that the commission, although thinking of itself as apart from and with different aims from the industry, will nonetheless be incapable of conceiving of or bringing about any radical changes in industry practices or structure.
>
> This opposition [to pay television] comes, as Dr. Frank Stanton of CBS told us, not because the industry has any "economic axe to grind," but because it would not be in the best interests of the public. It is, I think, a universal rule that businessmen never act from higher motives than when they are engaged in restricting potential competition.

Other observers are equally disillusioned about public utility control. Professor Massel is a good example:

> Public utility regulation in the United States is enveloped in a legalistic framework which provides few positive pressures for greater efficiency, more innovation or substantial cost reduction. The regulatory process has been evolved through the

---

Commission, and reward commissioners on a basis unrelated to their services to the carriers.

"Until the basic logic of political life is developed, reformers will be ill-equipped to use the state for their reforms, and victims of the pervasive use of the state's support of special groups will be helpless to protect themselves. Economists should quickly establish the license to practice on the rational theory of political behavior." *Id.* at 17–18.

[30] Daniel, *The Regulation of Private Enterprises as Public Utilities*, 34 Soc. Res. 347 (1967); Stigler, *The Process of Economic Regulation*, 17 Antitrust Bull. 207 (1972): "The specialized agency [regulatory commission], however, is as welcome to the regulated activity as it is necessary to the legislature: by constant association and pressure the regulator is brought to a cooperative and even complaisant attitude toward the regulated group."

[31] Coase, *The Economics of Broadcasting and Government Policy*, 56 Am. Ec. Rev. 440, 442, 446 (1966). See also Loevinger, *Regulation and Competition as Alternatives*, 11 Antitrust Bull. 101 (1966).

inherited superstitions of generations of lawyers, who have usually looked upon regulation as an exercise in legal procedures.[32]

In his view the commissions are constantly seeking a magic mechanical formula which can be applied to all situations. They refuse to consider the effects of their price policy on consumption or demand.[33]

Many other observers have called for a review of regulatory policies. They seek to find what the actual effects of regulations have been. The old complaint about combining legislative, executive, and judicial functions in one agency is by no means dead. It has been pointed out that the effort to "judicialize" the conduct of the agencies has led to many problems including inordinate delays.[34] Recurrent, however, is the theme that regulation is actually protective rather than regulatory in character:[35]

. . . without regulation the firm would face competition from neighboring firms which might encroach on its territory. To

---

[32] Massel, *The Regulatory Process and Public Utility Performance*, in TREBING, note 2 *supra*, at 113. He continued: ". . . the regulatory problems have been left largely in the hands of the lawyers with some help from the accountants. The legal profession has dominated the regulatory process in the companies, the legislatures, the commissions and the courts. Counsel for the companies and the regulatory agencies have had to carry on their battles with small assistance from other professions. Public considerations of the problems of regulation have usually been regarded as the domain of the lawyers, who have pursued their natural bent for improving procedures while issues of substance have fallen between the chairs." *Id.* at 114.

[33] *Id.* at 115–16. He complained further: "A natural result of the dearth of economic analysis has been a disregard of experience. Despite the many thousands of decisions which have been made, there has been little interest in examining the consequences of these rulings. Virtually no attention has been paid to the effects of the past proceedings on rate levels, volume of activity, efficiency, costs, and innovation. When a decision is made, the job is done."

[34] See, *e.g.*, Trebing, *Government Regulation and Modern Capitalism*, 3 J. ECON. ISSUES 94 (March 1969); PHILLIPS, THE ECONOMICS OF REGULATION: THEORY AND PRACTICE IN THE TRANSPORTATION AND PUBLIC UTILITY INDUSTRIES 712–13 (1965): "The independent regulatory commission combines in the same body legislative, judicial, and executive functions in regulation of an industry. A number of advantages were assumed to accrue to regulatory commissions, including continuity of policy, expertise, impartiality, experimentation, and flexibility in procedures. And independence was designed to gain for commissions the isolation from politics enjoyed by the judiciary. Today, however, all these supposed virtues have been challenged." He referred also to the inordinate delays in deciding cases. *Id.* at 730.

[35] Moore, *The Effectiveness of Regulation of Electric Utility Prices*, 36 SOUTHERN ECON. J. 365, 374 (1970).

the extent that this type of competition is possible, any removal of regulation would increase the elasticity of demand faced by a single firm above the elasticity of the market and so lead to lower prices.

It has been argued further that deregulation would not necessarily require the establishment of "pure" competition. Some degree of "workable" competition would suffice.[36]

In terms of specific regulatory agencies the Federal Power Commission has frequently borne the brunt of the attack. Professor MacAvoy's study of the effect of its regulation of the price of the gas at the well-head is devastating. He found that the result of the regulation was to divert the gas to unregulated consumers at the expense of domestic and commercial patrons.[37] Another calculation indicated that the cost of regulation of the price of natural gas ran to about 7 percent of the base price.[38] This is indeed a high expense for achieving a negative benefit.

The pioneer study of this type, and still one of the most important studies, was that carried out by Professor Stigler and Mrs. Friedland with respect to the rates of electric utilities. The public utility commission controls were found to be almost totally ineffective.[39] Here again, the consumer is the victim, both of regulation and of its expense.

Although somewhat rehabilitated from the iniquitous reputation it enjoyed a few years ago, the Federal Communications Commission has likewise come in for a large share of blame. Professor Ronald Coase declared that the task imposed on the commission could not be handled efficiently by any organization, however competent. He found that the principal reason for the FCC's poor performance was its method of allocating frequencies.[40] Other observers have

---

[36] Gies, note 2 *supra*, at 96; Lerner, *Toward an Improved Decision Framework for Public Utility Regulation*, 44 LAND ECON. 403 (1968).

[37] MacAvoy, *The Regulation-Induced Shortage of Natural Gas*, 14 J. LAW & ECON. 167 (1971).

[38] Gerwig, *Natural Gas Production: A Study of the Costs of Regulation*, 5 J. LAW & ECON. 69, 91 (1962).

[39] Stigler & Friedland, *What Can Regulators Regulate? The Case of Electricity*, 5 J. LAW & ECON. 1 (1962); see Stathas, *Some Future Considerations and Implications for Regulated Industries and Regulatory Agencies*, in THE ECONOMICS OF REGULATION OF PUBLIC UTILITIES 172, 173, 184, 185 (1969); Moore, note 35 *supra*, at 374.

[40] Coase, *Evaluation of Public Policy Relating to Radio and Television Broadcasting: Social and Economic Issues*, 41 LAND ECON. 161 (1965); ". . . it is my considered opinion that

condemned the FCC for its attempt to obstruct the so-called CATV industry in order to protect television licensees already in the market.[41] Many other uncomplimentary comments have been made about the Communications Commission, perhaps the most important being that it gave only minor attention to the vital questions of prices and costs.[42] The activities of the same commission in the television industry have also met with unfavorable response.[43] One student enumerated the following fundamental mistakes made by the commission:[44]

1. It has not solved the standard of subsidization.
2. Its studies have been inadequate to solve its problems.
3. It has not attacked the cost-benefit problem or established adequate guidelines for spectrum use.
4. Its case-by-case approach to various market problems is unlikely to constitute an effective method of coping with its tasks.

Professor Cramton raised the question whether regulation really did anything other than enrich lawyers and create vested property interests.[45]

Even the Interstate Commerce Commission, long the revered

---

the task imposed on the FCC could not be handled efficiently by any organization, however competent." Professor Coase wrote further: "The task of charting a sensible future for the broadcasting industry is not one which can be left to the industry, which has its own interests to protect. It cannot be left to the Federal Communications Commission, which cannot conceive of any future which is not essentially a repetition of the past. Who, therefore, is to perform this task? I suggest that it has to be assumed by academic economists. . . . I would not argue that academic economists are technically the best qualified to investigate what government policy should be toward the broadcasting industry. But unless they do it, no one else will." *Id*. at 446–47. Cf. Frech, *Institutions for Allocating the Radio-TV Spectrum and the Vested Interests*, 4 J. ECON. ISSUES 23, 30–36 (Dec. 1970).

[41] Barnett & Greenberg, *Regulating CATV Systems: An Analysis of FCC Policy and an Alternative*, 34 LAW & CONTEMP. PROB. 562 (1969); Park, *Cable Television, UHF Broadcasting and FCC Regulatory Policy*, 15 J. LAW & ECON. 207 (1972).

[42] Comanor & Mitchell, *The Costs of Planning: The FCC and Cable Television*, 15 J. LAW & ECON. 177, 180 (1972).

[43] Frech, *More on Efficiency in the Allocation of Radio-TV Spectrum*, 5 J. ECON. ISSUES 100 (1971).

[44] TREBING, note 2 *supra*, at 315, 317, 325. Arbitrary allocation of joint costs is another FCC mistake. *Id*. at 315. The list of mistakes is long. *Id*. at 314.

[45] Cramton, *The Effectiveness of Economic Regulation: A Legal View*, 54 AM. ECON. REV. 182 (1964).

object of adoration by advocates of intervention,[46] has been the subject of bitter abuse. In the eyes of Professor (as he then was) Felix Frankfurter, the Interstate Commerce Commission, with its long record of integrity, constituted the ideal method of coping with economic problems.[47] Today scarcely anyone has a good word to say about it.[48] One of the kinder comments is that of Professor Cramton, who wrote:[49]

> The Commission, understandably, concentrates its energies on the most manageable and specific of the tasks assigned to it by the legislature: protecting interests created in the past and moderating the effects of undesirable change. The Commission's attempts to prevent or ameliorate departures from the existing rate structure and traffic pattern—a kind of soft-hearted and backward-looking cartelism—indicate its true purpose and function as a conservative body fighting a rear guard action against the inevitable forces of change.

Professor Harper was more specific in his accusations:[50]

> Restrictions on the freedom to compete that are found in entry control, rate regulation, and other aspects of regulation can be a cause of economic inefficiency in our transportation system, since they can have the effect of slowing down decision making, making it difficult for carriers to adapt quickly to changes in their environment, misallocating traffic among modes, forcing empty back hauls in some situations, providing protection to the inefficient carrier, making rates higher than they would be without regulation, making single-carrier service over long hauls difficult, discouraging initiative, preserving excess capacity, and so on. The degree of inefficiency caused by regulation is, of course, not equally distributed among the several modes. And, in addition to the problem of inefficiency, it also appears that the goals of regulation have been lost sight of in the tangle of laws and commission and court decisions that have accumulated over the past eighty years.

---

[46] See 4 SHARFMAN, THE INTERSTATE COMMERCE COMMISSION 342 (1937).

[47] See also Frankfurter, *The Interstate Commerce Commission*, in OF LAW AND LIFE AND OTHER THINGS THAT MATTER 235 (Kurland, ed., 1967).

[48] See Huntington, *The Marasmus of the ICC*, 61 YALE L. J. 467 (1952).

[49] Cramton, note 45 *supra*, at 189.

[50] Harper, *Transportation and the Public Utilities: Discussion*, 59 AM. ECON. REV. 270, 271 (1969).

Other observers have pointed out that the notion of a "fair return on fair value" is misplaced when an industry is declining but that the ICC continues to utilize it.[51] It continues to adhere to cost formulas that inhibit the use of the market as a gauge for economic pricing when numerous competitors of different kinds are seeking the same traffic.[52]

More fundamentally, the critics claim that the ICC does not have a carefully reasoned and consistently applied philosophy of the meaning of "inherent advantage"—the statutory precept applicable to its activity. Furthermore, it pays little attention to matters not presented to it by carriers and shippers, disregarding the public's viewpoint insofar as it differs from those of the mentioned adversaries.[53] It is now said that we should recognize the fact that the commission was never designed to protect the public but rather to bring order to an industry by enforced cartelization.[54] Frequent comments are made to the effect that the regulators find it convenient and comfortable to be on cozy terms with the industries which they are supposed to regulate.[55]

IV. DISTORTION OF ECONOMIC ALLOCATIONS

In general terms the argument is that all regulatory activity induces a higher than optimal level of investment and thus fails to minimize cost. In more familiar language this might be termed "inflating the rate base" so as to justify higher prices.[56] Professor West-

---

[51] Hilton, *The Basic Behavior of Regulatory Commissions*, 62 AM. ECON. REV. 47 (1972). Hilton complained that ICC regulation misallocated resources in two ways. First, it promoted monopoly, and second, it insisted on producing services not desired by patrons. *Id.* at 47.

[52] Pegrum, *Should the I.C.C. Be Abolished?* 11 TRANSP. J. 5, 10 (1971). Pegrum complained that ICC regulation had lacked flexibility, adaptability, and imagination. It was so enmeshed in detail that it had become a vast bureaucracy, usurping the functions of both management and the market.

[53] Sampson, *Inherent Advantages under Regulation*, 62 AM. ECON. REV. 55, 57 (1972).

[54] Carson, *Ralph Nader Discovers the ICC*, 5 J. ECON. ISSUES 93, 97 (June 1971). Carson draws attention to the 1935 legislation curbing motor carriers to protect the railroads.

[55] Stigler, note 30 *supra*. Journalists recently reported that state regulation of insurance companies was a farce. Blundell & Meyer, *Toothless Tigers?*, WALL ST. J. p. 1, col. 6, 2 Aug. 1973.

[56] Sheshinski, *Welfare Aspects of a Regulatory Constraint*, 61 AM. ECON. REV. 175 (1971); Takayama, *Behavior of the Firm under Regulatory Constraint*, 59 AM. ECON. REV. 255 (1969).

field declared he had demonstrated that it could be in the interests of a regulated industry to pay a higher rather than a lower price for its plant and equipment.[57] Others have avoided adverse criticism of the structure of the regulated industries, particularly the railroads. But they would prefer to apply the strict anti-merger standards of the antitrust laws.[58] Still others refer to the "static character of the regulatory structure" and suggest that it has a stultifying effect.[59] The regulated monopolist may be even less efficient than the unregulated and, in any event, there is always a fringe area in which the regulated firms compete against those without constraints with attendant ill results. Optimum service is not achieved and minimum costs are neglected.[60]

Professor Demsetz, one of those who has found much fault with regulation, has suggested an interesting alternative:[61]

> At this juncture, it should be emphasized that I have argued, not that regulatory commissions are undesirable, but that economic theory does not, at present, provide a justification for commissions insofar as they are based on the belief that observed concentration and monopoly price bear any necessary relationship.

His suggestion is that the privilege of operating the public utilities be sold to the highest bidder and thus avoid the necessity for regu-

---

[57] Westfield, *Regulation and Conspiracy*, 55 AM. ECON. REV. 424 (1965). Professor Westfield's demonstration appears to require an inelastic demand for the utility's services. *Quaere*, whether this is always a sound assumption. He also argues that regulation creates an environment conducive to conspiratorial practices. *Id.* at 442–43. This argument is difficult to follow since, under regulation, the utility companies rarely encounter competition.

[58] Pegrum, note 52 *supra*, at 10.

[59] Shepherd, *Utility Growth and Profits under Regulation*, in SHEPHERD & GIES, note 2 *supra*, at 3; Cross, *Incentive Pricing and Utility Regulation*, 84 Q. J. ECON. 236 (1970); cf. TREBING, note 2 *supra*, at 7–8. A differing view is presented in Rosoff, *The Application of Traditional Theory to a Regulated Firm*, 4 BUS. ECON. 77, 80 (1969).

[60] Wilson, *The Effect of Rate Regulation on Resource Allocation in Transportation*, 54 AM. ECON. REV. 160, 170 (1964); Daniel, note 30 *supra*, at 351–52, 354; cf. Hilton, note 51 *supra*, at 50–51. Professor Gies has questioned the basic notion that public utility services are necessities rather than luxuries. Gies, note 2 *supra*, at 93, 94. In economic theory it is axiomatic that luxuries will sell at competitive prices. But cf. United States v. Container Corp., 393 U.S. 333, 336 (1969).

[61] Demsetz, *Why Regulate Utilities?* 11 J. LAW & ECON. 55, 61 (1968).

lation at all. In that way the heavy hand of regulation would be lifted and replaced by a form of taxation, but at the same time forces of competition would discipline the managements of the utility companies: [62]

> In the case of utility industries, resort to the rivalry of the market place would relieve companies of the discomforts of commission regulation. But it would also relieve them of the comfort of legally protected market areas. It is my belief that the rivalry of the open market place disciplines more effectively than do the regulatory processes of the commission. If the managements of utility companies doubt this belief, I suggest that they re-examine the history of their industry to discover just who it was that provided most of the force behind the regulatory movement.

V. A Handful of Loyalists

Not everyone is ready to abandon regulation. In the first place, even those who find much fault with the present system sometimes say that it is better than deregulation. Thus Professor Cramton wrote: [63]

> The record of performance in the transportation industries justifies the assertion that the present halfway house, despite its deficiencies, is superior to the more effective protectionism that would be the only likely result of centralized control and broader authority over the transportation industries, the proposal that is concealed under slogans of the need for increased "coordination" and integration in the transportation.

Professor Phillips is another student who has found that the growth rates of the regulated industries have been good and their prices lower, although he admits that enterprises in the transportation sector do not fully sustain his point of view.[64]

---

[62] *Id.* at 65. Cf. Frenkel & Pashigian, *Regulation and Excess Demand: A General Equilibrium Approach*, 45 J. Bus. 379 (1972).

[63] Cramton, note 45 *supra*, at 190. See also Telser, *On the Regulation of Industry*, 77 J. Pol. Econ. 937, 950 (1969). An imaginative defense of regulation has been presented by Professor Sheshinski. Note 56 *supra*.

[64] Phillips, note 34 *supra*, at 735–36; cf. Daniel, note 30 *supra*, at 348; Irwin, *Computers and Communications: The Economics of Interdependence*, 34 Law & Contemp. Prob. 360, 386 (1969); Sherman, *The Design of Public Utility Institutions*, 46 Land Econ. 51, 52 (1970).

Other students cling to the idea of regulation while voicing strong disapproval of the manner in which the various commissions have acted. One stalwart supporter of regulation is Professor Lewis, who wrote:[65]

> I believe firmly in the institution of public utility regulation but, along with many others, I have little enthusiasm for its performance. Public-utility regulation has not lived up' to its early-twentieth-century promise, and if that promise continues to fade, both regulation and private ownership in the utility industries are in deep trouble.

He went on to say that the United States Supreme Court was largely to blame for the sad state of regulation. His complaint is that the Court gave the commissions too much leeway and did not eliminate the cumbersome, inefficient, and cluttered methods employed by the regulatory bodies.[66] In a somewhat similar vein, Professor Parker found that the commissions were not adequate as a substitute for competition. Nevertheless, he found no reason to eliminate them.[67] One commentator, however, advised the regulatory agencies to employ better planning and to exercise a broader vision. While his view, of course, is tenable, it amounts to a counsel of perfection. He finds several reasons for the continuance of regulation but none of them is new.[68]

Finally, as one might imagine, some observers have published more sophisticated views of the effects and possibilities of regulation. For example, it is argued that nobody knows the exact cost of capital at any particular moment in time and, therefore, it is impossible to fix rates based thereon. On the other hand, the existence of rate controls may motivate the firm to increase its output and to take other steps beneficial to the economy as a whole.[69]

---

[65] Lewis, *Emphasis and Misemphasis in Regulatory Policy*, in SHEPHERD & GIES, note 2 *supra*, at 212, 213.

[66] *Id*. at 229.

[67] Parker, *The Regulation of Public Utilities*, 10 NAT. RES. J. 827 (1970); Pegrum, note 52 *supra*, at 12; Harper, note 50 *supra;* Sampson, note 53 *supra*. Specific suggestions are, however, meager.

[68] Trebing, *Government Regulation and Modern Capitalism*, 3 J. ECON. ISSUES 87, 103 (1969); Trebing, note 2 *supra*, at 300.

[69] Rosoff, note 59 *supra*, at 79; Frenkel & Pashigian, note 62 *supra*, at 384; Westfield, *Methodology of Evaluating Economic Regulation*, 61 AM. ECON. REV. 211, 214 (1971).

VI. Some Problems of Conflicts between the Two Concepts

Let us suppose that Mr. Justice Douglas's opinion in *Otter Tail* becomes accepted law. All public utilities then are subject to the constraints of the antitrust laws. In addition, of course, they are subject to the various state, federal, and municipal regulative statutes which control their rates, service, and financing.

A convenient starting point is the prohibition of monopoly by § 2 of the Sherman Act. It will be recalled that in the *Otter Tail* case the regulated public utility which refused to sell at wholesale to municipal power systems was held, over a dissent, to be in violation of that statute.[70] Several decisions dealing with nonregulated enterprises indicate that a defendant may be found guilty of enjoying monopoly power in violation of § 2 if he has 89 percent of a defined market.[71] It would be interesting to observe how few public utilities enjoyed less than 89 percent of the business in their geographic areas.[72] It would seem to follow, therefore, that most public utility companies, like Otter Tail Power, are in violation of § 2 of the Sherman Act. Hence they could be subjected to the civil and criminal penalties provided in the Sherman and Clayton Acts, including an injunction. But how would such an injunction be framed? Could the public utility company be dismembered? Such a suggestion leads to the old argument about duplicate and triplicate gas, water, and electric lines in the streets and the difficulties inherent therein. Such duplication of facilities would undoubtedly prove expensive as well as inconvenient.[73] It is hard to conceive of widespread public support for any such ruling.

Closely allied to the monopoly problem is that of division of territory. Most public utilities operate in a defined geographical

---

[70] Mr. Justice Stewart wrote: "With respect to decisions by regulated electric utilities as to whether or not to provide nonretail services, I think that in the absence of horizontal conspiracy, the teaching of the 'primary jurisdiction' cases argues for leaving governmental regulation to the Commission instead of the invariably less sensitive and less specifically expert process of anti-trust litigation." 410 U.S. at 391.

[71] United States v. Grinnell Corp., 384 U.S. 563 (1966); Denver Union Stockyard v. Denver Live Stock Commission Company, 404 F.2d 1055 (10th Cir. 1968).

[72] But cf. Illinois Motor Carrier of Property Law, Ill. Rev. Stat. c. 95.5, §§ 18–301 (existence of one carrier not a bar to issuance of certificate to another).

[73] Demsetz, note 61 *supra*.

area and do not attempt to invade the neighboring area of another utility company. We know from the famous *Sealy* case[74] that any agreement so to divide territories would be illegal and even in the case of public utilities the United States Supreme Court has insisted that natural gas pipelines must operate in the same areas and compete.[75] This, of course, is all at odds with the general theory of public utility regulation whereby, for example, the certificate issued to a common carrier must specify the routes and termini or territory which it will serve.[76] The carrier is not allowed to operate in other areas. Again, the question is whether problems of indivisibility and perhaps aesthetic considerations will indicate that only a single utility should serve in any one area. The only solution which has been offered for this dilemma is the suggestion of Professor Demsetz that the right to serve any territory should be auctioned off periodically and awarded to the highest bidder. This solution would not remove the element of monopoly but would presumably recapture monopoly profit.

Moving back to § 1 of the Sherman Act, we observe the familiar rule that price-fixing is unlawful thereunder. Indeed, in the *Container Corporation* case,[77] the mere exchange of price information, absent any agreement with respect thereto, was found to be illegal under the Sherman Act. This rule is directly at war with the common provision of public utility statutes that common carrier rates must be "established," filed, published, and posted. Even contract carrier rates must be filed with the regulatory commission.[78] Hence the prices of those utilities are public information available to competitors in direct contravention of the rule laid down in the *Container* case. A careful comment on this problem reached the conclusion that dual controls were not feasible:[79]

---

[74] United States v. Sealy, Inc. 388 U.S. 350 (1967).

[75] Cascade Natural Gas Corp. v. El Paso Gas Co., 386 U.S. 129, 135 (1967); see Shenefield, *Antitrust Policy within the Electric Utility Industry*, 16 ANTITRUST BULL. 681, 686, 693 (1971).

[76] Illinois Motor Carrier of Property Law, Ill. Rev. Stat. c. 95.5, § 18–301(d).

[77] United States v. Container Corp., 393 U.S. 333 (1969); see Hale, *Communication among Competitors*, 14 ANTITRUST BULL. 63 (1969).

[78] Illinois Motor Carrier of Property Law, Ill. Rev. Stat. c. 95.5, § 18–310, –501, –505.

[79] Pegrum, note 52 *supra*, at 12.

One proposal is to abolish the Commission [ICC] and transfer the responsibility for regulation to the Sherman and Clayton Acts with enforcement in the hands of the Antitrust Division and the Federal Trade Commission. This approach assumes separate and completely independent action by all the individual enterprises. This ignores the unique problems of transport, which have already been discussed, but it also ignores the fact that antitrust has had no experience whatsoever in dealing with transport problems.

Rate-making in transport requires cooperation on joint rates, through rates, joint routes, division of rates, interchange of traffic and equipment as well as cooperative use of facilities such as terminals. All this requires agreements that would find an inhospitable home under current interpretation of antitrust. Discrimination in pricing would impose a hopeless task on antitrust authorities under the present interpretation of the Robinson-Patman Act, and could not be dealt with in any case under concepts applicable to industry in general. Common carrier obligations and arrangements do not fall within the antitrust laws. Consolidation, at least among railroads, would face even greater barriers than it does today. The mergers that have been approved to date have been possible only because the I.C.C. does not have to meet the standards of the Clayton Act, and the Antitrust Division has been unsuccessful in imposing its concepts of the application of the Sherman Act.

In short, transportation does not fit into antitrust interpretation, even though in some areas the I.C.C. could bring its policies more into line with the philosophy of antitrust. Transportation is a mixture of public utility and competitive economics that is not amenable to antitrust jurisdiction alone.

Tying arrangements have been the subject of vigorous condemnation under the antitrust laws. Perhaps the most striking decision is *Fortner v. United States Steel Corporation.*[80] In that opinion it was declared that U.S. Steel had unlawfully "tied" the sale of its prefabricated houses to the extension of credit for the purchase thereof. The logic of this holding would appear to prohibit any seller from extending credit to any customer. As in the case of other esoteric decisions, extrapolation apparently has not taken place. Nevertheless, the principle of the decision would appear to prohibit a grocer from providing both vegetables and meats. Carried far enough, perhaps a railroad could not haul more than a single commodity;

---

[80] 394 U.S. 495 (1969). See Dam, *Fortner Enterprises v. United States Steel: "Neither a Borrower, Nor a Lender Be,"* 1969 SUPREME COURT REVIEW 1.

and an electric utility could be forbidden to offer 220 volt service in addition to 110 volt service. It seems unlikely that any such determination would be acceptable to public opinion.

Another vicious practice forbidden under the antitrust laws is that of reciprocity. A manufacturer is not allowed to purchase his supplies from persons who happen to be his customers.[81] As applied to public utilities, such a holding might prohibit an electric generating company from purchasing wire from a patron whose plant it served. This problem could probably be obviated by finding another source of supply in a more distant area but it would also add to the costs of the public utility.

In fairly recent years we thought that an acquisition by a firm in the free market sector could only be attacked if some anticompetive effect resulted therefrom. Recent decisions, including the famous *Procter & Gamble* case,[82] appear to have altered that view in some degree. If applied to an electric utility company, therefore, *Procter & Gamble* might suggest that the company should divest itself of water, gas, or other services it may be providing. On the other hand, a recent empirical study indicates that there is no demonstrable adverse effect on rates when the public utility supplies both electricity and gas.[83]

A few years ago no one saw harm in vertical mergers—and some still don't. The courts, however, have found them to be vicious instruments of "foreclosure."[84] We have mentioned above the last phase of the *Northwest Pipeline*[85] case which forbade vertical integration by a public utility. Now we find that despite state regulation and possibly Civil Aeronautics Board regulation, a merger of airlines can be attacked under § 7 of the Clayton Act.[86] A logical extrapolation of these holdings would require one public utility company to generate electricity and a separate one to distribute it to consumers. Here again the cost of breaking up a public utility system may seem high in comparison with whatever benefits may possibly be derived therefrom.

---

[81] F.T.C. v. Consolidated Foods Corp., 380 U.S. 592 (1965).

[82] F.T.C. v. Proctor & Gamble Co., 386 U.S. 568 (1967).

[83] Pace, *The Relative Performance of Combination Gas-Electric Utilities*, 17 ANTITRUST BULL. 519 (1972).

[84] Ford Motor Co. v. United States, 405 U.S. 562 (1972).

[85] Cascade Natural Gas Corp., note 75 *supra*.

[86] United States v. Pacific Southwest Airlines, 358 F. Supp. 1224 (C.D. Calif. 1973).

Closely allied to the subject of merger is that of joint ventures. They, too, have been found to be in violation of § 7 of the Clayton Act.[87] Hence, it is not surprising to find that § 7 was also applied to a joint venture by gas distributing companies to build a common pipeline to producing areas. Further, we have learned that § 7 of the Clayton Act must be applied to joint ventures among utilities such as the operation of a common electric generating plant.[88] Here again the cost of competition may soon seem excessive.

In the private sector of the economy a seller may stop doing business with one distributor and take on another so long as he does not enter into a conspiracy.[89] Public utility firms, however, are obliged by law to serve any responsible patron. Here is an application of the antitrust laws which would work a result contrary to the import of those described above. It seems unlikely that the courts are ready to abandon the doctrine that a public utility must serve any patron within its territory.

We have saved to the last the most glaring example of the clash between the commands of the antitrust laws and those of public utility regulation. We are referring, of course, to enforcement of § 2 of the Clayton Act, commonly referred to as the Robinson-Patman Act. In a recent Supreme Court decision a Robinson-Patman Act claim was sustained on the ground that the defendant was selling pies at lower prices in some areas than in others.[90] If applied to a public utility this might mean that the nearby patrons would be compelled to subsidize extension of mains or lines to a distant patron. In the *Utah Pie* case, again the court claimed that the defendant had failed to "cost justify" its prices.[91] Public utility rate structures with their separate schedules for interruptible and firm service, their demand charges for larger customers, and their sharp reduction of charges with volume of use would require wholesale revision to fit into the mysteries of Robinson-Patman compliance. We know from a recent case, for example, that § 2 of the Clayton Act reaches

---

[87] United States v. Penn-Olin Chemical Co., 378 U.S. 158 (1964).

[88] Northern Natural Gas Co. v. F.P.C., 399 F.2d 953 (D.C. Cir. 1968); Municipal Electric Ass'n v. S.E.C., 413 F.2d 1052, 1057–59 (D.C. Cir. 1969); cf. Shenefield, note 75 *supra*, at 714.

[89] Joseph E. Seagram & Sons, Inc. v. Hawaiian Oke, Ltd., 416 F.2d 71 (9th Cir. 1969); cf. United States v. Arnold, Schwinn & Company, 388 U.S. 365 (1967).

[90] Utah Pie Co. v. Continental Baking Co., 386 U.S. 685 (1967).

[91] *Id*. at 694–95.

discrimination against a plaintiff who received deliveries of lumber more slowly than other customers.[92] *Quaere*, how this could be applied to distant patrons of public utility companies. Furthermore, the entire rate structure administered by the Interstate Commerce Commission is known to discriminate against high value commodities. Coal moves for much less per ton than jewels. Here again the system of regulation is wholly different from that imposed by § 2 of the Clayton Act. For that reason, presumably, one court has declared the quantity discounts of an electric utility to be exempt from antitrust controls.[93]

A final specter is the possibility that suits against public utilities might result in huge treble damage awards. In private litigation, judgments running into the millions are no longer uncommon.[94] As applied to a public utility such a judgment might constitute a discrimination against the nonfavored patrons; they would, in effect be compelled to pay higher rates in order to keep the utility solvent. This very idea was expressed many years ago by the United States Supreme Court in the *Keogh* case[95] in which damages under the antitrust laws were refused in a suit against railroads. The court expressly referred to the possibility that such damages could constitute an illegal rebate.[96]

VII. Conclusion

Application of the antitrust laws to regulated industries presents many promising possibilities. As noted above, many observers are weary of direct controls and would prefer pushing the utilities into the free market.[97] The case against regulation has been so con-

---

[92] Centex-Winston Corp. v. Edw. Hines Lumber Co., 447 F.2d 585 (7th Cir. 1971).

[93] Gas Light Co. of Columbus v. Georgia Power Co., 440 F.2d 1135, 1137–38, 1140 (5th Cir. 1971).

[94] Philadelphia Electric Co. v. Westinghouse Electric Co., CCH Trade Cases ¶ 71, 123 (E.D. Pa. 1964); cf. Simpson v. Union Oil Co., 377 U.S. 13 (1964), 396 U.S. 13 (1969).

[95] Keogh v. Chicago & North Western Railway, 260 U.S. 156 (1922).

[96] *Id.* at 162.

[97] Shenefield, note 75 *supra*, reviews cases applying antitrust law to electric utilities and finds no objection unless increase of costs, etc., are shown. Owen, *Monopoly Pricing in Combined Gas and Electric Utilities*, 15 Antitrust Bull. 713, 722 (1970); Daniel, note 30 *supra;* Irwin, note 64 *supra*, at 381; Park, note 41 *supra*, at 230.

vincingly stated that only a handful of students continue to place faith in interventionist regulation. Moreover, technological developments, as mentioned above, possibly are working in the direction of market freedom.[98] Even if the only savings were to relieve the utilities and their patrons of the burden of filing and examining thousands upon thousands of tariff schedules, there would seem to be a net benefit.

One is, of course, attracted to the solution suggested by Professor Demsetz. As indicated above, he has proposed a system of bidding for the right of supplying utility service in situations wherein duplication of facilities would be onerous. Thus, there would remain only one distributor of gas in any area and only one set of gas mains in the streets, but the identity of the proprietor of the system might change from time to time depending on who would pay the highest price for the privilege of becoming the sole supplier.[99] On the other hand, there are some problems with respect to Professor Demsetz's suggestion, one being that it may not be the right remedy for a decreasing cost industry.[100]

The bland assumption that antitrust laws can be applied to utility companies while interventionist controls remain in effect seems naive.[101] There is always the danger that application of the antitrust laws to pervasively regulated industries might turn into a protectionist program designed to shelter existing firms.[102]

As pointed out above, many conflicts occur between the commands of public utility commissions and their organic laws, on the one hand, and the antitrust statutes, on the other. The uncertainty over which set of controls might be applicable to any given situation would be costly and time-consuming. Almost any move by a public utility firm could be questioned under both means of control. This is scarcely a time—if ever there was one—to add needless costs to public utility service. Long periods of uncertainty, possibly

---

[98] Trebing, note 2 *supra*, at 308–09.

[99] Demsetz, note 61 *supra*, at 65.

[100] Telser, note 63 *supra*, at 939, 950; Pace, *Relevant Markets and the Nature of Competition in the Electric Utility Industry*, 16 ANTITRUST BULL. 725, 729 (1971).

[101] Northern Natural Gas Co. v. Federal Power Comm'n, 399 F.2d 953, 959 (D.C. Cir. 1968).

[102] Hale & Hale, note 1 *supra*, at 52; Hale & Hale, *Regulation: A Defense to Anti-Merger Litigation?* 54 KY. L. J. 683, 715 ff. (1966).

extending for five or more decades, might be required to ascertain what activities of the utilities remained under interventionist regulation and which would be attacked under the antitrust laws. In short, the utility companies can scarcely be expected to serve two masters. Hence the issue should be put to the legislative branch of government for resolution. If the Congress were to abolish the federal system of utility regulation—and we think it should—state legislators should also act. In a word, the cry is: Repeal!

RUSSELL WHEELER

EXTRAJUDICIAL ACTIVITIES OF

THE EARLY SUPREME COURT

Neither law, political science, nor history has looked with favor upon the pre-Marshall Supreme Court. There is a widely held notion that until Marshall came to the Supreme Court, the Court did nothing. It did nothing, it is said, in part because its members so preoccupied themselves with nonjudicial duties that work on the Court was distinctly secondary. Historians have, of late, taken another look at the pre-Marshall Court and have concluded that its judicial work was not as unimportant as has been believed.[1] Yet the suspicion remains that the early judges were more anxious to be politicians than judicial statesmen.[2]

It is surely true, and often noted, that Jay and Ellsworth served as diplomats, that Bushrod Washington and Chase made partisan speeches. What deserves recognition, though, are the occasions on which the members of the early Court rejected demands for extra-judicial service, and why they did so. The Jay Court faced a President and Congress anxious to adopt a basic assumption of the English constitution, the assumption that judges were obligated to

Russell Wheeler, Assistant Professor of Political Science, Texas Tech University, (on leave), is a Fellow of The Federal Judicial Center, Washington, D.C.

AUTHOR'S NOTE: I am pleased to express my thanks to Professor Herbert J. Storing for his careful examination of my argument.

[1] See MORRIS, JOHN JAY, THE NATION AND THE COURT, esp. cc. 2 & 3 (1967).

[2] Note the acid comment of Professor Alpheus T. Mason: "During the Federalist era, politicians and statesmen bivouacked in and out of the Chief Justiceship on their march from one position to another." *Pyrrhic Victory: The Defeat of Abe Fortas*, 45 VA. Q. REV. 19, 22 (1969).

serve the nation extrajudicially in various ex officio capacities in which their judicial skills would be of use. When faced with demands for extrajudicial activity they thought would violate the American philosophy of separation of powers, the judges refused to comply. Yet they did not regard obligatory extrajudicial service as unconstitutional per se. The American Constitution created a unique judicial office, and it fell to the Jay Court to explain its character. Thus, not only was the early Court a special kind of "schoolmaster," teaching the "people how to be good republicans,"[3] it also lectured the high officials of the government, teaching them of the limits that the American philosophy of government placed on judges. This teaching should be explored for an adequate understanding of the Supreme Court's history.

Certainly their teaching was not entirely effective. The notion that judges are obliged to serve the government in extrajudicial capacities has recurred throughout the history of the Court, despite Tocqueville's observation that the American judge "performs his functions as a citizen by fulfilling the precise duties which belong to his profession as a magistrate."[4] Congress has made occasional ex officio assignments, such as the Chief Justice as a Regent of the Smithsonian Institution[5] and the appointment of five Justices to the Electoral Commission of 1876.[6] Moreover, extrajudicial activity not undertaken ex officio has often been discussed in terms of the obligations of the office. Court of Appeals Judge John Parker justified Jackson's mission to Nuremberg with the claim that there are occasionally calls "for a judge to do something for his country which no one but a judge can do so well." In such a situation, Parker wrote, the judge is obligated to perform the task.[7] According to Chief Justice Warren, President Johnson thought that "no less a person-

---

[3] Lerner, *The Supreme Court as Republican Schoolmaster*, 1967 SUPREME COURT REVIEW 127, 178.

[4] 1 TOCQUEVILLE, DEMOCRACY IN AMERICA 107 (Vintage ed. 1955).

[5] Act of 10 Aug. 1846, ch. 178, §§ 1, 2, 9 STAT. 102–03. The Chief Justice still serves as a regent. See 20 U.S.C. §§ 41, 42.

[6] For the history of the 1876 Commission, see WOODWARD, REUNION AND REACTION 161–62 (2d ed. rev. 1956). Justice Hughes obeyed a 1911 directive that he serve on a commission to investigate aspects of the postal service. 1 PUSEY, CHARLES EVANS HUGHES 296 (1951).

[7] Parker, *The Judicial Office in the United States*, 23 N.Y.U.L.Q. REV. 225, 237–38 (1948). This was a self-serving statement; Parker himself served at Nuremberg.

age than the Chief Justice . . . should head up" the investigation of President Kennedy's assassination.[8] On the other hand, Chief Justice Taft saw the "proper standing and function of the Court in the governmental structure" as a prohibition on extrajudicial activity,[9] at least so far as others were concerned. Chief Justice Fuller said that "the nature of the office" dictated "that the Chief Justice should not participate in public affairs."[10]

This debate might be clarified by examining the course it took in the years immediately after the Constitution was ratified, when Americans were first faced with squaring obligatory extrajudicial activity with the Constitution's new scheme of separated powers and functions. Statesmen of the founding period necessarily trod on virgin constitutional soil. They did not have the gilded luxury of refusing or accepting extrajudicial activity by a cavalier reference to "tradition" or "propriety." Instead, as Donald Morgan has noted, citizens and officials of the "early constitutional period . . . when contemplating measures of governmental action, probed constitutional issues [and] demonstrated knowledge and insight in the two fields of government and law."[11] They did so to a degree unique in American political history.

What follows is an examination of the pre-Marshall Court's response to demands that Supreme Court Justices serve the government in official but extrajudicial capacities. Not treated here is extrajudicial activity which was not ex officio, such as the diplomatic activity of Jay and Ellsworth and the electoral politics of Jay, Cushing, Washington, and Chase.[12]

I. WHAT THE FOUNDERS INTENDED

American political dialogue and diatribe abounds with references to "the founders' intentions," references that often reveal in-

---

[8] Quoted in Lewis, *A Talk with Warren on Crime, the Court, and the Country*, N.Y. TIMES MAG. 34, 134 (19 Oct. 1969).

[9] Quoted in MASON, HARLAN FISKE STONE 705 (1956).

[10] Quoted in KING, MELVILLE WESTON FULLER 247, 254 (1967).

[11] MORGAN, CONGRESS AND THE CONSTITUTION vii (1966).

[12] Such "ad hoc" off-the-court political involvement surely merits study. I have attempted an analysis of it elsewhere. Wheeler, Extrajudicial Activities of United States Supreme Court Justices: The Constitutional Period, 1790–1809; esp. chs. 7 and 8 (unpublished Ph.D. dissertation, University of Chicago, Department of Political Science, 1970).

adequate understandings of those intentions.[13] Thus, Eugene Mc-
Carthy was certain that President Johnson's appointment of Chief
Justice Warren to chair the Kennedy assassination investigation
"could in no way be squared with the intention of the framers of
the Constitution."[14] An analysis of the Constitutional Convention's
debates suggests, to the contrary, that many of the framers expected
judges to make off-the-court contributions to the government, and
furthermore that they viewed such a prospect favorably.

To be sure, there was in the constitutional period a common
conviction that the separation of powers was an essential barrier
to tyranny and that judicial independence was an essential in-
gredient in the separation of powers. Furthermore, political and
legal theorists stressed that judicial independence would be secured
by providing the judges with tenure during good behavior and salaries that could not be lowered during their incumbency. Indeed, the
crown's refusal to allow American judges these historic English
protections was a major cause of the Revolution.[15]

On the other hand, there was very little fear of extrajudicial activity, and such activity was common both in England and the
American colonies. It was standard practice in colonial America for
governors to attempt to control the legislatures by the promise of
places within their appointment power. Judgeships were freely distributed in this manner.[16] Objections to plural officeholding, including that by judges, found occasional expression in the colonial period[17] and in the post-colonial state constitutions.[18] It would appear,
however, that these objections were based primarily on a desire to
avoid the system of influence that had corrupted Parliament in the

[13] For a good discussion of one popular misconception, see Martin Diamond's excellent
analysis, *What the Framers Meant by Federalism*, in Goldwin, ed., A Nation of States
24–41 (1963).

[14] McCarthy, First Things First 41 (1968).

[15] See Bailyn, The Ideological Origins of the American Revolution 74 *passim*
(1967); Ervin, *Separation of Powers: Judicial Independence*, 35 Law & Contemp. Prob.
108–27 (1970).

[16] See Labaree, Royal Government in America 100–02 (1930); Greene, The
Quest for Power 186 *passim* (1963).

[17] See Spurlin, Montesquieu in America, 1760–1801 30 (1940); 5 Colonial Laws
of New York 73 (1770); Brennan, Plural Office Holding in Massachusetts,
1760–1780 80–105 (1945).

[18] See the various documents in both volumes of Poore, ed., The Federal and State
Constitutions (1877).

eighteenth century, and to restrict "the monopoly of political power by the upper classes."[19] For example, the reason the New Jersey Constitution barred from the legislature "Judges of the Supreme or other Courts, Sheriffs, or any other person or persons possessed of any post of profit" was so that the legislature "may, as much as possible, be preserved from all suspicion of corruption."[20]

Majority sentiment in the 1787 Constitutional Convention toward extrajudicial activity is hard to discern, but it is obvious that more than a few of the prominent delegates felt it quite proper to require some type of extrajudicial service by the nation's highest jurists. Two proposals were made to prohibit all extrajudicial plural officeholding by judges, but neither ever reached a vote.[21] Most notable of the proposals for obligatory extrajudicial service were Madison's plan for a council of legislative revision and a proposal by Pinckney for advisory opinions. Other types of service, however, were suggested. Gouverneur Morris submitted a plan to the Committee of Detail which would have made the Chief Justice the second ranking member of a council of state. He would have recommended laws to promote judicial administration, "and such as may promote useful learning and inculcate sound morality throughout the Union."[22] Morris's plan reflects a conviction that those who held the judicial office had skills of statesmanship which they were obliged to put extrajudicially to the nation's service.

This same conviction is reflected in the debate over Madison's

---

[19] DOUGLASS, REBELS AND DEMOCRATS 26 (1955); see also COLBOURN, THE LAMP OF EXPERIENCE, esp. chs. 3 and 9 (1965). Massachusetts seems to have made a concerted effort to limit judges to the performance of the judicial function. Whether this reflects a zeal to protect judicial independence is problematic, however, since Massachusetts judges were notorious beneficiaries of the "fruits of political control." See DOUGLASS, *supra* at 149 and chs. 9–11; BRENNAN, note 17 *supra*.

[20] N.J. CONST. art. 20 (1771); 2 POORE, note 18 *supra*, at 1313.

[21] The proposed prohibitions are found in the New Jersey Plan's judiciary provision and in a set of propositions submitted by Charles Pinckney to the Committee of Detail. Paterson's proposal would have prohibited judges from "receiving or holding any office or appointment during their time of service, or for thereafter [*sic*]." 1 FARRAND, THE RECORDS OF THE FEDERAL CONVENTION 244 (rev. ed. 1937) (hereinafter cited as FARRAND). Pinckney's proposal was in a section banning plural officeholding by all executive and judicial members of the government. 2 *id.* at 341. In the interest of legislative integrity, legislators were banned from an executive or judicial post in the government. U.S. CONST. art. 1, § 6. Neither may any officer of the government be a presidential elector. Art. 2, § 1.

[22] 2 FARRAND at 342–44, 427. A somewhat similar proposal by Ellsworth can be found *id.* at 328–29.

proposal for a Council of Revision, to be comprised of the President "and a convenient number of the National Judiciary, . . . with authority to examine every act of the National Legislature before it shall operate" as well as the then-contemplated congressional veto of any state laws.[23] Although the proposal was decisively rejected, arguments made on its behalf are noteworthy, for they indicate that some of the prominent framers wanted to have American judges assume roles similar to those of their English counterparts. Proponents of judicial participation in the council first satisfied themselves that the judges, when expounding the laws, would not be influenced by the part they had had in creating them.[24] More important for our purposes are the advantages which Madison and others thought would come from employing the judges in extrajudicial service. The "Code of laws," Madison said, would receive "perspicuity, . . . conciseness, and . . . systematic character" from exposure to "the Judiciary talents."[25] Gerry, however, did not want to make "Statesmen of the Judges."[26] Morris countered by pointing to England, where "the Judges . . . had a great share in the Legislation. They are consulted in difficult and doubtful cases. . . . They are or may be members of the privy Council."[27] Gorhum charged that judges "are not to be presumed to possess any peculiar knowledge of the mere policy of public measures."[28] Mason responded that the nature of the judges' vocation and the institutional protections they enjoy foster in them special qualities: "the habit and practice of considering laws in their true principles, and in all their consequences."[29] "Laws," Wilson said, might be "unjust, . . . unwise, . . . dangerous, . . . destructive; and yet not be so unconstitutional as to justify the Judges in refusing to give them effect"[30] if they arose in adjudication. He supported Madison's move to have the judges "counteracting, by the weight of their opinions the improper views of the Legislature."[31] Judges, in other words, had a wisdom which should not be limited to adjudication.

---

[23] 1 *id.* at 21.

[24] The argument, basically, was that a conflict would not arise so often as to be dangerous. See, *e.g.*, King's objection to the Council and Madison's response, 1 *id.* at 98, 138–39.

[25] 1 *id.* at 139.

[26] 2 *id.* at 75.

[27] *Ibid.*

[28] 2 *id.* at 73.

[29] 2 *id.* at 78.

[30] 2 *id.* at 73.

[31] *Ibid.*

This recognition of special judicial skills appropriate for extrajudicial use was not confined to the proponents of the Council of Revision. Even some opponents of the Council of Revision urged that judges be assigned extrajudicial tasks. Charles Pinckney also proposed bans on extrajudicial plural officeholding, once as a convention delegate and again in 1800, in response to the diplomatic activity of Jay and Ellsworth.[32] Yet Pinckney seconded Morris's motion for a Council of State.[33] More important, he proposed that President and Congress have authority "to require the opinions of the supreme Judicial Court upon important questions of law, and upon solemn occasions."[34] The proposal reflected the English practice whereby the Executive or Parliament could request legal advice from the judges.[35] Participation on the council, Pinckney had argued, would give "a previous tincture" to the judges' opinions because it would "involve them in parties."[36] Presumably the mere rendering of advisory opinions would not create this bias, because it would not involve the judges in the legislative process. Furthermore, Pinckney evidently envisioned judges giving advice to President and Congress on other than mere legal questions. The phrase "upon solemn occasions" is inserted in the sentence so as to describe when the judges could be called upon for advice. And the Constitutional Convention did not reject Pinckney's motion, as is often assumed.[37] The motion simply did not emerge from the Committee of Detail, to which he submitted it. This could well mean that the committee assumed that the President and Congress could and would seek the judges' opinions in accord with Anglo-American practice, which indeed they did.[38] The important thing is that even staunch opponents of judicial membership on the Council of Revision thought that judges should perform some extrajudicial tasks. It does not appear entirely true, as Professor Lerner argues, that the defeat of the Council of Revision indicates a "notion that judges

---

[32] 2 *id.* at 298, 341. Pinckney's proposed constitutional amendment can be found at 10 ANNALS OF CONGRESS 41–42 (1800) (hereinafter cited as ANNALS).

[33] 2 FARRAND 342.   [34] 2 *id.* at 341.

[35] See, *e.g.*, Frankfurter, *Advisory Opinions*, in 1 ENCYC. Soc. SCI. 475–78 (1930).

[36] 2 FARRAND 298.

[37] See, *e.g.*, Frankfurter, note 35 *supra*, at 476; SCIGLIANO, THE SUPREME COURT AND THE PRESIDENCY 61–62 (1971).

[38] See text *infra*, at notes 97–118.

should do—and only do—what they are trained for."³⁹ Or, at the least, many delegates felt that judges were "trained for" more than simply deciding cases and controversies. Many delegates shared Mason's conviction that it was proper that "further use be made of the judges."⁴⁰

While this conviction did not produce any extrajudicial assignments in the Constitution, it led to the adoption of numerous measures after the Constitution was ratified. The basic principles that guided the judicial response to these various demands for ex officio extrajudicial service were outlined by Chief Justice Jay in a charge delivered to grand juries on his first riding of the eastern circuit.⁴¹ In the charge, Jay expressed his strong support for the separation of powers doctrine, although he admitted that certain of its principles were "theories unconfirmed by practice." Yet, its basic soundness was manifested in its tendency to have each department check the excesses of the other two. It is, Jay continued:⁴²

> universally agreed to be of the last importance to a free people, that they who are vested with executive, legislative, and judicial powers should rest satisfied with their respective portions of power, and neither encroach on the provinces of each other, nor suffer themselves to intermeddle with the rights reserved by the Constitution to the people.

Jay referred specifically to the officeholders, to those "who are vested with" the powers of government. His reference leads to an initial conclusion that he felt any extrajudicial activity would compromise the independence of the judiciary and thus should not be undertaken. Closer reading makes clear that Jay had two distinct kinds of transgressions in mind.

The officers of the general government should not "suffer themselves to intermeddle" with the people's rights. They should, in other words, avoid active and passive interference in personal liberties. They should be careful not to be led into or forced into such interference. On the other hand, Jay used "encroach" to describe deleterious interbranch relations. Officers of each branch of gov-

---

³⁹ Lerner, note 3 *supra*, at 177.

⁴⁰ 2 FARRAND at 78.

⁴¹ The charge is in 3 JOHNSTON, ed., CORRESPONDENCE AND PUBLIC PAPERS OF JOHN JAY 387–95 (1891) (hereinafter cited as JOHNSTON). For information on the grand jury charge in the early period, see Lerner, note 3 *supra*, at 129–35, *passim*.

⁴² 3 JOHNSTON at 389.

ernment should avoid active interference in the business of the other two. The fact that Jay here substituted "encroach" for "suffer" suggests that officeholders in the various branches could be called upon to aid each other in their respective duties.

To be more specific, judges might respond to requests that they serve the government extrajudicially. In fact, as an officer of the government, a judge would presumably have an obligation to respond to a request to serve that government. This obligation, however, was clearly subordinate to the demands of the separation of powers principle. Obviously, judges should not "encroach" on the business of the other branches, but instead should only respond to requests for service. Moreover, Jay put a premium on the departments' checking each other. The judges should avoid any extrajudicial activity which would threaten their ability to judge impartially. It was, Jay asserted elsewhere, neither "illegal [n]or unconstitutional, however it may be inexpedient, to employ [judges] for other purposes, provided the latter purposes be consistent and compatible with the" judges' basic function.[43] It is at bottom a question of discretion whether the judge can maintain judicial independence while serving the nation off the bench. That discretion belongs in some degree to those seeking the judges' services. But it belongs primarily to the judges. The question is: how did the judges of the constitutional period exercise it?

II. JUDGES AS FACT-FINDERS: THE LIMITS OF HAYBURN'S CASE

In the constitutional period and beyond, Congress called on judges to perform, while on the bench, a variety of tasks other than the primary judicial function. This function James Wilson defined as "applying . . . the constitution and laws to facts and transactions in cases, in which the manner or principle of this application are disputed by the parties interested in them."[44] Under English and colonial practice, judges were also assigned duties other than deciding law cases. It is often thought that the 1792 action popularly referred to as *Hayburn's Case*[45] put a stop to such assignments. In

---

[43] Draft of a letter by Jay, intended for Washington, enclosed with a letter from Jay to Iredell, 15 Sept. 1790, 2 McREE, THE LIFE AND CORRESPONDENCE OF JAMES IREDELL 292, 294 (1857).

[44] McCLOSKEY, ed., 1 WORKS OF JAMES WILSON 296 (1967).

[45] 2 Dall. 409 (1792). A common interpretation is in HAINES, ROLE OF THE SUPREME COURT IN AMERICAN GOVERNMENT AND POLITICS, 1789–1835 128–131 (1944).

Hayburn's Case, judges of the federal circuit courts refused to comply with a statute directing them to pass on the validity of pension applications by allegedly ill Revolutionary War veterans. This refusal must not, however, blind us to a substantial number of tasks about which there appears to have been little controversy. Congress assigned, and judges evidently willingly performed, many duties in which they employed judicial skills in the service of the executive and legislative branches. These tasks were performed on the bench but did not involve the decision of law cases. Judges were asked, in some instances, merely to certify documents or evidence, and in others to investigate evidence and determine the existence of facts. The judges evidently complied with these directives except in *Hayburn's Case,* where it appeared that judges were asked to subordinate themselves, as judges, to a nonjudicial administrative hierarchy. Even then, however, the judges were willing to perform the task extrajudicially as ex officio commissioners.

Before examining the *Hayburn's Case* controversy, it might help to explore the wide variety of congressionally assigned tasks which the judges performed on the bench, tasks which did not involve the decision of law cases. In each instance, "further use" was made of the judges' skills in fact-finding and/or their judicial attributes of trustworthiness and honesty. For example, a 1792 law directed federal district judges to attend, in certain circumstances, to the salvaging of French ships shipwrecked or stranded on the American coast.[46] Congress, no doubt, was aware of the controversy over the amount of material which a salvager could claim from stranded ships.[47] It acted to find individuals who could be trusted to oversee the salvage and prevent, in the words of the Franco-American convention, "all kinds of dispute and discussion."[48] A 1790 law directed judges to receive applications from ships' crews who alleged their vessels were unsafe. The judges were to have maritime experts examine the complaints. Upon their reports, the judges

---

[46] Act of 14 Apr. 1792, ch. 24, § 1, 1 STAT. 254. The duty arose out of obligations created by the Franco-American consular convention of 1788. See Convention on Defining and Establishing the Functions and Privileges of Consuls and Vice-Consuls, § 9, 14 Nov. 1788: SCOTT, THE CONTROVERSY OVER NEUTRAL RIGHTS BETWEEN THE UNITED STATES AND FRANCE, 1797–1800 480 (1917).

[47] See 1 BLACKSTONE, COMMENTARIES ON THE LAWS OF ENGLAND 283–84 (1st ed. 1765).

[48] SCOTT, note 46 *supra.*

would decide "whether the ship [was] fit to proceed on the intended voyage."[49] Another statute provided that when congressional elections were contested, a judge was to examine witnesses about the election and forward his findings to Congress.[50] District judges are still required to receive copies of electoral college ballots and hold them in case of disputed elections.[51] In each case, Congress made "further use" of judges' skills in fact-finding and attributes of trustworthiness.

Two statutes reveal especially well the extent to which judges were relied upon to render competent non-case-related judicial service. A 1790 law authorized the Secretary of the Treasury to remit fines or forfeitures paid by individuals guilty of unintentional customs law violations.[52] The law was recommended by Hamilton[53] and patterned after a British statute which put similar powers in the hands of the customs commissioners.[54] The American statute differed however, in that it directed claimants to file their petitions with a district judge. He would investigate the facts of the violation "in a summary manner" and send the results of the inquiry to the Treasury Secretary, who would decide if the fine should be remitted. Although the judges' duties under the statute did not involve the decision of cases or controversies, they were truly judicial. As Justice Story said, the judge exercised "his judicial function" in investigating the facts, and in stating "the facts, as they judicially appear before him." The judge did not merely state the evidence, but instead drew a "legal conclusion" from the evidence "as to the existence of those facts."[55] To put it another way, the "evidence" had to "satisfy the judicial conscience of the judge that [the facts were] true."[56] Whether or not the remission was

---

[49] Act of 20 July 1790, ch. 29, § 3, 1 STAT. 132.

[50] Act of 23 Jan. 1798, ch. 8, § 1, 1 STAT. 537.

[51] Act of 1 Mar. 1792, ch. 8, § 4, 1 STAT. 240; 3 U.S.C. § 13.

[52] Act of 26 May 1790, ch. 12, 1 STAT. 122–23. The statute was reenacted in essentially the same form in 1797 and in 1800 it was extended in force without limit. Act of 3 Mar. 1797, ch. 13, 1 STAT. 506–07; Act of 11 Feb. 1800, ch. 6, 2 STAT. 7.

[53] See 1 ANNALS 1066–67 (1790).

[54] 27 Geo. III, ch. 32, § 15 (1787).

[55] The Margaretta, 16 F. Cas. 719, 721, No. 9,072 (C.C.D. Mass., 1815).

[56] District Judge Ware in The Palo Alto, 18 F. Cas. 1062, 1065, No. 10,700 (C.D. Maine, 1847). The ambiguity in *Hayburn's Case* eventually made its mark. See Mactavish v. Miles, 263 F. 457, 458 (D. Md., 1920), in which District Judge Ross refused to

granted, however, was an administrative decision, "submitted to the [Treasury Secretary's] sound discretion."[57]

In 1795, Congress delegated to the courts the responsibility to naturalize aliens.[58] The Congress established rules for naturalization, as was its responsibility,[59] but delegated to judges the task of determining if aliens met the requirements. Congress chose judges to perform a fact-finding function which Parliament had evidently kept to itself.[60] The act specified residency requirements for the alien and also provided that "it shall further appear to [the judge's] satisfaction that during that time, he has behaved as a man of good moral character, attached to the principles of the constitution of the United States, and well disposed to the good order and happiness of the same." Thus, while the naturalization proceeding was not a case or controversy,[61] it was nevertheless an exercise by the judge of his fact-finding abilities.

Marshall confirmed this in 1830.[62] A District of Columbia Court of Appeals had found an alien to be entitled to citizenship and had issued a citizenship decree. The decree was contested on the grounds that a residency certificate submitted in the proceedings was defective according to statutory criteria. On appeal to the Supreme Court, Marshall upheld the decree, concluding that citizenship was to be granted through the "judicial process," and that

---

proceed under the codified and expanded version of the forfeiture remission statute, because he believed Story was wrong in *The Margaretta* and *Hayburn* allowed judges to refuse to hear such petitions.

[57] Justice Story, in *The Margaretta*, note 55 *supra*.

[58] Act of 29 Jan. 1795, ch. 20, 1 STAT. 414–15. The statute was revised on several occasions. See Act of 18 June 1798, ch. 54, 1 STAT. 566–69; Act of 14 Apr. 1802, ch. 28, 2 STAT. 153–55; Act of 26 Mar. 1804, ch. 47, 2 STAT. 292–93. District judges still participate in the naturalization process, although much of the fact-finding work is done by administrative personnel. See 8 U.S.C. §§ 1421(a), and 1443(a).

[59] U.S. Const. art. 1, § 8, ¶ 4.

[60] See 7 Jac. ch. 2 (1609); 1 BLACKSTONE, note 47 *supra*, at 362.

[61] In Tutun v. United States, 270 U.S. 568 (1926), Justice Brandeis asserted that the naturalization proceedings were indeed "cases or controversies," which were thus reviewable in the courts of appeals. It is noteworthy that the element of the proceeding which gave it its character as a case or controversy in 1926 was missing from the earlier proceedings. Brandeis noted that the 1906 Naturalization Act makes the United States a potential "adverse party," reserving to it the "full rights of a litigant." *Id.* at 577. This provision did not exist in the earlier acts. The judge was to weigh the evidence using his judicial discretion—but did not have the benefits of the adversary proceeding which give "cases" their peculiar quality.

[62] Spratt v. Spratt, 4 Pet. 393 (1830).

naturalization was a judicial rather than a ministerial act. Congress decided to "submit the decision on the right of aliens to courts of record. They are to receive testimony, compare it with the law, and then judge on both law and fact." The certificate was merely "evidence which ought indeed to be required to satisfy the judgment of the court, but the want of which cannot annul that judgment." Then, he added "it seems to us, if it [*i.e.*, the citizenship decree] be in legal form, to close all inquiry, and like every other judgment, to be complete evidence of its own validity."[63]

The naturalization proceedings are especially revealing, for through them the courts were directed to find facts of the highest order. The courts were directed to determine if the alien had "behaved as a man of good moral character, attached to the principles of the constitution of the United States, and well disposed to the good order and happiness of the same."[64] Through normal judicial proceedings of examining witnesses and the alien himself, the court was to decide nothing less than whether the alien had potential for good citizenship. Judges were seen as proper officers to judge men on the basis of an understanding of what human characteristics are necessary for the maintenance of the political system established by the Constitution. Why judges? Because judges, in Mason's words, "are in the habit and practice of considering laws in their true principles, and in all their consequences."[65]

The judges, however, did not acquiesce in any congressionally assigned task. In *Hayburn's Case*, they thought that an assignment called for more than the exercise of judicial skills. They regarded the statute in question as an attempt to put the judges to nonjudicial use. The judges refused to perform this nonjudicial task on the bench. They did recognize an obligation for extrajudicial service, and thus agreed to perform the task, not as judges, but as ex officio commissioners. Their performance, however, raises questions about the wisdom of having judges perform nonjudicial tasks ex officio.

Hayburn's Case involved a 1792 statute, in which Congress directed the judges of the circuit courts to evaluate the pension appli-

---

[63] *Id.* at 406–08.　　　　　[64] Act of 29 Jan. 1795, ch. 20, 1 STAT. 414–15.

[65] 2 FARRAND at 78. Evidence suggests that the judges tended to become lax in the performance of the naturalization function, which brought about the 1906 statute. It may be that the problem was created in part by the performance of the task by many state and local judges, some of whom were little more than clerks. See FRANKLIN, LEGISLATIVE HISTORY OF NATURALIZATION IN THE UNITED STATES (1906).

cations of veterans injured in the Revolutionary War.[66] The applicant was to submit certain documents to the judges to prove he was indeed a veteran. The judges would then examine his wound and determine, based on its seriousness, the portion of his military salary to which each veteran was entitled as a pension. They were then to send their findings to the Secretary of War, who would place the veteran on the pension list at the recommended rate, unless he suspected "imposition or mistake," in which event he could report the matter to Congress and recommend reversal of the judges' recommendations.

Why were the judges selected for this task? They were selected, evidently, because Congress wanted to make "further use" of the judges' honesty as well as their ability as intelligent and capable fact-finders. Secretary of War Knox had proposed that judges be directed to receive certain documents from the veterans and certify them for Congress.[67] To this task, Congress merely added another: actual examination of the petitioners. Congress demanded, as Hart and Wechsler noted, that applicants assert their pension claims before a trustworthy judge who was more able than officials in Philadelphia "to appraise the personal good faith of claimants and the extent of their disability."[68]

Judges of three circuit courts wrote to Washington explaining why they could not comply with the statute.[69] In the first place, as Wilson wrote for the Pennsylvania court, "the business directed by this act is not of a judicial nature. It forms no part of the power vested by the constitution in the courts. . . ." Jay wrote that the "duties" were not "properly judicial" and they were not "to be

---

[66] Act of 23 Mar. 1792, ch. 11, 1 STAT. 243–45. Actually the circuit courts had no separate judges. Supreme Court Justices and district judges sat together as judges of the circuit courts. See Act of 24 Sept. 1789, ch. 20, § 4, 1 STAT. 74–75.

[67] *Report of the Secretary of War to the House of Representatives*, 25 Feb. 1791, in 1 FRANKLIN, ed., AMERICAN STATE PAPERS, Class 9 (Claims), No. 19 (1834) (hereinafter cited as AMERICAN STATE PAPERS, with appropriate class).

[68] HART & WECHSLER, THE FEDERAL COURTS AND THE FEDERAL SYSTEM 100 (1st ed. 1953).

[69] The letters are at 2 Dall. 410. Thus, strictly speaking, *Hayburn's Case* was not a "case." The term refers to the refusal of the Pennsylvania circuit court to consider a pension application of William Hayburn. Two other circuit courts refused to proceed under similar applications. Attorney General Randolph's suit to have the Supreme Court mandamus the Pennsylvania circuit court to hear Hayburn's application was the "second *Hayburn's Case*." See 2 Dall. 409 (1792), and Farrand, *The First Hayburn Case, 1792*, 13 AM. HIST. REV. 281–85 (1908).

performed in a judicial manner." A distinct second reason why the judges refused to act was that their recommendations would be subject to nonjudicial review.[70]

The judges did not specifically say what it was about the pension duty that made its performance by judges unconstitutional. Yet their refusal is explainable in terms of the separation of powers theory. Taking the second reason first, courts should not have their actions checked by nonjudicial officers. More important, however, a determination of the proper pension rate seemed to require the exercise of other than judicial discretion. Congress told the judges not only to find facts of a medical disability, but also to recommend a pension rate which they "may think just." But the statute gave no legal standards by which the judges were to determine if the applicant deserved a pension, or what pension rate would be "just," beyond the vague standard of "comparability" with the applicant's "degree of disability."[71] The fact that the Secretary of War, and Congress, were to review the judge's determinations of "just" pension rates no doubt confirmed suspicions that more than a judicial discretion was to operate.

And, while the judges may have been unaware of it, the background of the 1792 pension act indicates that its sponsors did indeed want a certain administrative policy to guide the granting of pensions. When Secretary of War Knox proposed that a pension system be established, he urged Congress to keep close rein on the granting of pensions. Knox knew that many veterans who would claim pensions "were not conspicuously entitled" to them. A policy of hard skepticism was necessary because it was "easy, from the influence of humanity, to obtain plausible [pension] certificates, even from men of good character."[72] The judge, insulated from executive and legislative control and contact, might well be unable

---

[70] It is sometimes thought, as Chief Justice Taney thought, that "when the decision of the court was subject to the revision of a Secretary and Congress, it was not the exercise of a judicial power. . . ." Gordon v. United States, 117 U.S. 697, 703 (app.) (decided 1864, reported 1886). A close reading of the various opinions renders this interpretation unacceptable. For example, the Pennsylvania court said that it could not proceed "1st. Because the business directed by this act is not of a judicial nature. . . . 2d. Because, if upon that business the court had proceeded its judgments . . . might, under the same act, have been revised and controlled by the legislature, and by an officer in the executive department." 2 Dall. at 411.

[71] Act of 23 Mar. 1792, ch. 11, 1 Stat. 243–45.

[72] Note 67 supra.

to exercise this administrative discretion conformable to the policy desires of the politically responsible officials.

Later actions of the judges give credence to this speculation. Aware of public sympathy for the veterans, some of the judges decided to implement the act by tortuously interpreting it as having appointed them "commissioners for the purpose mentioned in it, by official instead of personal description."[73] Of course, the judges elected to accept the appointments they had devised. (Indeed, that the judges resorted to this labored interpretation indicates how common was the acceptance in the constitutional period of an ex officio extrajudicial service.)[74] Yet, as commissioners "by official description," the judges still benefited from the political insulation of their judicial office and, in fact, did a poor job as pension commissioners. They bore out Knox's warnings when they gave play to the "good character" qualities of sympathy and kindness, rather than review the pension applications skeptically. Insulated from any political control, the judge-commissioners saw the legislative and executive purpose of the act as aiding "many unfortunate and meritorious individuals whom Congress have justly thought proper objects of immediate relief."[75] They were so kind and sympathetic, in fact, that Congress quickly changed the pension system by relieving the judges of the task of receiving the applications. A House Committee noted that "very improper grants of pensions have been made." Continuing to allow the judges to review pension applications, one congressman warned, would "increase the pension list in such a manner, as ten times the present revenues of the United States would not be adequate to supporting."[76]

---

[73] Both New York and southern circuit judges so interpreted the act. When the Pennsylvania judges refused to do so, they were warned in the public press that they should have "pursued the prudent line of conduct of the Circuit Court of New York." Letter from Camden, Aurora General Advertiser (Philadelphia), 21 Apr. 1792 (hereinafter cited as Aurora).

[74] It is true that the Court decided in 1794 that the pension act could not be interpreted as appointing commissioners, but this says nothing about the constitutionality of ex officio appointments per se. See United States v. Todd, reported by Chief Justice Taney in 1851, as a note to United States v. Ferreira, 13 How. 40, 52 (1851). See also note 77 infra.

[75] 2 Dall. at 414.

[76] Thus, the common impression that Congress changed the pension statute in response to the judges' unofficial declaration that it was unconstitutional is in error. For debate on the 1793 statute, see 3 ANNALS 734 (1792). See also the statement by Congressman

This brief review of the pension business illustrates that the federal judicial office, like others established by the Constitution, is structured so as to influence the conduct of its incumbent. The judicial office, with its constitutional guarantee of life tenure and irreducible salary, is structured to insure an impartial finding of facts and application of law. As the early Congresses realized, this fact-finding need not be limited to the decision of cases and controversies. The very protections which encourage impartial fact-finding, however, can discourage the proper performance of nonjudicial tasks. It is noteworthy that Jay and Cushing later agreed that their performance of the duty as commissioners was not warranted by the statute. This might well mean that they belatedly realized that judges do not make good administrative officers when they hold the office "by official description."[77]

III. Ex Officio Service of the Chief Justice

Congress and the Executive also acted in the constitutional period to make "further use" of Supreme Court Justices (notably the Chief Justice) in certain ex officio capacities. These tasks differ from those assigned to lower court judges in that the duties assigned to the Chief Justice were to be performed ex officio but were not to be performed on the bench. The assignments of the Chief Justice were based on assumptions much like those that led Madison to propose judicial participation in the Council of Re-

---

William Eustis, ten years later, in debating a bill imposing similar pension duties on the judges. The judges had, Eustis noted, already "objected" to "similar duties." And, it was best they not exercise such duties, because "[w]hen an applicant appeared before them, . . . his wretchedness . . . would be too powerful an address to their sensibilities as men to [allow them to] resist his demands; and they would generously and magnanimously allow him, without rigid inquiry what he claimed." Eustis proposed a military commission. 12 Annals 514 (1803).

[77] A 1793 pension law ordered the Secretary of War and the Attorney General to bring litigation to determine if the claims passed on by the judge-commissioners were valid. Act of 28 Feb. 1793, ch. 17, § 3, 1 Stat. 325. Without giving a written opinion, the Court ruled that they were not. United States v. Todd, note 74 *supra*. Taney said that in *Todd*, Jay and Cushing realized that they had given, in 1792, "a construction to the law which its language would hardly justify." 13 How. at 53. It is doubtful that it took the judges two years to realize that their strained interpretation was invalid. More likely, the judges realized that judge-commissioners were not qualified to determine the pension claims and that, as a consequence, many undeserving applicants had been placed on the pension list.

vision. That is to say, judges, by dint of their training and experience, had a certain element of wisdom and statesmanship which could properly be tapped for duties other than deciding law cases. Moreover, this involvement of the Chief Justice would create public confidence in the government operations with which he was associated.

The Chief Justice was assigned ex officio membership in two administrative bodies.[78] One superintended the reduction of the Revolutionary War debt, and the other inspected the operation of the United States Mint. Upon Hamilton's recommendation, Congress directed that sample coins annually "be assayed under the inspection of" a group including the Chief Justice, the Secretary and Comptroller of the Treasury, the Secretary of State, and the Attorney General.[79] The Chief Justice's association with such activity had clear English precedents, namely the "Trial of the Pix," before, among others, the Lord Chancellor.[80] While less important than the Sinking Fund duty, the Mint inspection duty was still noteworthy. For one thing, the integrity of the United States coins was a pressing political and economic question in the constitutional period. Moreover, the presence of defective coins was to be reported to the President, who would dismiss the appropriate officers of the Mint.

More significant was the Chief Justice's membership on the Sinking Fund Commission. Congress authorized this agency as part of Hamilton's plan to reconsolidate and fund the national war debt. The Chief Justice, along with the Vice-President, the Secretaries of State and Treasury, and the Attorney General were placed in charge of earmarked revenues with which they were to purchase

---

[78] Note, also, that other assignments were considered and rejected, such as having the Justices determine what compensation was due individuals who were granted patents. 2 ANNALS 1519 (1790). The House considered putting the Senior Associate Justice in the line of ascension to the presidency. 3 id. at 401 (1792). Anticipating the 1876 Electoral Commission, the so-called Ross election bill of 1800 would have made the Chief Justice the chairman of a twelve-man congressional committee empowered to determine the validity of electoral votes. The bill is printed in full in Aurora, 19 Feb. 1800.

[79] Act of 2 Apr. 1792, ch. 16, § 18, 1 STAT. 250. Hamilton proposed the plan in his *Report on the Establishment of a Mint*, 28 Jan. 1791, 7 SYRETT, ed., PAPERS OF ALEXANDER HAMILTON 570–607 (1963) (hereinafter cited as SYRETT).

[80] See id. at 606–07.

evidences of the debt.[81] These "Sinking Fund Commissioners" were clearly expected by Congress to exercise administrative discretion. The statute directed that their purchases of the debt be "made in such manner and under such regulations as shall appear to them best calculated to fulfill the intent of this act."[82]

Hamilton drew on two sources for his idea of a Sinking Fund and a commission to spend it. In the first place, England had had sinking funds since the seventeenth century. The most recent legislation was that of 1786, wherein Parliament, at Pitt's suggestion, established a "Board of Commissioners of the Sinking Fund," comprised of ex officio officers with financial or revenue responsibilities.[83] The Chief Justice's place on the American commission has some comparability to the Chancellor of the Exchequer's place on the English commission. The latter was a judicial officer who had extensive administrative duties as well, all of which related to revenue matters.[84] The Chief Justice was understood by Hamilton, and by Congress, to bring a special knowledge of legal-financial affairs to the commission's deliberations.

Hamilton also relied on some suggestions about sinking funds put to him by Gouverneur Morris.[85] Morris felt that it was extremely important that the public have confidence in the administrators of the fund, "both for the public security and for the reputation of the Ministers." Therefore he suggested they not be limited to financial officers, but include "the President and the other principal officers of State, such as the Secretary at War, and of Foreign Affairs." Such an arrangement, Morris wrote, would provide the public with "every advantage of wisdom, activity, and integrity."[86] Hamilton and Congress saw the Chief Justice as an individual who would enhance the operation of the Sinking Fund Commission and increase public trust in it.

---

[81] Act of 12 Aug. 1790, ch. 47, 1 STAT. 186. The commissioners retained their responsibilities until 1834, when the Treasury Secretary assumed sole responsibility for the small debt remaining. See Ross, *Sinking Funds*, 7 PUBS. AM. ECON. ASS'N 319, 346 (1892).

[82] Act of 12 Aug. 1790, ch. 47, § 2, 1 STAT. 186.

[83] 2 Geo. III, ch. 31, § 14 (1786); see also, Ross, note 81 *supra*, at 324.

[84] 1 HOLDSWORTH, HISTORY OF ENGLISH LAW 233–40 (7th ed. 1956).

[85] There is no reason to doubt that Hamilton relied on Morris. See the editorial note on *Report on Public Credit*, 6 SYRETT 51, 63.

[86] *Observations on the Finances of the United States*, 8 May 1789, 3 SPARKS, LIFE OF GOUVERNEUR MORRIS 469, 476 (1832).

At no time in the debate on the controversial funding plan or its operation was opposition expressed to this "further use" of the Chief Justice.[87] Despite the controversy over such extrajudicial activity as diplomatic missions, making "further use" of the judges by way of ex officio extrajudicial activity was generally accepted.[88] In fact, in 1806, when John Randolph proposed a ban on plural officeholding, he exempted such ex officio service. He specifically noted the Chief Justice's Sinking Fund Commission activity as quite proper, because the commissioners "are not, strictly speaking, officers. The duties they discharge are *ex officio*, . . . and, as Commissioners, they receive no salary."[89] Randolph's concern was with tyrants seeking personal power and wealth. He favored making ex officio "further use" of the judges.

Jay's response to this assignment is best examined in light of his grand jury charge of 1790. Jay assumed an obligation to attend Sinking Fund Commission meetings, but he made clear that his primary obligation was to his judicial duties. His attitude was revealed in 1792 when he was attending circuit court in New York. The commission, which met in Philadelphia, was deadlocked over a point respecting its operational authority. Since Jay's presence was "indispensable," the commission "request[ed his] attendance . . . as speedily as possible."[90] Jay, however, refused to come, because the hazardous roads could prevent his returning to New York in time to attend court.[91] In a separate letter to Hamilton, Jay elaborated on the theme of conflicting duties. He regarded his "Duty to attend

---

[87] See, *e.g.*, 2 ANNALS 1762, 1766 (1791). Other criticisms of the funding plan were also devoid of attacks on the Chief Justice's association with it. See, *e.g.*, the six featured articles by "Brutus" in the National Gazette (Philadelphia), 15, 19, 22, 26 Mar. and 5, 9 Apr. 1792, and Gallatin, *A Sketch of the Finances of the United States*, in FURGESON, SELECTED WRITINGS OF ALBERT GALLATIN 31–61 (1967).

[88] Jay was criticized extensively for improper extrajudicial activity when he was appointed special envoy to England in 1794. Those critics occasionally mentioned his Sinking Fund Commission membership, but they did so to attack his ties with Hamilton, not to criticize his extrajudicial service. See, *e.g.*, the letter signed "Q" in Aurora, 23 May 1794, and the article *For the General Advertiser*, id. 7 June 1794.

[89] 15 ANNALS 929 (1806).

[90] Adams to Jay, 21 Mar. 1792, 11 SYRETT at 159–60.

[91] Jay to John Adams, 23 Mar. 1792, John Jay Collection, Columbia, University Library, New York (quoted with permission).

the Courts as being in point of legal Obligation primary, and to attend the Trustees as secondary."[92] But, he added, he could "conceive that the Order would be sometimes inverted if only the Importance of the occasion was considered."

Jay's statement of primary and secondary obligation was not a simple question of statutory interpretation. The judiciary act in force at the time allowed for a circuit court quorum of two of the three judges and provided for postponement if the quorum was not met.[93] Jay, moreover, knew that the March business of the Sinking Fund Commission might have been more important than the March court session. Thus, he gave a relatively unimportant and nonessential session of the circuit court priority over a meeting of the Sinking Fund Commission at which his attendance was deemed essential by the other commissioners. Jay made it clear that as a judge he would serve other branches of government but that his primary obligation was to decide law cases. (It may be that Jay was led to assert his independence from obligatory Sinking Fund attendance in part because of lingering irritation about the pension assignment, over which he had battled only a month earlier.)

The commissioners allowed Jay to issue an opinion in writing because the question at issue turned on "the mere words of law" and Jay's "attendance as a trustee . . . would interfere with his attendance as a judge, on the circuit courts now near at hand."[94] Although the commission did not want this incident to be a precedent for obtaining votes by writing, their recognition of Jay's judicial duties as a legitimate cause for his absence set the precedent all the same. Furthermore, sketchy notes of the commission's minutes indicate that later Chief Justices also regarded their obligation to the commission as secondary and attended the meetings irregularly. Ellsworth was evidently consulted often by Treasury Secretary Wolcott,[95] but it is not clear whether he attended meetings regularly. There are minutes which suggest that Jay, and to a

---

[92] Jay to Hamilton, 23 Mar. 1792, 11 SYRETT at 172–73.

[93] Act of 24 Sept. 1789, ch. 20, §§ 4, 6, 1 STAT. 74, 76.

[94] Minutes of the Sinking Fund Commission, 26 Mar. 1792, 1 AMERICAN STATE PAPERS, Class 3 (Finance), No. 53 at 236 (1832).

[95] Oliver Wolcott to Washington, 3 Aug. 1796, 1 GIBBS, MEMOIRS OF THE ADMINISTRATIONS OF WASHINGTON AND JOHN ADAMS 374 (1846).

greater degree Marshall, attended the commission's meetings infrequently.[96]

Is it possible to square Jay's response to the 1792 pension statute with his response to the Sinking Fund assignment? In accepting the latter position, Jay acted consistently with the letter of his 1792 opinion in *Hayburn's Case*. He did not perform the nonjudicial duty in his official capacity. But was the Sinking Fund role consistent with the constitutional principles of his *Hayburn* opinion? It has been argued above that when the judges acted as ex officio pension commissioners, they violated the principles of *Hayburn's Case*. It has also been suggested that Jay came to realize this. As commissioners, the judges were responsible to no administrative authority, although they were performing an administrative task. In the same fashion, the Chief Justice was under no political pressure to see that the debt was reduced properly. On what grounds might Jay have justified this evident inconsistency? The most obvious answer lies in the fact that the pension task depended for its successful performance on numerous judges' following administrative directives which the protections of their office allowed, almost encouraged, them to resist. The Sinking Fund duty, on the other hand, was assigned to only one officer, the Chief Justice. Jay probably felt that the Chief Justice could be trusted to avoid a laxness which his judicial office might encourage. Nevertheless, in the final analysis, the Chief Justice's performance of the task depended on individual integrity and wisdom, not on any established line of political responsibility.

IV. Advising the Executive

Formal ex officio service was not the only "further use" envisioned for Supreme Court Justices in the constitutional period. There were also attempts to employ the judges as official advisers to the Executive and Congress on matters of policy and law. It is

---

[96] Jay's attendance is indicated at 1 American State Papers, Class 3 (Finance), No. 53 at 236–38, and No. 55 at 252–70 (1832). Marshall's is shown at 1 Rhodes, The Papers of John Marshall: A Descriptive Calendar 457–59 (1969). How often the Chief Justices attended the Mint assays is hard to determine, but at any rate, the Chief Justice was relieved of this responsibility when the capital was moved to the District of Columbia. His task was assigned to a district judge, who still has the assignment. Act of 3 Mar. 1801, ch. 21, 2 Stat. 111; 31 U.S.C. § 363.

well known that the Justices declined to render an advisory opinion to President Washington in 1793. While this incident has become a precedent for an important principle of constitutional law,[97]
it has not been studied closely. Marshall related the event in his
Life of Washington, but he was evidently unaware of the letter
from the Justices to Washington in which they explained their
refusal to advise him.[98] Justice Story based his interpretation on
Marshall's account and concluded that the judges found a constitutional prohibition against any "extrajudicial interpretations of
law."[99] Story's view has become the basis for the standard interpretation of the 1793 incident.[100] While not incorrect, Story's rendition
of the event, and later references to it based on that rendition, fail
to convey adequately the reasons that motivated the judges in 1793.

The general understanding during that period was that federal
judges, like their English counterparts, were to render advice to the
executive and legislative branches. Such advice-giving was advocated even among those who opposed judicial participation in legislative revision.[101] Washington certainly assumed that it was proper
for him to include the Chief Justice as one of his advisers. Jay and
Washington had a personal acquaintance that persisted into the new
government. That Jay advised Washington purely out of a spirit
of friendship, however, is doubtful. Indeed, Washington gives the
contrary impression. In 1790, he wrote LaFayette that many of the
Frenchman's "old acquaintances and Friends are concerned with me
in the administration of the Government." "By having Mr. Jeffer-

---

[97] See United States v. Evans, 213 U.S. 297, 301 (1909); Muskrat v. United States,
219 U.S. 346, 354 (1911).

[98] The letter is dated 8 Aug. 1793, but Marshall writes that in late July "it is probable
that the difficulties felt by the judges ... were communicated to the executive." 5
MARSHALL, LIFE OF WASHINGTON 441 (1807). A letter requesting the advice was printed
in 1847 in 10 SPARKS, THE WRITINGS OF WASHINGTON 359-60, 542-45. The full correspondence, however, was evidently not printed until 1891 in 3 JOHNSTON at 486-89.

[99] 3 STORY, COMMENTARIES ON THE CONSTITUTION § 1771, at 651 (1833).

[100] Chief Justice Fuller cited it as authority in United States v. Evans, 213 U.S. 297,
301 (1909).

[101] See the discussion of Pinckney's attitude, in the text, *supra*, at notes 33-37. Eldridge
Gerry also opposed the Council of Revision but as a congressman said that the President
and Senate could consult with the judges for advice on constitutional questions. See 1
ANNALS 504-05 (1789).

son at the Head of the Department of State, Mr. Jay of the judiciary, Hamilton of the Treasury and Knox of that of War, I feel myself supported by able Co-adjutors who harmonize extremely well together."[102] Washington understood that the Judiciary was not a "Department" in the same sense as "Treasury, War and State," into which Congress had divided "all the business of a domestic nature."[103] He knew he had no official "control over the proceedings of the Judges."[104] Yet, the LaFayette letter shows that Washington obviously understood that the Chief Justice in his official capacity was to work with the executive officers. Other events show how encompassing the Chief Justice's obligation was understood to be.

For example, in January 1790 Washington was told of counterfeiting in New York. He wrote back to his informer: "In order that the most prudential steps might be taken on the subject," his letter "was laid before the Chief Justice of the United States," who recommended forwarding it to the governor of New York.[105] In February 1790 Washington was uncertain about his power to appoint a certain officer without Senate consent. Thus he "desired to take the opinion of the Chief Justice of the United States" as well as the Treasury and War secretaries, "and let me know the result."[106] During the "War Crisis of 1790" Washington turned for advice to "the Chief Justice" as well as his other advisers, on what action should be taken if the British marched across the United States to battle Spanish forces.[107] Washington and others also

---

[102] 3 June 1790, 31 Fitzpatrick, ed., Writings of Washington 44–46 ("Bicentennial Ed.") (hereinafter cited as Fitzpatrick). Similarly after the 1794 cabinet turnover and Jay's resignation from the Court, Adams noted that "the offices are once more full. But how different than when Jefferson, Hamilton, Jay, etc., were here!" 8 Feb. 1796, in 2 Adams, ed., Letters of John Adams to His Wife 194, 195 (1841).

[103] To Jefferson, 21 Jan. 1796, 30 Fitzpatrick at 509–11, 510 (1939).

[104] Jefferson, quoting Washington, in a letter to Washington, 28 Mar. 1792, 6 Ford, ed., Works of Jefferson 456 (1904).

[105] Washington to David Forman, 21 Jan. 1790, 30 Fitzpatrick at 509 (1939). It is true that Jay at that time was continuing to supervise the State Department pending Jefferson's return from France. The fact is, though, that Washington said he turned to Jay as Chief Justice rather than as Secretary of State.

[106] 3 Fitzpatrick, ed., Diaries of Washington 90 (1925).

[107] For various references to the Chief Justice, see id. at 42; Boyd, The War Crisis of 1790, 17 Boyd, ed., Papers of Thomas Jefferson 35–108 (1965).

viewed the judges as proper sources of advice on judicial administration and reform.[108]

In 1790 and in 1791, Washington sought Jay's advice when he was preparing his State of the Union address. The 1790 correspondence especially reveals the degree to which Washington saw Jay, the Chief Justice, as one of his official advisers.[109] When he planned the 1790 address, Washington wanted to know "every matter which may occur to the heads of Departments."[110] Thus, he wrote Jay, asking for "anything in the judiciary line, anything of a more general nature," which should be in the speech. He asked for the submission "with the freedom and frankness of friendship." Yet he also asked that they be sent to arrive with "the communications from the other great Departments, and with such matters as have been handed immediately to me from other quarters."[111] Washington obviously turned to Jay as a "friend." But officially he turned to him as the Chief Justice, as he turned to the Treasury Secretary and the other cabinet members, as a head of one "of the great Departments," not as a man "from other quarters."[112] On all these occasions, "Mr. Jay of the Judiciary" was cooperating and "harmonizing" with the officers of the emerging executive cabinet, in "support" of the President in the "administration of this Government."

It is unclear whether the pre-1793 Court, or at least its more vocal members, had a definite conception of their responsibility to render advice. Jay's advice to Washington was private, and may have been given reluctantly and merely to help Washington in his trying times

---

[108] For Washington, see text *infra* at notes 101–12. Recall the Morris plan, text *supra* at notes 21–22. Congressman William Smith, among others, wanted to give the judges prime responsibility for the structure of the new judicial system. 1 ANNALS 1104 (1790). This suggests that the advisory relationship which Murphy traced from the nineteenth century had even earlier precedents. See MURPHY, ELEMENTS OF JUDICIAL STRATEGY cc. 4 & 5 (1964).

[109] For the 1791 exchange, see the letter from Washington to Jay, 4 Sept. 1791, 31 FITZPATRICK at 354 (1939), and Jay's response of 23 Sept. 1791, 2 JAY, LIFE OF JOHN JAY 205 (1833).

[110] Washington to Knox, 19 Nov. 1790, 31 FITZPATRICK at 156–57 (1939).

[111] Washington to Jay, *id.* at 155–56.

[112] Jay responded with advice on a wide range of subjects appropriate for legislation. The letter in question is dated 13 Nov. 1790, and appears in 3 JOHNSTON at 405–08. This letter seems an obvious reply to Washington's request, dated 19 November, and thus one is led to believe that Johnston or Jay misdated the response.

as the first President. Other instances of judicial advice-giving or lack of it are no more helpful in divining the early attitudes of the Justices. Jay declined a suggestion by Hamilton that the Court speak out against state resolutions condemning national economic policies. Jay's reason, however, was simply that discreet silence was a better tactic than heavy denunciation.[113] Some historians of the Court have concluded that the Justices initially favored public advisory opinions on legal issues, and only changed their mind in 1793. For example, Washington informed the Justices that he would appreciate receiving advice from them on the operation of the circuit court system.[114] Jay composed, for the Justices, a letter stating that the Constitution was "plainly opposed" to having them sit also as circuit judges, and he anticipated that Washington would publicize the letter by sending it to Congress.[115] Scholars since Justice Story have taken the letter to mean that the Justices initially looked favorably upon advisory opinions.[116] It appears, however, that the letter was never sent, thus leaving unclear the attitudes of the Justices.[117] They did write to Washington about the circuit riding duty. But the closest thing to a legal opinion was a comment that the dual judging sanctioned by the act was "unfriendly to impartial justice," and thus to confidence in the courts.[118] The various letters condemning the constitutionality of the 1792 pension act were advisory opinions in one sense, but they were written with much reluctance. The pre-1793 record, then, is ambiguous as to whether the early Justices looked favorably on advisory opinions.

Two questions were at issue in 1793. First, could Washington

---

[113] See, e.g., Hamilton to Jay, 13 Nov. 1790, and Jay's response, 28 Nov. 1790, id. at 404–05, 409–11.

[114] 3 Apr. 1790, 31 FITZPATRICK at 31.

[115] See the draft letter from Jay to Washington, note 43 supra.

[116] See 3 STORY, note 99 supra, at 437–38 n.1; cf. HART & WECHSLER, note 68 supra, at 79.

[117] Hart and Wechsler seem to rely on Story's assertion that the letter was sent. Story, though, misread his source, a contemporary law journal. It reprinted the letter but noted that a desire to avoid embarrassing the operation of the government led the Justices to mute their doubts and continue to ride circuit. See Constitution and the Supreme Court 4 AM. JUR. & LAW MAG. 293 (1830). The letter is not in the Washington Papers at the Library of Congress (microfilm edition), nor is its reception noted in Fitzpatrick's edition of Washington's works, the most complete printed collection, note 102 supra.

[118] See the judges' letter of August 1792, in 1 AMERICAN STATE PAPERS, Class 10 (Misc.), No. 32, at 52 (1834).

and his cabinet ask the Justices of the Court to announce principles of international law by which America could conduct her relations with France? More significant, though, was it proper to view the judges of the Supreme Court as permanent advisers to the executive branch on questions of law and policy? The Justices declined to accept the broad extrajudicial role which the government sought to impose on them, but they did not state categorically that all extrajudicial advising was unconstitutional. Their view was more complex than latter-day observers would have it appear.

The 1793 request for extrajudicial advice was made after it became clear to Washington that the French would not accept the American view of international law vis-à-vis American treaty obligations to France.[119] The federal district court in Philadelphia refused to extend its maritime jurisdiction to incidents arising out of French seizures of British ships in American waters and, consequently, refused to interpret the treaties. Thus, Washington, "desirous of having done what shall be strictly conformable to treaties of the United States and the laws . . . determined to refer the questions therein to persons learned in the laws." Those persons were the two Supreme Court Justices who were in Philadelphia at the time. Letters were sent to them on 12 July, requesting their presence before the cabinet on 18 July, "to give their advice on certain matters of public concern."[120] Both factions in the cabinet had no doubt that the advice would be forthcoming. Jefferson confidently promised Monroe to "write [him] what the judicial determination is."[121] He and his contemporaries knew that in "England . . . such questions are referred regularly to the Judges of the Admiralty."[122] They obviously expected the English precedent to control in America. Although Lodge maintains that Hamilton "objected to a reference to the judges on the ground that the matter was not within

---

[119] One can review the debate from the Genet-Jefferson correspondence in 1 AMERICAN STATE PAPERS, Class 1 (Foreign Relations), No. 65, at 147–48 (1832), and THOMAS, AMERICAN NEUTRALITY IN 1793 (1931).

[120] Cabinet opinion, 12 July 1793, 15 SYRETT at 87; letters from Jefferson to Jay, and to Patterson, 12 July 1793, 90 JEFFERSON PAPERS Nos. 15479–80 (Library of Congress, microfilm ed., reel 31).

[121] 14 July 1793, 7 FORD, WORKS OF JEFFERSON 446, 448 (1904).

[122] Jefferson to Judge Tucker, 11 Aug. 1793, in CONWAY, OMITTED CHAPTERS OF HISTORY DISCLOSED IN THE LIFE AND PAPERS OF EDMUND RANDOLPH 191 (1888).

the province of the judiciary,"[123] Hamilton's reluctance grew from a conviction that the questions should not be referred to the "animadversion and decision of the Courts of Justice" because "the whole is an affair between the Governments of the parties concerned—to be settled by reason of state, not rules of law."[124] Others have said that Washington was hesitant about seeking an advisory opinion, for he knew "he was treading on swampy ground."[125] This assumption is based on some cautionary passages in a letter which Jefferson wrote for the cabinet on 18 July, asking if it was proper that the Justices issue public advice and noting that there might be questions which "circumstances might, in their opinion, forbid them to pronounce on."[126] Yet, that cautionary tone was a direct result of Jay's oral intimations to Washington that the advice he sought might not be forthcoming. The cabinet had merely presumed that the Justices would present themselves as requested. Then Jay told Washington on 17 July that they would first have to decide "whether the business which it is proposed to ask their opinion on is, in their judgment, of such a nature that they can comply." Washington in turn asked Jefferson to "draft something . . . that will bring the question properly before them."[127] Jefferson did so by the letter of 18 July. On 20 July, the Justices wrote that their response would have to wait until the full Court assembled. By late July, it was obvious that the advice would not be given and by letter of 8 August the Court detailed the reasons for their refusal.[128]

The actual correspondence between the cabinet and the Court is important because it illustrates the constitutional understanding on which the Court acted. By his letter of 18 July, Jefferson asked basically for an extension of the advisory relationship between President and Chief Justice which Washington had established. By his response, Jay gave notice that the relationship needed to be restricted rather than expanded. Jefferson pointed to the war in Eu-

---

[123] 5 LODGE, ed., WORKS OF HAMILTON 16, n.1 (1904).

[124] Hamilton to Washington, 15 May 1793, 14 SYRETT at 454–60 (1969).

[125] ROSSITER, ALEXANDER HAMILTON AND THE CONSTITUTION 90, 294, n. 103 (1964).

[126] Jefferson to Jay, 18 July 1793, 3 JOHNSTON at 486–87.

[127] The words are Washington's relaying to Jefferson his conversation with Jay, by letter of 18 July 1793, 37 FITZPATRICK at app. 575.

[128] 3 JOHNSTON at 487–89.

rope, from which arose questions "of considerable difficulty, and of greater importance to the peace of the United States." Their answers would depend on "construction of our treaties, on the laws of nature and nations, and on the laws of the land." Yet, they often arose "under circumstances *which do not give a cognisance of them to the tribunals of the country.*" Thus Washington would be "much relieved if he found himself free to refer questions of this description to the opinions of the judges of the Supreme Court." Why? First, because the judges, competent in the fields of law and statecraft, could be depended upon to "secure us against errors dangerous to the peace of the United States." Furthermore, however, "their authority [would] insure the respect of all parties." Thus, Jefferson asked whether "the public may, with propriety, be availed of their *advice on these questions,*" and if so, whether the cabinet might "present, for their advice, the abstract questions which have already occurred, or may soon occur, from which they will themselves strike out such as any circumstance might, in their opinion, forbid them to pronounce on."[129]

Jefferson's letter reveals the commonly held assumption of the period that judges were possessors of a certain legal-political wisdom of which the nation should take advantage. While the questions prepared for the judges' attention were legal questions,[130] Jefferson was evidently looking for more than mere points of law. For he expected that the judges' advice would "secure us against errors dangerous to the peace of the United States." Yes or no answers to the questions would only clarify the law. Answers to help to preserve the peace would have to be more. The judges would have to call on what Mason termed their "practice of considering laws in their true principles, and in all their consequences."[131]

Note also that Jefferson asked for much more than answers to a specific list of questions. He asked instead whether the Court would become a permanent executive adviser on questions of law and

---

[129] 3 JOHNSTON at 486–87.

[130] For example, "Do treaties . . . authorise France *as of right* to erect Courts within the Jurisdiction of the U States for the trial and condemnation of Prizes made by armed vessels in her service? Do the laws and usages of Nations authorise her as of right to erect such Courts for such purposes" (Emphasis in original.) These are questions 9 and 10 of *Draft of Questions to be Submitted to Justices of the Supreme Court*, 18 July 1793, 15 SYRETT at 110, 113.

[131] 2 FARRAND at 78.

policy. When he asked if he could refer "questions of this description" to the judges, he was referring to important and complicated legal questions. If the Justices agreed to help in 1793, their successors would surely be asked to help when questions of "this description" arose in the future, as they surely would. Furthermore, Jefferson did not ask simply for a confidential advisory relationship. He asked "whether the public may . . . be availed of their advice on such questions." Justices of the Supreme Court were authorities by whom the President could justify his policies to the public and "ensure the respect of all parties."

Yet, the judges refused to assume the task because they regarded it as inconsistent with the American version of the separation of powers. For one thing, they surely disagreed with Jefferson's suggestion that the question at issue would not arise in the courts.[132] Thus, they realized they would be setting a precedent for public advice-giving on legal questions which could arise before them in litigable form. This they declined to do. In 1793, Jay sought to protect the judiciary's "checking" function, of which he had spoken in his 1790 grand jury charge. Specifically, the Court said, in 1793, that the three branches of government were "in certain respects checks upon each other." This, along with the Justices' role as a "court in the last resort," were "considerations which afford strong arguments against the propriety of our extrajudicially deciding the questions alluded to."[133]

Advice-giving poses several threats to judicial independence. Certainly the judges were aware that the Court's prestige would be compromised. Presidents would tend to rely on the Court for public advice whenever they were sure that the advice would support their policies, making the Court appear an executive appendage. If the Court's advice were not followed the Court would appear weak, and if a case arose based on such an action there would be a tendency for the public to interpret a decision opposed to the President as vindictiveness and to regard a decision upholding him as obsequiousness.

The advisory relationship for which Washington and Jefferson

---

[132] For example, the Gideon Henfield controversy was actually in the courts. See, *e.g.* 1 WARREN, SUPREME COURT IN UNITED STATES HISTORY 112–15 (rev. ed. 1926). And in 1794 the Court indeed did accept jurisdiction in a case growing out of Genet's activities. Glass v. Sloop Betsy, 3 Dall. 6.

[133] 3 JOHNSTON at 488.

hoped also threatened the judicial process itself. For one thing, in stating the law extrajudicially, the Court would not be stating the law through the process best designed to secure a true interpretation of it. Courts reach decisions through a process designed to formulate the issues sharply. They are aided by counsels' debate, which in the early period at least consisted of well-considered arguments lasting sometimes for days.[134] Absent those arguments, the decisions stood a greater chance of being in error.

More important, the Justices thought that they would retain a bias toward an opinion once publicly stated. English judges gave advisory opinions because they were confident their opinions would not affect their judicial decision making. They believed that they could "without difficulty" change their minds if legal arguments showed that an earlier advisory opinion was in error.[135] The American judges simply did not trust themselves, or later judges following their precedent, to be able to change their opinion so easily. While they did not comment on this danger in the 1793 letter, there is ample evidence that this indeed was their conviction. Jay, for example, had warned in 1790 that judges were reluctant to "relinquish sentiments publicly, though perhaps, too hastily given." Such reluctances "not infrequently infuse into the minds of the most upright men some degree of partiality for their official and public acts."[136] Justice Iredell was reluctant to write Washington extrajudicially that he considered the 1792 pension act unconstitutional. For, if he did receive a pension application while on the bench, he would have to reconsider the statute's constitutionality, and he knew "how liable the best minds are, notwithstanding their utmost care, to a bias, which may arise from a preconceived opinion, even unguardedly, much more, deliberately, given."[137] Justice Blair referred to "the difficulty of changing opinions, once deliberately formed."[138]

Not only were the Justices of the early Court afraid of their susceptibility to bias, they found that the public would suspect such a bias. In 1790 Jay had quoted a "celebrated writer" to the effect

---

[134] See MORGAN, note 11 *supra*, at 87; WARREN, note 132, *supra passim*.

[135] Sackville's Case, 2 Eden's Ch. 371–72 (1760).

[136] See the draft letter from Jay to Washington, note 43 *supra*, at 293.

[137] 2 Dall. at 414.

[138] Penhallow v. Doane, 3 Dall. 54, 109 (1795).

"that 'next to doing right, the great object in the administration of public justice should be to give public satisfaction.'" If Justices were forced to consider their extrajudicial statements in their judicial capacity, "much room would be left . . . to suspect that an unwillingness to be thought and found in the wrong had produced an improper adherence" to the previous statement.[139]

The 8 August letter conveyed more than a refusal by the Court to become a standing body of official executive advisers. Jay also told Washington that his view of the Chief Justice as a semiofficial executive adviser would have to be abandoned. The message was given subtly. One of the reasons the Justices would not give the advice was: "especially as the power given by the Constitution to the President of calling on the heads of departments for opinions seems to have been purposely as well as *expressly* united to the *executive* departments."[140] Yet Jefferson's letter had in no way intimated that the judges' advice was being sought on the basis of Article II, § 2, which authorizes the President to seek written opinions from "the principal officers of each of the Executive departments." Jay evidently saw the request as a product of the view that the Chief Justice had an official responsibility to advise the President on the legal and policy aspects of executive branch activities.[141]

Note, however, that the judges' purpose was to separate themselves from the other branches, not to insulate themselves from all nonjudicial activity. They did not claim that the Constitution forbade all extrajudicial service; it only "afford[ed] strong arguments against the propriety of our extrajudicially deciding the questions alluded to."[142] The judges still felt obligated to render what extrajudicial service they could, provided that they would not be led to endanger the separation of powers. They were "not only disposed but desirous to promote the welfare of our country in every way that may consist with our official duties."[143] This left it to the

---

[139] Draft letter from Jay to Washington, note 43 *supra*, at 294.

[140] 3 JOHNSTON at 487.

[141] All this should make abundantly clear that it is untrue that the judges refused to answer simply because they were intimidated by the amount and intricacy of the advice sought, as Thayer suggested in his oft-cited essay, *Advisory Opinions*. THAYER, LEGAL ESSAYS 53–54 (1908).

[142] 3 JOHNSTON at 488.   [143] *Ibid.*

judges' discretion when extrajudicial service could be undertaken consistent with the judicial function. For example, Jay obviously thought that his participation as a Sinking Fund commissioner would not threaten judicial independence because Sinking Fund matters would rarely arise in litigable form. He did not stop advising Washington in 1793.[144]

Jay evidently did not even mean to suggest that all formal advisory opinions were unconstitutional, and later actions show that he did not think they were. To be specific, as governor of New York in 1801, Jay sought a formal advisory opinion from the state judiciary. The notion of separation of powers, of widespread popularity in the period, had long been championed by Jay during New York's constitutional history, and there is no reason to suppose that he was any less attached to it in state affairs in 1801 than he had been in national affairs in 1793. Indeed, Jay had occasion to speak in 1801 of the high importance to "free states, that the different departments and officers of government should exercise those powers only which are consititutionally vested in them." [145]

Specifically, Jay asked the chancellor and judges of the New York Supreme Court to settle once and for all whether the New York Constitution gave the governor the exclusive power to nominate individuals for the Council of Appointment to accept or reject.[146] The question had arisen constantly under the 1777 Constitution and had never been successfully resolved.[147] Yet, Jay's request for advice differs in crucial respects from Jefferson's in 1793, and the differences illustrate the more limited conception which Jay had of the obligations of judges to serve their government extrajudicially. In the first place, Jay's request for advice

---

[144] See MONAGHAN, JOHN JAY 347 (1935).

[145] 4 JOHNSTON, note 41 *supra*, at 289. Jay was referring to his dispute with the legislature, about which he sought the advisory opinion, but his words have broader impact. It is true that the New York Constitution appointed judges, ex officio, to a Council of Revision, which approved legislation before it could take effect. Yet judicial participation in the council was not an authorization to give advisory opinions, and Jay did not contend that it was.

[146] Jay's correspondence with the judges is printed, along with an accompanying message by Jay to the legislature, in a special supplement to the Albany Centinel, 31 Mar. 1801.

[147] See N.Y. Const. art. 23 (1777), which may be found in 2 POORE, note 18 *supra*, at 1336. See also 1 LINCOLN, CONSTITUTIONAL HISTORY OF NEW YORK 599 (1906); SPAULDING, HIS EXCELLENCY, GEORGE CLINTON 257 (1938).

was qualified; he asked for the advice *"unless* a mode of having [the question] judicially determined should occur to you, and *in that case,* that you will be pleased to indicate it."[148] Moreover, unlike Jefferson in 1793, Jay made it clear that his request for advice extended only to the interpretation of the specific question at hand. Jay made no suggestion that he wanted to be able to refer all kinds of problems to the judges for extrajudicial interpretation.

Thus, while Jay did not mean to foreclose all extrajudicial advice-giving, he clearly tried to limit the contemporary view that extensive advice-giving was proper. Advice-giving which committed the judge to a particular legal-political position which might have come before him on the bench was inconsistent with the place of the judiciary in the American scheme of separation of powers. This points to the conclusion that private, informal consultation between Justices and Presidents is inconsistent with the 1793 precedent, if such consultation concerns matters with potential for litigation. If we adhere to Tocqueville's observation that, in America, every political question eventually becomes a judicial question,[149] the range of subjects appropriate for informal executive-judicial consultation becomes quite narrow.[150]

Neither Chancellor Livingston nor the New York Supreme Court judges provided Jay with the advice he sought. Livingston refused for fear of setting a precedent that would draw judges into other political disputes, and the other judges refused to answer simply because their answer would be "without effect." They did state that they saw no way that the question could be resolved judicially, although they added the English qualifier that they would "not presume there cannot be any."[151]

Perhaps the most interesting aspect of this exchange is the absence of any reference to the 1793 incident as precedent for refusal

---

[148] Jay to New York Supreme Court judges, 18 Mar. 1801, in special supplement to the Albany Centinel, 31 Mar. 1801. (Emphasis in original.)

[149] Tocqueville, note 4 *supra,* at 290.

[150] It is, of course, an open question whether judges become biased by giving advisory opinions. An advisory opinion and an on-the-bench opinion may well both grow from the same political or judicial conviction. If so, informal executive-judicial consultation, while inconsistent with the letter of 1793 from the judges, note 133 *supra,* may nevertheless not alter on-the-bench activity.

[151] Chief Justice John Lansing, and other New York Supreme Court judges, to Jay, 26 Mar. 1801, in Albany Centinel, note 148 *supra.*

to act in 1801. One might well have expected Livingston, given his antipathy toward Jay, to charge some sort of inconsistency in the actions of Chief Justice Jay and Governor Jay. His failure to do so suggests that the 1793 incident became the well-known precedent it is today only through a gradual process. While several newspapers were aware of Jefferson's letter to the judges in 1793, none carried a report of the Justices' refusal to advise the Executive. In fact, two years later a leading paper reported that the President could "ask the opinions of the Judges on points of law."[152] Adams and Jefferson evidently had little contact with the judges.[153] But an advisory opinion proposal by Justice Chase in 1802[154] and the 1822 correspondence between Monroe and some of the Supreme Court Justices[155] suggests that only gradually did the incident become firm

---

[152] Connecticut Courant, 15 Aug. 1795, quoted in WARREN, note 132 *supra*, at 110 n.1. Newspapers reporting the request for advice included the Aurora, 17 July 1793, the National Gazette (Philadelphia), 27 July 1793, and the Boston Gazette and Country Journal, 12 Aug. 1793.

[153] There is, in the Washington Papers, a letter from newly confirmed Chief Justice Ellsworth to Senator Jonathan Trumbull, but it obviously was not solicited by Washington, nor was it part of the cabinet deliberations at hand, namely, the constitutional right of the House to see certain executive documents. See letter of 13 Mar. 1796 in the Washington Papers, ser. 4 (Library of Congress, microfilm ed., reel 108), and a letter from Washington to Wolcott, 25 Mar. 1796, in GIBBS, note 95 *supra*, at 310.
Jefferson evidently kept a healthy distance from the Justices. His papers show only occasional letters to them, dealing mainly with personal incidentals. In fact, in 1808, Justice Johnson sent Jefferson some seeds and botanical observations. Jefferson did not even acknowledge their receipt from his close friend and judicial appointee until 1810. If this incident is any guide, Jefferson's personal, not to mention political, contact with the Justices was extremely slight. William Johnson to Jefferson, 6 Mar. 1808, 65 Jefferson Papers, No. 31083 (Library of Congress microfilm ed., reel 66), and Jefferson to William Johnson, 17 Mar. 1810, 190 *id.* No. 33783 (reel 73).

[154] Chase wrote to Marshall that he was convinced that the Judiciary Act of 1802 was unconstitutional. He proposed that the Justices meet in August. If they shared his constitutional interpretation, "it would be proper to lay the result before the President, as our predecessors did in a similar case." Recall however that the earlier Justices had omitted any constitutional interpretation from their letters of 1792 and 1794. Chase obviously intended that the letter he proposed contain such interpretations, for they were the entire substance of his letter to Marshall. The letter is dated 24 April 1802 and is in the William Paterson Papers, Bancroft Transcripts, Manuscript Division, The New York Public Library, Astor, Lenox and Tilden Foundations (quoted with permission).

[155] Monroe sent a copy of a veto message to the Justices in 1822. Johnson responded for himself and three others that they were "deeply sensible of the mark of confidence bestowed on them in this instance and should be unworthy of that confidence did they attempt to conceal their real opinion." Undated letter in MORGAN, JUSTICE WILLIAM JOHNSON, THE FIRST DISSENTER 123-24 (1954). See also MURPHY, note 108 *supra*, at cc. 5 & 6.

precedent. And it is Justice Story's 1833 interpretation of the event which has come to control the current understanding of the 1793 correspondence.

On reexamination, it seems obvious that the direction of Story's interpretation is true. Yet, the 1793 incident was more than a refusal to give advice. It was part of a broader attempt by the early Supreme Court to deemphasize the obligatory extrajudicial service concept, so widely held in the early period. It was—along with *Hayburn's Case* and Jay's bout with the Sinking Fund Commission—an attempt to point out to non-judges and future judges that the duties of the American judge were best limited to judging cases and controversies. It remained for later judges, most notably Marshall, to show how encompassing that single duty could be.

RICHARD A. EPSTEIN

SUBSTANTIVE DUE PROCESS

BY ANY OTHER NAME:

THE ABORTION CASES

In its recent decisions in the abortion cases—*Roe v. Wade*[1] and *Doe v. Bolton*[2]—the Supreme Court has demonstrated anew its ability to make daring innovations in constitutional law. While it is now clear that the Burger Court will not emulate its predecessor in a large number of areas—obscenity,[3] school finance,[4] and criminal procedure[5] immediately leap to mind—it is equally clear that it is prepared to adopt a very broad view of its own constitutional powers.

The decisions in the abortion cases held that neither the traditional statutes on abortion nor the modern substitutes patterned on the Model Penal Act can withstand scrutiny under the Due Process

---

Richard A. Epstein is Professor of Law, The University of Chicago.

AUTHOR'S NOTE: I should like to thank Gerhard Casper, David Currie, Geoffrey Stone, and Frank Zimring for their helpful comments on an earlier draft of this article.

[1] 410 U.S. 113 (1973).

[2] 410 U.S. 179 (1973).

[3] Miller v. California, 93 S. Ct. 2607 (1973); Paris Adult Theatre I v. Slaton, 93 S. Ct. 2628 (1973); United States v. 12 200-ft Reels of Super 8mm. Film, 93 S. Ct. 2665 (1973).

[4] See, *e.g.*, San Antonio Independent School District v. Rodriguez, 411 U.S. 1 (1973).

[5] See, *e.g.*, Harris v. New York, 401 U.S. 222 (1971); Kirby v. Illinois, 406 U.S. 682 (1972); United States v. Ash, 93 S. Ct. 2568 (1973); Schneckloth v. Bustamonte, 412 U.S. 218 (1973).

Clause of the Fourteenth Amendment. The doctrinal basis for the Court's conclusion was first suggested in the opinion almost in passing:[6]

> This right of privacy, whether it be founded in the Fourteenth Amendment's concept of personal liberty and restrictions upon state action, as we feel it is, or, as the District Court determined, in the Ninth Amendment's reservation of rights to the people, is broad enough to encompass a woman's decision whether or not to terminate her pregnancy.

Any study of the abortion cases must pay great attention to the internal logic of the Court's opinion on the substantive issue. But there is an antecedent issue: the Court's treatment of the technical questions of standing and mootness. Its attitude on these problems also provides important clues to the Court's current view of its institutional role.

I. Standing and Mootness

The Court begins its brief, indeed cryptic, examination of the standing question by noting with approval the rationale offered by Mr. Justice Brennan in *Baker v. Carr*.[7] In Brennan's view the requirement is designed to insure that the plaintiff has "such a personal stake in the outcome of the controversy as to assure that concrete adverseness which sharpens the presentation of issues upon which the Court so largely depends for illumination of difficult constitutional issues."[8]

Whatever its merits in general, this proposition rings false in the abortion cases. It may be granted that a plaintiff with an immediate financial or personal stake in the outcome of a case will have a

---

[6] 410 U.S. at 153. The reliance on the Due Process Clause was confirmed when the Court summarized its position. *Id*. at 164.

[7] 369 U.S. 186 (1962).

[8] *Id*. at 204. This theme was reiterated in Flast v. Cohen, 392 U.S. 83, 106 (1968): "The taxpayer's allegation in such cases would be that his tax money is being extracted and spent in violation of specific constitutional protections against such abuses of legislative power. Such an injury is appropriate for judicial redress, and the taxpayer has established the necessary nexus between his status and the nature of the allegedly unconstitutional action to support his claim of standing to secure judicial review. Under such circumstances, we feel confident that the questions will be framed with the necessary specificity, that the issues will be contested with the necessary adverseness and that the litigation will be pursued with the necessary vigor to assure that the constitutional challenge will be made in a form traditionally thought to be capable of judicial resolution."

strong incentive to press upon the courts all arguments that help advance his position. But that kind of stake is by no means necessary to insure that the plaintiff will act in that fashion. It is beyond doubt that many people, as a matter of general principle, have strong, indeed intense, beliefs about the proper social response to the abortion problem, beliefs that they are prepared to support with both time and money, even though they do not have any prospects for immediate financial or personal gain. Indeed, the abortion cases leave the distinct, if undocumented, impression that the nameless plaintiffs were parties to the case only because the persons and organizations that wished to overturn the abortion statutes sought them out as a means to mount their challenge. Given their energy and determination, it seems dubious here, and perhaps in the general case, to insist that the standing requirement is necessary to protect the Court from ill-prepared suits by indifferent parties. Financial costs involved may serve that function as well.

There is also little reason in the context of the abortion cases to prize the "concreteness" which compliance with the standing requirement is said to bring to a lawsuit. That requirement might well make sense if the model of the constitutional lawsuit were the private action at common law—with Professor Jaffe's Hohfeldian plaintiff—where the parties are content to let precedent take care of itself so long as they vindicate their private rights in litigation.[9] But in so many areas the Supreme Court today views constitutional litigation as a means of settling the great conflicts of the social order. Given its level of aspiration, the "concreteness" of a factual situation may well prove to be an embarrassment that can only work to limit the comprehensive sweep of the Court's pronouncements, for the details of a case could well reveal narrow grounds for a decision on the merits.[10] The particulars of the personal situation of each

---

[9] See, generally, Jaffe, *The Citizen as Litigant in Public Actions: The Non-Hohfeldian or Ideological Plaintiff*, 116 U. Pa. L. Rev. 1033 (1968).

[10] Indeed, it could well have proved awkward for the Court even to learn at what period in her pregnancy Roe brought her suit. As Mr. Justice Rehnquist noted in his dissent: "Our previous decisions indicate that a necessary predicate for such an opinion is a plaintiff who was in her first trimester of pregnancy at some time during the pendency of her law suit. While a party may vindicate his own constitutional rights, he may not seek vindication for the rights of others. . . . The Court's statement of facts in this case makes clear, however, that the record in no way indicates the presence of such a plaintiff. We know only that plaintiff Roe at the time of filing her complaint was a pregnant woman; for aught that appears in this record, she may have been in her last trimester of pregnancy as of the date the complaint was filed." 410 U.S. at 171.

plaintiff was a matter of complete indifference to the Court when it struck down on their face the operative portions of the abortion statutes. Concreteness, then, is not always a virtue and, if so, it becomes difficult to see why it should afford a rationale for the standing requirement. These observations, I believe, explain why there is so little relationship between the Court's decision on the standing question and the rationalizations used by the Court to defend the decision's unhappy place in constitutional history. I turn, therefore, to the particular plaintiffs in the abortion cases on the assumption that the standing requirement, whatever it is, must be satisfied only because it is there. The discussion at this point must take on a technical cast, and I must proceed in the knowledge that the doctrine has effects that are apt to be as unfortunate as the basic doctrine itself.

The first of the parties was Jane Roe,[11] and to all appearances her case is one of classic mootness. She alleged that, at the commencement of the suit in 1970, she was single and pregnant; that she wanted to get an abortion within the state of Texas; and that she could not have the abortion because it was prohibited under Texas law except in the one case, not applicable here, where the abortion is necessary to save the life of the mother. There could be no doubt that as of the time of the complaint the plaintiff had standing. But clearly, in the nature of things, the question of abortion *vel non* must become moot after the end of the term of pregnancy.[12] It appears, then, that she had only the interest of a concerned citizen who wants to attack a law that she dislikes.[13]

Nonetheless, Mr. Justice Blackmun held that, under the circumstances, the case should not be dismissed as moot. His argument ran as follows: The plaintiff could well become pregnant again; and, when pregnant, could desire an abortion then as she did in this case. Her only recourse under the law, unless the abortion statutes were changed in the interim, would be to bring an action of the very same kind that she brought here. But if this action were dismissed on mootness grounds, then it would follow that the subse-

---

[11] 410 U.S. at 124–25.

[12] Roe alleged that she represented a class of women similarly situated. 410 U.S. at 120. But if her case was moot, the same must be true for the others in that class, for be they ever so many, they are each pregnant for only 266 days or so.

[13] See Sierra Club v. Morton, 405 U.S. 727, 739 (1972), where the point was made in connection with standing under the Administrative Procedure Act, § 10, 5 U.S.C. § 702.

quent action must suffer the same fate, because the legal issues, then as now, could not be resolved fully in a nine-month period. "Pregnancy provides a classic justification for a conclusion of nonmootness. It truly could be 'capable of repetition, yet evading review.' "[14]

That argument has force if the necessity exception to the mootness rule operates to insure that a given plaintiff or class of plaintiffs should be entitled to press its objections in the courts. That exception had, however, been construed in earlier cases on which the Court relied to apply only when there was a danger that the Court could not deal with the issues raised in the case if the present plaintiff were unable to proceed.[15] Now one could opt for the first view of the standing requirement on the theory that it is fairer to allow pregnant women to challenge the claim, a result which must be greeted with favor by those, like myself, who see little value in an independent standing requirement. But if there are valid institutional reasons for the retention of the standing rules in the face of private claims to the contrary, then those must operate at an institutional level, which implies that the exception applies only where necessary for the Court to reach the substantive issue. It therefore becomes relevant to ask whether other parties could raise the constitutional issues in proper time. This question may be answered by looking at the other

---

[14] 410 U.S. at 125.

[15] The internal quotation was taken by the Court from a passage that reads in full: "In the case at bar the order of the Commission may to some extent (the exact extent it is unnecessary to define) be the basis of further proceedings. But there is a broader consideration. The questions involved in the orders of the Interstate Commerce Commission are usually continuing (as are manifestly those in the case at bar) and their consideration ought not to be, as they might be, defeated, by short-term orders, capable of repetition, yet evading review, and at one time the Government and at another time the carriers have their rights determined by the Commission without a chance of redress." So. Pac. Terminal Co. v. I.C.C., 219 U.S. 498, 515 (1911). It is at least arguable that the switch in contexts is of some importance, because the ICC has permanent regulatory power over railroads that makes short-term orders inappropriate. Again, note the shift in the "it." In the full quotation "it" seems to refer to the legal questions, but in the Court's opinion "it" seems to refer to pregnancy.

The Court also cited Moore v. Ogilvie, 394 U.S. 814 (1969), in support of its position. The appellants in that case were independent electors who sought declaratory or injunctive relief from the Illinois State Board of Electors that would require it to put their names on the ballot. The objection was pressed that the case was moot because the 1968 election had been concluded. The Court held, without much discussion, that it was not because the problem "reflects a continuing controversy in the federal-state area where our 'one man, one vote' decisions have thrust." Id. at 816. In both cases, then, the Court's continuing supervisory role (difficult to justify, perhaps, in Moore v. Ogilvie) lay behind this exception to the mootness doctrine. By no stretch of the imagination is it present here.

parties in *Roe v. Wade* who sought to challenge the abortion statutes.

The first of these challenges was by Dr. Hallford, who, in his petition for intervention, alleged that he was subject to prosecution in the state of Texas for alleged violations of its abortion law.[16] It must be conceded that the doctor could raise his constitutional objections to the statute in the course of his defense to the criminal prosecution. The issue here then was whether he could go into federal court in order to get an early determination of the constitutional question which would forestall the need for the criminal trial in state court. On this point, one clearly distinguishable from the pure standing question, the Court broke no new ground but applied in mechanical fashion its decisions in *Younger v. Harris*[17] and *Samuels v. Mackell*,[18] which held he could not.

The important point here is that the presence of Dr. Hallford shows that the Court was mistaken when it held that the mootness requirement must be relaxed in the abortion cases because they present questions which will constantly arise yet be incapable of review. The criminal trial of the doctor would provide him with every opportunity to challenge the abortion statute on its face. True, the posture of the criminal case might not be an ideal one in which to raise the issue, but it would still be possible for other doctors, not subject to pending criminal prosecution, to seek a declaratory judgment to the same effect.[19] These doctors would not have interests in all respects identical with those of pregnant women, but since they too would seek to upset the statute on its face, it is hard to see what arguments would not be available to them that would be available to the women, particularly since the doctors could assert the rights of their patients in support of their own case.[20]

Again, the treatment by the Court of the second set of plaintiffs

---

[16] 410 U.S. at 125–27.

[17] 401 U.S. 37 (1971).   [18] 401 U.S. 66 (1971).

[19] See the opinion of Mr. Justice Brennan in Perez v. Ledesma, 401 U.S. 82, 93–130 (1971). Indeed Dr. Hallford tried to make a case in those terms when he argued that he represented a class of doctors who were potential defendants in abortion cases. But the Court dismissed that portion of the argument because the pleadings were defective, and because Dr. Hallford was subject to prosecution, which meant that to allow him to make the claim was to upset the comity. 410 U.S. at 127, n.7.

[20] Griswold v. Connecticut, 381 U.S. 479, 481 (1965).

in the case, the Does, also casts doubt on the decision to give Roe standing within the framework of existing law.[21] The Does were a married couple who claimed that the statute acted as a constant threat to the happiness of their marital relations. Mrs. Doe suffered from some kind of "neurochemical" disorder which, in her opinion and that of her physician, made the continuation of the pregnancy undesirable, even though it did not present a serious risk to her life. They could only avoid the possible impact of the statute if they were prepared to abstain from normal marital relations.

In effect, their position was little different from that of the physicians found to have standing in *Doe v. Bolton* who wanted to advise their patients to have abortions but were afraid to do so because of the possible impact of the Georgia statute.[22] It is true that the Does were not in the business of having abortions, but for purposes of standing the existence of the personal stake and not its characterization ought to be decisive. While the Court could have dismissed their claim (having allowed Roe's) by describing their interest as "future," "speculative," and "uncertain," those words were inapposite, no matter how familiar, because the couple objected, not to the prospective effect of the statute in the event that Mrs. Doe became pregnant, but to its current effect upon their marital relations. Their asserted interest appears to be stronger than that of Roe, for they do not claim the right to challenge the statute solely because Mrs. Doe might become pregnant at some future time. If Roe had standing, then the Does had standing. And if the Does had standing, there was no need to make an exception to the mootness requirement on behalf of Roe.[23]

The question of the Does' standing could have been approached

---

[21] 410 U.S. at 127–29.

[22] "The physician is the one against whom these criminal statutes directly operate in the event he procures an abortion that does not meet the statutory exceptions and conditions. The physician-appellants, therefore, assert a sufficiently direct threat of personal detriment. They should not be required to await and undergo a criminal prosecution as the sole means of seeking relief." 410 U.S. at 188. The Court distinguished Poe v. Ullman, 367 U.S. 497 (1961), on the ground that *Poe* was a "ripeness" case. The Connecticut statutes that prohibited the dissemination of information about contraceptives had never been relied upon in a criminal prosecution.

[23] The point, moreover, retains its force even if the Does had not joined Roe in the suit. It is quite enough, if we take the standing requirement seriously, that the issue would be raised at some future time. Roe had no personal stake, and there was no need to concern ourselves with her feelings. Roe, of course, would have standing, if any person were allowed to attack a criminal statute on its face. But that is not the case.

from a different direction—one not mentioned by the Supreme Court—but without a change in result. Of late the Court has developed in connection with the Administrative Procedure Act a new test of standing. That test dispenses with the traditional requirement that the plaintiff must show that the statute sanctions an invasion of his legally protected interests. The new test requires the plaintiff only to show, first, that he has suffered an "injury in fact, economic or otherwise" and, second, that "the interest sought to be protected by the complainant is arguably within the zone of interests to be protected or regulated by the statute or constitutional guarantee in question."[24]

The first question, that of injury of fact, confronts the Court with the persistent problem of remoteness of damages. But if the recent decision in *United States v. SCRAP*[25] furnishes any guide to the Court's posture on the question, then the Does must be entitled to challenge the abortion law. *SCRAP* decided that a group of law students had a sufficient interest to challenge a determination by the Interstate Commerce Commission that allowed railroads a 2.5 percent increase in their freight rates on all goods, including "recyclable" materials. The students claimed that they "directly suffered" injury on the ground that the rate increase would "lead to" an increased use of nonrecyclable commodities in preference to recyclable ones, that in turn could "result in" a complex chain reaction ending in an increase of litter and refuse that would find its way into the parks of the Washington area used by the students.[26]

The Court accepted, although its conclusion could easily be disputed, that these allegations referred to a "perceptible harm" suffered by the plaintiff, and held, in regard to their truth, that the railroads had to demonstrate the hollowness of the allegations. The Court noted as well that a "trifle" should do the work of an "interest," but without explanation of how this reinterpretation of the standing requirement identified the "proper" plaintiff for a lawsuit.[27]

---

[24] Data Processing Service v. Camp, 397 U.S. 150, 152, 153 (1970).

[25] 412 U.S. 669 (1973).   [26] *Id.* at 685.

[27] *Id.* at 689. n. 14. Nor is any reason for the retention of the trifle requirement given by Professor Davis. The authority relied upon by the Court was DAVIS, ADMINISTRATIVE LAW TEXT, §§ 22.09-5, 22.09-6 (Supp. 1970). Davis gives an excellent short statement of why the common justifications for the requirement make no sense. *Id.* at § 22.04. Perhaps the notion of unrestricted standing put forward by Professor Jaffe, note 9 *supra*, should be expressly revived, though it was rejected in Sierra Club v. Morton, 405 U.S. 727, 736–41 (1972).

The ultimate strengths of *SCRAP*, however, are not our immediate concern, for on the narrow question at hand it seems that the
Does must satisfy the first branch of the standing requirement even
if *SCRAP* represents the current status of the law.

The Does appear to fall as well into the class of persons whose
interests are arguably regulated by the statute. As a general proposition, it is difficult to see what is gained by the addition of this test
to the law of standing once it is decided that the plaintiff need not
show an invasion of his legally protected interests.[28] Until the Court
finds the case in which the test excludes from standing a plaintiff
otherwise entitled to it, it is best to regard the requirement as a
temporary adornment to the law,[29] an impression only reinforced
in *SCRAP*, where the test was mentioned in passing but neither
discussed nor applied.[30]

II. When Is a Person?

Before Mr. Justice Blackmun was ready to deal with the
constitutional issues, he found it necessary to burden his opinion
with an exhaustive history of abortion from ancient times until the
present day.[31] It is difficult to see what comfort he could draw
from his researches, for at no point do they lend support for the
ultimate decision to divide pregnancy into three parts, each subject
to its own constitutional rules. All that the study accomplished was
to prove what we already knew, that legal rules and social attitudes
on the question of abortion vary much by time and place. Even in
ancient times abortions were subject to severe criminal sanctions
in some places, while in others they were resorted to as a matter of
course. The history of the last two thousand plus years covered
greats and near greats—Hippocrates, Galen, Bracton, Coke, Blackstone, and the American Medical Association—but it demonstrated
only that it is possible to adopt and defend positions which fall un-
easily between the two extremes. Those who wish to check the
footnotes in Mr. Justice Blackmun's history of the law and practice
of abortion are free to do so, but they are warned that neither the
mass nor the antiquity of the sources can conceal their essential
irrelevance to the constitutional inquiry. Our society remains as

---

[28] For an effective attack on the concept, see Davis, note 27 *supra*, at § 22.07.

[29] See Jaffe, *Standing Again*, 84 Harv. L. Rev. 633 (1971).

[30] 412 U.S. at 690.   [31] 410 U.S. at 129–52.

divided today as before on the questions when abortions should be made criminal and when they should be permitted. In the months that have passed since the decision in *Roe v. Wade*, its troubled logic has added a new dimension to a burning controversy. The diversity of opinions on all aspects of the abortion question might have suggested that the Court should have been careful not to foreclose debate on the issue by judicial decision, and more careful still not to use constitutional means to resolve the question.[32] Anyone can quote Holmes in *Lochner v. New York*.[33] But not everyone can apply the Holmes doctrine when his views are not embodied in the legislation under review.

The important question concerned the circumstances, if any, in which a state would be entitled to prohibit an abortion.[34] In order to answer that question Mr. Justice Blackmun, speaking for the Court, invoked an extended but unarticulated notion of a constitutional right to privacy.[35] It is true that privacy is nowhere expressly mentioned in the Constitution, but the right has been en-

---

[32] "As an exercise of raw judicial power, the Court perhaps has authority to do what it does today; but in my view its judgment is an improvident and extravagant exercise of the power of judicial review which the Constitution extends to this Court." 410 U.S. at 222. White, J., dissenting.

[33] "We bear in mind, too, Mr. Justice Holmes's admonition in his now vindicated dissent in Lochner v. New York, 198 U.S. 45, 76 (1905): '[The Constitution] is made for people of fundamentally differing views, and the accident of our finding certain opinions natural and familiar or novel and even shocking ought not to conclude our judgment upon the question whether statutes embodying them conflict with the Constitution of the United States.'" 410 U.S. at 117. For a comparison of *Roe* with *Lochner*, see Ely, The *Wages of Crying Wolf: A Comment on* Roe v. Wade, 87 YALE L. J. 920, 937–43 (1973).

[34] One inconsequential argument can be quickly dismissed. The plaintiff in *Roe* contended that the abortion statute passed by the Texas legislature in 1854 was not designed to protect the life of the unborn child, but instead was designed to protect the mother against the hazards of nineteenth-century medical practice. Accordingly, they argued that the statute should be struck down because it was no longer needed for the purpose for which it was enacted. 410 U.S. at 148. Even on the merits of the case, this argument is a doubtful one if only because the statute was reenacted without any substantial change as late as 1911 after the advent of safe surgical procedures. Even if the plaintiff could show both that the original intent was solely to protect the mother and that the statute had never been reenacted, the statute should still not be vulnerable on this ground. New justifications can be advanced for old statutes, as they can for old rules at common law. There is no reason to require a legislature to protect or rehabilitate an old statute with a new preamble.

[35] The arguments in the main opinion were paralleled in large measure in the concurrence of Mr. Justice Douglas in Doe v. Bolton, 410 U.S. at 213. The criticisms directed against the Court's opinion apply with equal force to Douglas's concurrence.

shrined in constitutional theory,[36] and it was enough for Mr. Justice Blackmun to list the disparate situations to which it had been applied. The right of privacy under the First Amendment protects the possession of obscene materials in the home.[37] A long line of search-and-seizure cases have vindicated a right of privacy under the Fourth Amendment.[38] Laws have been struck down, perhaps in the name of privacy, that prohibited parents from sending their children to private schools.[39] Notions of privacy have been invoked as well to strike down state laws which prohibited miscegenation,[40] which sought to prohibit procreation,[41] or which, as in *Griswold v. Connecticut*,[42] would prohibit the use of contraceptives.

Of these cases, *Griswold* appears to be closest to the instant problem, because it is at least arguable that there is but a short jump from contraception to abortion. Nonetheless the Supreme Court appeared to go out of its way to distinguish *Griswold* from the abortion cases, treating it as just one of many cases that recognized the right of privacy. I believe that the tactical decision was a sound one. The language of the opinions in *Griswold* gave a great deal of attention to the special place that marital privacy enjoys among the "rooted traditions" of our people.[43] That rationale of the case does

---

[36] See Kalven, *Privacy in Tort Law—Were Warren and Brandeis Wrong?* 31 LAW & CONTEMP. PROB. 326 (1966), for an excellent skeptical account of privacy. Indeed the misuse of the concept at the hands of the Court only confirms Professor Kalven's views of the utility of the concept

[37] Stanley v. Georgia, 394 U.S. 557 (1969).

[38] Here the Court cited: Terry v. Ohio, 392 U.S. 1 (1968); Katz v. United States, 389 U.S. 347 (1967); Boyd v. United States, 116 U.S. 616 (1886); and Brandeis's dissent in Olmstead v. United States, 277 U.S. 438, 471 (1928). There was no discussion of the particular points raised in any of these cases.

[39] Pierce v. Society of Sisters, 268 U.S. 510 (1925).

[40] Loving v. Virginia, 388 U.S. 1 (1967).

[41] Skinner v. Oklahoma, 316 U.S. 535 (1942). Note that the *Skinner* opinion should not be read to say that there is an inviolate right to have offspring, even though a portion of Mr. Justice Douglas's opinion tends to support that result. 316 U.S. at 541. The gist of the opinion was not that the state could not sterilize on account of repeated criminal offenses, but that it could not choose to do so in connection with larceny when it refused to do so in connection with embezzlement. Again, the concurrence of Chief Justice Stone, which rested upon Due Process Clause grounds, did not deny that the state could sterilize in individual cases, but only insisted that a hearing be given in the case to see if it involved a person whose criminal tendencies were indeed inheritable. 316 U.S. at 544-45.

[42] 381 U.S. 479 (1965). The Court also cited Eisenstadt v. Baird, 405 U.S. 438 (1972).

[43] 381 U.S. at 478, where Justice Goldberg in his concurrence quoted from Snyder v. Massachusetts, 291 U.S. 97, 105 (1933).

not account for the subsequent development in *Eisenstadt v. Baird*, where the Court appeared to hold that an unmarried person also had a right under the Constitution to use contraceptive devices.[44]

It is possible to think of subtle reinterpretations of *Griswold*, with emphasis upon the elusive but prevalent notions of "fundamental rights," that might explain the results in both *Griswold* and *Baird*. It does not follow that any effective reconciliation of these two cases could aid the Court in deciding the abortion cases in the manner that it did. Both *Griswold* and *Baird* studiously avoided discussion of the possible claims that any putative child could make on behalf of anticontraception legislation. Yet it is precisely the claims of the fetus and its status to assert them that raise the greatest difficulties in the abortion cases. In the end, therefore, it does seem fruitless to look to *Griswold* for either guidance or authority. Any reliance upon it would require the rationalization of two difficult decisions instead of one.

Once it is settled that *Griswold* was not of special importance in the abortion cases, then it is difficult to see how the concept of privacy linked the cases cited by the Court, much less to explain the result in the abortion cases. It takes an astute mind to see how the disposition of a search-and-seizure case could guide the Court when the state wants to regulate procreation or to deny parents the right to send their children to private schools, and a fanciful one to intuit the relationship between the common aspects, if any, of these questions with problems of obscenity. It is nice to be able to make constitutional generalizations; it is also dangerous to make constitutional overgeneralizations which use isolated words as slogans to solve hard questions raised by the Bill of Rights.

If we must hazard an attempt to find the common thread which runs through all of these cases, however, it might well be the principle of classic liberalism: the state is entitled to restrict the liberty of any individual within its jurisdiction only where necessary to protect other persons from harm.[45] On the strength of that principle it is possible to argue that there is no state interest in the prohibition of marriage between persons of different races because no

---

[44] The Court, of course, recognized the matter of the conflict between *Griswold* and *Baird*. 405 U.S. at 453–54.

[45] "The only purpose for which power can be rightfully exercised over any member of a civilized community against his will, is to prevent harm to others." MILL, ON LIBERTY, c.1.

one could be shown to be harmed by that act. But that conclusion will be defensible only if we accept as a constitutional principle that a dislike of the practice by third persons, however intense and for whatever reason, is not to be treated as a harm, as that term is used in our general rule. Again it is possible to view the cases which give parents a right to send their children to a private school of their own choice as cases which involve no harm to third persons. But we must first decide that the child himself would not be stunted in his social and moral development for want of, say, exposure to children of different backgrounds. Second, we must decide that there is no harm to other children denied the benefits of association with the children sent off to private schools because their parents dislike people of different races, creeds, or colors. The case of a man who views obscene materials in his own home poses precisely the same problems. To apply the general principle, it is necessary to decide that no one is harmed even though there are those who believe, perhaps without absolute proof, that the vast proliferation of obscene materials contributes, at the very least, to widespread social decay and stagnation which threaten to engulf us all. And the situation is little different with the general use of contraceptives, for general permissiveness can easily be seen as a harm to others.[46] These objections, however, need not be fatal to the general proposition, for it is not unreasonable to give an account of harms—one that emphasizes physical, proprietary, and financial loss central to older notions of standing—which insures that the exception will not swallow the rule.[47] Thus we could reject accounts of harm to others based on their displeasure at our actions, or on deprivations of beneficial associations, or on fears for the future of civilized life. But the general principle will have only an empty exception if "harm to another" does not cover the death of another person. Let it be accepted that the unborn child is a person (or even is to be treated like one), and it is clear beyond all question that abortion cases fall not within the general rule that protects the liberty of each person to do as he pleases but within the exception that governs the infliction of harm to others. And the case, moreover, becomes instantly distinguishable from that posed by the state regulation of contra-

---

[46] "Finally, it should be said of the Court's holding today that it in no way interferes with a State's proper regulation of sexual promiscuity or misconduct." 381 U.S. at 498–99.

[47] See Hart, Law, Liberty, and Morality 45–46 (1963), for a strong statement on the need to limit the account of the term "harm."

ception, because no one claims that there is a person before contraception.

The statement of the general proposition thus compels us to face the definitional question: who is a person? That task is not a happy one because we cannot resolve it either by scientific investigation or by social convention. The question pushes us to the uncharted areas of language and perception, and forces a decision in black and white when there are only grays. It would be nice to say that the "unborn" belongs to some special third category, complete with its own set of rights tailored to its own special status. But how do we determine the content of these rights, and what possible form could they take if the mother were allowed to terminate her pregnancy at will? If the "unborn" is to be protected, it must be because it will become a person (with no qualifications) in the ordinary course of its development. Once that much is conceded, then why is it not entitled to the full protection enjoyed by everyone else? To put the matter yet another way, if we do recognize that third category, how do we decide without reference to the first two categories the extent of its entitlements? We may start with three categories, but in the end we are reduced to two, person or no person, and it is only after the category question is answered that we can apply the test that governs the scope of individual liberty.

We should also reject the suggestion, however tempting, that the problem should be left to individual choice because it is too hard to be solved by collective means. The preference for individual choice is quite proper when we ask whether a person should take advantage of a liberty that is his, but it cannot be accepted where the very question raised concerns the appropriate social limits to be placed upon individual choice. Suppose the mother believes that the fetus is not a person, but the person next door thinks otherwise. Can the mother have the abortion, or can that third person interfere, claiming the general privilege of the criminal law to act in the defense of third persons? The point must be decided one way or the other for both parties, who cannot be allowed to make individual decisions. The criminal law in general does not allow an individual to decide which of its collective pronouncements it will honor and which it will not, and that rule must apply in hard cases as well as easy ones. The problem must be met. We must do the best that we can. Here the "best" is an examination of the views taken both inside the law and beyond it on the question—and here the very act of phrasing is crucial—is this unborn, or unborn child, or fetus, or embryo, or whatever, a person?

The most obvious place to begin is, of course, the criminal law, and there we find that abortion is classified, perhaps uncritically, as an offense against the person.[48] Abortion, however, was not a crime at common law, but was only made such by statute. Indeed when made criminal, it was not treated simply as an instance of murder, but was classified as a separate and distinct offense, with its own scale of penalties. All this, however, need not be decisive against the claims of the fetus, because the belated statutory protection could be treated as a considered extension of the criminal law, much like the extension of crimes against property to cover cases of embezzlement. And the unique set of penalties could be regarded, though not without difficulty, as an expression of the uneasiness of the judgment that the unborn should be treated as a person. Apart from the statutes, moreover, there was limited protection of fetal life at common law. Thus it was murder to attack the mother with the intent to kill the unborn child, but only if the child were born alive and died in consequence of its injuries.[49] Although the law has not gone further,[50] it is none too difficult to argue that nothing should turn on the accident of the time of death, and nothing, more ominously, on whether the mother was victim or author of the attack. The inferences from the criminal law, then, are at best uncertain.

Tort law, too, has generally treated the unborn child as a person, in those cases in which it has been born alive. There is, to be sure, some old authority which held that an infant born alive could not recover for injuries it suffered before birth for the technical reason that it was not a person to whom a defendant could owe a duty

---

[48] PERKINS, CRIMINAL LAW xiii (1969).

[49] The position dates back to Lord Coke, 3 INSTITUTES 50, and is taken up by Blackstone, 1 COMMENTARIES *125–*26.

[50] See, e.g., Keeler v. Superior Court, 2 Cal.3d 619 (1970), cited by Mr. Justice Douglas, 410 U.S. at 218 n.7, in support of the proposition that there is no offense if the child is stillborn from the attack. The decision, however, does not turn as much on the general theory of criminal responsibility as it does on the niceties of statutory interpretation under the California Penal Code. The California Supreme Court was at pains to note that a narrow construction was demanded in criminal cases in order that the accused may have notice of the nature of the offense, 2 Cal.3d at 631, 634–35, even though § 4 of the California Penal Code expressly states that the common law rule that criminal statutes are to be strictly construed has no application to the code.

of care.[51] That position has, as the Court noted, been rejected without hesitation in the last twenty-five years. More to the point, the right of action of the infant does not turn on the moment during pregnancy at which the injury was inflicted. Mr. Justice Blackmun noted that it "is said" that recovery is permitted "only if the fetus was viable, or at least quick, when the injuries were sustained."[52] Yet Prosser, his authority for the proposition, reports that "when actually faced with the issue for decision, almost all of the jurisdictions have allowed recovery even though the injury occurred during the early weeks of pregnancy, when the child was neither viable nor quick."[53] The limitation to persons born alive is not of theoretical importance here, because it need not stem from the conviction that only children born alive are persons. No dead person, be he born or unborn, has ever been able to maintain an action on his own behalf, a limitation beyond the power of any court to change. The crucial issue, therefore, is whether the parent could maintain in principle an action for the wrongful death of his child even if stillborn. Mr. Justice Blackmun noted the recent trend in that direction, only to dismiss the cases that allow it as indirect attempts "to vindicate the parent's interest." Parents, of course, have actions of their own to protect their own interest, so it is at least respectable to argue that the movement is designed to do exactly what it says: treat the unborn child as a person even when stillborn.

The last stop in the Cook's tour is the law of property, but it provides little support for the Court's position because it operates on the general principle that the unborn child will be treated as a person whenever that will be to its benefit.[54] To give but one simple example, an unborn person is treated as a life in being under the rule against perpetuities in order to preserve the validity of an interest left to it by will or by deed.[55] The principle should be sufficient to afford it the general protection of the criminal law so that it might be born.

This brief examination of the treatment of the "unborn child"

---

[51] See, for the first decision on the point, Dietrich v. Northampton, 138 Mass. 14 (1884) (Holmes, J.).

[52] 410 U.S. at 161.

[53] PROSSER, THE LAW OF TORTS 337 (4th ed. 1971).

[54] HARPER & JAMES, THE LAW OF TORTS 1029 (1956). The authors note that the rule should be of general application, even though it arises in a property context.

[55] GREY, THE RULE AGAINST PERPETUITIES §§ 931-47.

at common law is in a sense consistent with Mr. Justice Blackmun's conclusion that "the unborn have never been recognized in the law as persons in the whole sense."[56] But it remains true that for many purposes they, the unborn—Mr. Justice Blackmun studiously avoids "person"—are regarded as persons, and it remains true as well that recent judicial trends have expanded, not limited, their rights. Even if an unborn child is not treated as just another person, it is still necessary for Mr. Justice Blackmun to explain why the unborn child is not treated as a person in abortion cases, when it has been so regarded in other legal contexts.

The alternative tack is to forsake legal sources and to see how the question of the status of the unborn child is treated by others than lawyers. Here, too, the fruits of the investigation provide Mr. Justice Blackmun with little comfort. One prominent view has it that the life of the person begins at the point of conception. A variation on this theme is that, even if the unborn child is not a person at the time of conception, it should be treated as though it were, on the simple ground that it will become a person in the ordinary course of its development. Another position is that life, qua person, begins at quickening, when the fetus shows signs of its independent life. Viability, too, might well be the moment, although one dependent upon medical technology, for by then it is quite possible that the fetus could survive outside the womb. And, finally, birth itself could be viewed as the point at which life begins.

I do not propose at this point to debate which of those views is correct. It is enough to note that each of them has been maintained by some people who have thought long and hard about the question, and that the principled application of the general proposition about harm to others concealed by references to the right of privacy requires at the very least a selection among them. Indeed, when the decision is made on constitutional grounds, the necessity for choice is even more apparent. The legislature could make and defend the choice, though not with complete comfort, on the grounds that its choice represents in imperfect fashion the will of the people: representative government is still worth something. But no appointed court can rest its strength on an appeal to the democratic principle when it invokes the doctrine of judicial review.[57] In the

---

[56] 410 U.S. at 162.

[57] BICKEL, THE LEAST DANGEROUS BRANCH (1962).

case of the Supreme Court only principled grounds for decision
stand between it and the charge of arbitrary decision based upon
its naked political preferences.

Either the Court faces the question of what counts as a person,
or it lets all abortion statutes stand by declining to decide the case
on its merits. Mr. Justice Blackmun cannot take comfort in the
bland declaration that the Court "need not resolve the difficult
question of when life begins,"[58] and still invoke a notion of privacy
to decide the case. It may be well to note that philosophers, theo-
logians, and physicians all have not reached agreement on the matter, but they do not have, nor do they pretend to have, the power
to decide the question for us all. The Court admits to their ignorance. Is it too much to ask the Court to share their impotence?

The importance of the question—Does an unborn child count as
a person?—moreover, is demonstrated anew when we examine the
reasons that Mr. Justice Blackmun gave for why abortions should,
at least in some circumstances, be allowed as a matter of constitutional law. The Justice made his case in what are no doubt familiar
terms:[59]

> The detriment that the State would impose upon the pregnant
> woman by denying this choice altogether is apparent. Specific
> and direct harm medically diagnosable even in early pregnancy
> may be involved. Maternity, or additional offspring, may force
> upon the woman a distressful life and future. Psychological
> harm may be imminent. Mental and physical health may be
> taxed by child care. There is also the distress, for all concerned,
> associated with the unwanted child, and there is the problem of
> bringing a child into a family already unable, psychologically
> and otherwise, to care for it. In other cases, as in this one, the
> additional difficulties and continuing stigma of unwed mother-
> hood may be involved. All these factors the woman and her
> responsible physician necessarily will consider in consultation.

These rationales may have their intuitive appeal. But as a matter
of theory they have the unhappy distinction of being either insufficient or unnecessary. If the unborn is not a person, and an abortion
is, to use the phrase of Mr. Justice Stewart, only a simple "surgical
procedure,"[60] it is difficult to see why either the woman who requests it or the doctor who performs it owes anyone an explanation

---

[58] 410 U.S. at 159.

[59] *Id.* at 153.   [60] *Id.* at 170.

for their decision. There is no harm to any other person, no need for state intervention. The decision to end pregnancy is but an exercise of personal preference which needs no justification, because prima facie it suggests no wrong. Remove a hangnail, terminate a pregnancy, it is all the same thing. In both cases, the woman need only want the service, and perhaps have the means to pay for it. Third persons may object to the removal of hangnails, as they do to the performance of abortions, but their views are entitled to no more protection in the one case than in the other.

The case assumes a different complexion if we decide that the unborn child is, or should be treated as, a person. At this point, we can no longer speak of the exercise of natural liberties but must find some justification for the deliberate killing of a human being. Clearly, had the child been born, the mother would not be allowed to kill it at birth for the reason that a child might cause her mental distress and tax her with the burden of care. Nor could she kill her sick mother for a similar reason. These purported justifications for deliberate killing are, in a word, brutal. If the unborn child is indeed a person, then the logic of Mr. Justice Blackmun's position collapses.

The parallels can be extended in a more disquieting manner, even if we put Mr. Justice Blackmun's logic to one side. Take, for example, the justifications for the termination of pregnancy allowed under the Georgia statute, which was patterned on the Model Abortion statute and invalidated by *Doe v. Bolton*. That statute permits the termination of pregnancy in three sets of circumstances. Thus, it is allowed under the Model Penal Code when the physician "believes there is substantial risk . . . that the child would be born with a grave mental or physical defect."[61] But suppose the child had been born with these same defects. Would there then be grounds for putting it to death just after it was born? If so, then the abortion statute makes good sense but there is no need for a special rule, for the problem could be handled as well by the application of the general criminal law. But if not, then we have to accept one set of justifications for the killing of unborn persons and another for the killing of persons already born—the very alternative that is

---

[61] A.L.I., MODEL PENAL CODE, Proposed Official Draft, § 230.3(2) (1962). The Georgia statute struck down in *Doe v. Bolton* differs from the model act only insofar as it requires "a grave, permanent and irremediable mental or physical defect." Criminal Code of Georgia, § 26-1202(2).

ruled out if we decide that an unborn child should be treated as a person.

The same kinds of argument apply with equal force to the second of the three justifications for abortions permitted under the Model Penal Code statute: the case where "pregnancy resulted from rape, incest, or other felonious intercourse."[62] There is no question but that, with the child born, it could not be killed for the reasons set out in the statute. If we apply the major premise that the unborn child is a person, it at best follows that in this circumstance the mother is justified in putting the child out for adoption after it is born.

We must extend this analysis to the third possible justification for abortion, which, in the language of the Model Act, provides that a licensed physician may terminate a woman's pregnancy in cases where "there is a substantial risk that continuance of the pregnancy would gravely impair the physical or mental health of the mother."[63] At this point the statute seems to echo the general pattern of the criminal law, for the plea is the familiar defense of the person against external threats. But even here the parallel is not exact. If the child were alive, there is no doubt but that the mother could not be permitted to kill it even if she could show that the burdens of its continued care threatened either her life or her physical or mental health. In all cases the appropriate response is to take the child from the mother and place it in the care of another. That option is, of course, not possible during the pregnancy, and we are therefore pushed back to the two hard alternatives, and here it is at least possible to argue that the mother should be required to bear at least the risk of mental or physical distress (death is quite another matter, particularly if it might occur before the end of the term) because the alternative is the certain death of another person, the unborn child. The choice of the Model Abortion statute therefore is a hard one to make, but by the same token it is a hard one to criticize. In any case, the statutory justification requires proof of more than loose references to the "psychological harm" or the emotional "dis-

---

[62] MODEL PENAL CODE at § 230.3 (2). The Georgia statute requires that the "pregnancy resulted from forcible or statutory rape." Criminal Code of Georgia, § 26-1202(3).

[63] MODEL PENAL CODE at § 230.3 (2). The Georgia statute allows the abortion where "[a] continuation of the pregnancy would endanger the life of the pregnant woman or would seriously and permanently injure her health." Criminal Code of Georgia, § 26-1202(1).

tress," which so moves the Court. And it surely means that we are not allowed to take into account, as Mr. Justice Blackmun would have us do, the harm that follows only if the mother is required to keep the child after birth, for by then other alternatives for its care are feasible.

The arguments from principle, then, show how uneasy are the positions that search for intermediate grounds that justify some abortions and prohibit others. None of these arguments turns on the language of the Constitution. At most, each calls for an application of traditional legal principles to a most difficult substantive issue. The salient, and tragic, point to note about *Roe v. Wade* is that the rules of the game change the moment the debate is framed in constitutional terms. What seemed to make sense as a matter of principle to a lot of people and a lot of lawyers is all of a sudden suspect. In effect, therefore, we are required by the logic of Mr. Justice Blackmun's argument to retrace our steps and to ask, but with one crucial variation, our first question: What counts as a person under the Constitution? To this question, Mr. Justice Blackmun responds, as is his wont, by listing all the clauses of the Constitution which contain the word "person."[64] Without discussion, he then concludes that it is not at all clear whether the term, as used in these clauses, was meant to include the unborn child. And it does seem fair to say that the problem was not one discussed at the Constitutional Convention. But what follows from the conclusion? Mr. Justice Blackmun is quite troubled because he thinks it possible that once an unborn child is treated as a person under the Due Process Clause, then the Constitution forbids all abortions, even those performed to save the life of the mother.[65]

There are several reasons why the Court's position must be rejected. In the first place, the Due Process Clause still has its state action limitations.[66] There is no reason to suppose that the performance of an abortion by a private physician must constitute state action under the Constitution. Nor should medical licensing of phy-

---

[64] 410 U.S. at 157.

[65] *Id*. at 157, n.54. "[I]n any event, the argument that fetuses lack constitutional rights is simply irrelevant. For it has never been held or even asserted that the state interest needed to justify forcing a person to refrain from an activity, *whether or not that activity is constitutionally protected*, must implicate either the life or the constitutional rights of another person." Ely, note 33 *supra*, at 926.

[66] Moose Lodge No. 107 v. Irvis, 407 U.S. 163 (1972).

sicians and hospitals change that result, so long as no agent of the state makes the decision to perform the abortion.

Again, even if one adopts an expansive view of the state action requirement, it still does not follow that the unborn child has a right to life guaranteed to it under the Constitution. The Constitution does not prescribe a body of absolutes. "Balance of interest" tests are commonplace, given modern views on constitutional interpretation. Witness the elaborate rules which the Court lays down to govern the legality of abortions. That process of balancing can take place even if the unborn child is treated as a person under the Due Process Clause. Let abortions be unconstitutional per se, and we might as well conclude that self-defense never should be treated as a justification for the deliberate killing of another person under the law of either crime or tort. No one could believe that the constitutional right to life extends that far. And if it does not, it seems incredible that a Justice should believe that he is compelled by his role to decide that abortions (at least within the first trimester) are either per se lawful or per se unlawful under the Constitution. The frail language of the Due Process Clause does not give the Supreme Court license to rewrite the substantive criminal law. We could decide that the unborn child is a person under the Constitution and still leave it to state law to decide what complex of rights and duties attach to that status.

But Mr. Justice Blackmun did not believe that the problem is one which is best left to legislation. Contrary to his position in the capital punishment cases,[67] he believed it his duty to interfere in the abortion area because the legislation before him in both the Texas and the Georgia cases had not set the proper balance. He, therefore, proposed his definitive solution to the abortion problem, superior to the others only because it now has the force of law. We need not, however, be a defender of the bulk of the current legislation to note that there are internal difficulties in both the content and rationalization for the comprehensive legislation which Mr. Justice Blackmun (with the concurrence of six brethren) has enacted in the name of the Due Process Clause of the Constitution.

Mr. Justice Blackmun has stated that we must divide the term of pregnancy into three trimesters in order properly to accommodate the interests of the state, the mother, and the unborn child. (The

---

[67] Furman v. Georgia, 408 U.S. 238 (1972).

interests of the father are left unanswered in a footnote.)[68] During the first trimester, the Court concluded that "the abortion decision and its effectuation must be left to the medical judgment of the pregnant woman's attending physician."[69] But that result does not seem to be a fair implication of the right of privacy, the only suggested basis for the decision. The privacy to be protected must be that of the pregnant woman and not that of some attending physician.[70] In most cases, of course, the odd twist in the formula will have no practical consequences. If a woman does not know whether she wants an abortion, she might well consult her physician before she makes up her mind. But if she has already made up her mind for personal reasons, then she will clearly choose a physician who is prepared to perform abortions. It is either pretense or folly to assume that the decision to have an abortion will be made for the most part by physicians on the basis of "their best medical judgment."[71] The operation is quite simple and safe, and the interests of the unborn child can be disregarded. The usual grounds on which to caution a patient do not apply, and the patient's will must control. There is no medical question, and hence no place for medical judgment.

With that point to one side, it is still necessary to balance the "interest" of the woman against those that compete with it. True, the woman has a right to privacy, which indeed is a counterweight in the balancing of interests. But what about the interests of the unborn child and the state? Mr. Justice Blackmun, it should be recalled, believes that he "need not resolve the difficult question of when life begins." That conclusion is no doubt correct if the state is left free to regulate abortions as it will, whether or not the un-

---

[68] 410 U.S. at 165, n.67.   [69] 410 U.S. at 164.

[70] Thus, the Court recognized, in *Eisenstadt*, "the right of the individual, married or single, to be free from unwarranted governmental intrusion into matters so fundamentally affecting a person as the decision whether to bear or beget a child." 405 U.S. 438, 453 (1972). The proposition, relied upon by Mr. Justice Stewart in his concurrence, 410 U.S. at 169–70, seems inconsistent with the assertion that the right is shared by the woman with her physician. The liberty of the physician is fully protected if he is not required to perform an abortion against his will.

[71] Mr. Justice Blackmun, however, appeared to think otherwise: "*Roe* v. *Wade* . . . sets forth our conclusion that a pregnant woman does not have an absolute constitutional right to an abortion on her demand." 410 U.S. at 189. The statement makes sense only if it is taken to mean that a patient cannot compel a given physician to perform the abortion against his own will.

born child is regarded as a person under the Due Process Clause. But it is clearly wrong if the abortion question has, as Mr. Justice Blackmun insisted, its own irreducible constitutional dimension. He conceded that the "potential" life of the unborn child must be taken into account in order to make the constitutional rules to govern abortions. But is there not a potential life in the unborn child from the moment of conception? And, if so, how do we take its measure? It makes no sense to hold in conclusionary terms that "by adopting one theory of life, Texas may [not] override the rights of the pregnant woman that are at stake."[72] That formulation of the issue begs the important question because it assumes that we know that the woman's rights must prevail even before the required balance takes place. We could as well claim that the Court, by adopting another theory of life, has decided to override the rights of the unborn child which the law of Texas tries to protect. The Justice simply cannot strike the balance for the first trimester of pregnancy unless he has some theory of life of his own which shows that there is no "compelling" interest of the unborn child. His exhaustive history of the abortion question indicates quite clearly that there is no consensus on the question, and it is simple fiat and power that gives his position its legal effect.

Mr. Justice Blackmun was no more successful when he attempted to take into account the interest of the state during the first trimester of a woman's pregnancy. As always, he purported to balance interests when he concluded that the state was in no circumstance entitled to regulate either the decision to have the abortion or the manner and means of its performance in that first trimester. That result appears to be odd even within the balancing framework, for it is too late in the day to argue that the right of privacy makes unconstitutional all state schemes that wish to regulate the practice of medicine and surgery. Nor did he advance his argument against the propriety of state regulation during the first trimester by noting that the risks attendant on an abortion are less than those which are attendant on the normal birth of the child at the end of term.[73] If that statement is correct where the abortion and the birth are both performed under optimum standards, it does not follow that unregulated abortions will be as safe as regulated ones. Is this the place for the judicial resurgence of laissez-faire? Does the Court really

---

[72] 410 U.S. at 162.   [73] *Id.* at 163.

want to constitutionalize the right to a backroom abortion even by a licensed physician? It is quite beside the point to argue that a hands-off rule is necessary to prevent the passage of state regulations over abortions in the first trimester, on grounds that they will be used to frustrate the Court's constitutional scheme. Should any such scheme be passed with that intent or even have that effect, the Court could strike it down on the grounds that it upsets the delicate balance required in *Roe v. Wade*. At the very least, it should have allowed the states to pass such legislation before it concluded in advance that all regulation of the manner and mode of an abortion during the first trimester of the pregnancy impermissibly restricts the right of a woman (with her physician) to have her abortion.

The second period for constitutional purposes runs from the end of the first trimester to the onset of viability. In this period, too, the Court was obliged to find that magic way that accommodates the interests of all the claimants in question, the woman, the state, and the fetus. (The father is still in a footnote.) But again the purported balance must be regarded as a failure. The first point to be faced here concerns the power of the state to regulate the manner and the means of the abortion, conceding for a moment their general propriety.

On this issue, the Court finds a "compelling state interest" in the protection of the woman's life that justifies the state intrusion into her privacy, now belatedly revealed to be of a totally different sort from that protected in the other contexts in which notions of privacy have been invoked.[74] The reason given for this result was that after the first trimester the risk from abortions exceeds that which is associated with the normal childbirth at the end of term.[75] The problem with the argument is simple: it gives no reason why the degree of risk associated with normal childbirth provides the measure for a compelling state interest. It is at least as arguable that some absolute figure is appropriate. And in any event, the Court did not explain why the differences in degree, which may be but

---

[74] "The pregnant woman cannot be isolated in her privacy. She carries an embryo and, later, a fetus, if one accepts the medical definitions of the developing young in the human uterus. See Dorland's Illustrated Medical Dictionary 478–79, 547 (24th ed. 1965). The situation therefore is inherently different from marital intimacy, or bedroom possession of obscene material, or marriage, or procreation, or education, with which *Eisenstadt*, *Griswold*, *Stanley*, *Loving*, *Skinner*, *Pierce*, and *Meyer* were respectively concerned." *Id.* at 159.

[75] *Id.* at 149, 163.

incremental as the pregnancy runs its course, are insufficient to support a compelling state interest in the first trimester only to support one immediately thereafter. Perhaps the state has a rational purpose for only the regulations in question, the sort sufficient to justify state intervention if the fundamental rights of the woman are not involved. The Court should not be able to manufacture a "compelling" interest simply by showing that the case at hand is closer to the line than a case which has already been disposed of. Yet that is exactly what was done in its purported reconciliation of the claims of the state with those of the woman.

The same problem in essence emerges in connection with the Court's attempts to balance the claims of the woman against those of the fetus. The Court conceded that there is some difference between the status of the unborn child between the moment after its conception and the onset of the second trimester, yet nonetheless holds that the difference is not strong enough to allow the state to protect its interest. It is a case where more is still nothing. Yet there is absolutely no explanation why the differences in the status of the unborn are not great enough to warrant a difference in result, particularly in light of the importance attached to quickening at common law.

The mystery deepens when the Court applies its invisible standards to the period of pregnancy that extends from viability to birth. At this point it allows the state regulation of manner and mode to continue as before in the event that abortions are allowed at all: doubtless the risks of abortion are greater now than at any previous time. Yet its position regarding the interest of the unborn child can only be described as astonishing: the Court holds that the state is entitled, but not required, to protect its, the unborn child's, interest. The reason for the entitlement is that the fetus is now capable of an independent life outside the mother. But the problem is, why should not the claims of the fetus be sufficiently strong to require, and not merely to permit, the state to intervene for its protection? After the Court expressed such firm views on the proper balance until the onset of viability, it gave no explanation why the state must be allowed to make its own choice after that time.

Roe v. Wade is symptomatic of the analytical poverty possible in constitutional litigation. Even in cases that do not give rise to the devilish questions of what counts as a person, the term "compelling state interest" is an analytical snare of no modest proportions. But

1ere, where the question is not "how much" but "whose," the
phrase is but a plaything of the judges, an excuse but never a reason
for a decision. Thus in the end we must criticize both Mr. Justice
Blackmun in *Roe v. Wade* and the entire method of constitutional
interpretation that allows the Supreme Court in the name of Due
Process both to "define" and to "balance" interests on the major
social and political issues of our time.

The Court has over the years labored with good effect to insure
that the political process will be as open and fair as the inexact art
of government will permit. In this regard, the reapportionment
decisions of the Court, to take but one example, have done much to
make state governments responsive to the majority of its citizens.
Given its decision in the abortion cases, one wonders, at least for
the moment, why they bothered. The Texas statute, the Georgia
statute, and a host of possible alternatives are not monuments to the
ignorance of man. They are uneasy but reasonable responses to
most troublesome questions. They should not be struck down
as unconstitutional by the Supreme Court, particularly in an
opinion that avoids in the name of privacy the hard questions that
must be faced to reach that result. The reaction to the decision has
been strong. The foes of abortion may not have sufficient strength
to overturn *Roe v. Wade* by constitutional amendment. But if they
fail, it will not be because they are persuaded by anything the Court
said.

SYLVIA SNOWISS

THE LEGACY OF JUSTICE BLACK

Professor Paul Freund, speaking on the desired characteristics of Supreme Court appointees, called for individuals who "are sensitive to the climate of the age, not the weather of the day or the weather of the year." He then characterized the climate of this age as one of "increasing sensitivity toward human rights" and "large conceptions of equality under law."[1]

At first glance Justice Hugo Lafayette Black seems not merely to be part of the climate of our age but to be largely responsible for bringing it into existence. He was the acknowledged leader in the battle for incorporation of the Bill of Rights in the Fourteenth Amendment, probably the most significant development in recent constitutional law, and in the development of the judiciary's "increasing sensitivity toward human rights." This achievement alone would be sufficient to earn a secure place for Justice Black among the most influential Supreme Court Justices and to identify him as the commanding figure of the Warren Court. There is more. The Court has either adopted or moved close to his original dissenting positions in freedom of speech and freedom of association cases.[2]

Sylvia Snowiss is Associate Professor of Political Science, California State University, Northridge, California.

AUTHOR'S NOTE: I am grateful to Professor Herbert J. Storing, who read and criticized the entire manuscript. My original research on Justice Black was supported by an American Association of University Women fellowship (1964–65).

[1] N.Y. Times, 26 Nov. 1971, p. 23, cols. 2–3.

[2] On Communist affiliation and labor union leadership, see his dissent in American Communications Assn. v. Douds, 339 U.S. 382, 445, (1950); United States v. Brown, 381 U.S. 437 (1965); on Communist affiliation and public school employment, see his dissent in Adler v. Board of Education, 342 U.S. 485, 496 (1952); Keyishian v. Board of

The law of libel and obscenity reflects the standards he strongly and consistently enunciated.[3]

Justice Black's efforts to broaden Fifth Amendment protection is not so well known as is his First Amendment absolutism, yet current Fifth Amendment controversy and much Fifth Amendment law was first charted in his dissents. He always viewed police interrogations without counsel as secret inquisitions in violation of the Fifth Amendment's ban on self-incrimination, and he spoke out in dissent foreshadowing *Miranda*[4] as early as 1951.[5] His dissenting position in *United States v. Kahriger*,[6] in opposition to the federal gambling registration statute, was adopted by the Court fifteen years later in *Marchetti v. United States*.[7] *Murphy v. Waterfront Commission*[8] accepted his dissent in *Feldman v. United States*[9] and extended the protection available to those giving testimony under immunity statutes. Although Justice Black's opposition to the use of what the Court calls noncommunicative testimony remains a dissenting position, his dissents are major statements in a still open debate.[10]

Still other areas of Bill of Rights and Fourteenth Amendment adjudication reflect Justice Black's leadership. *Griffin v. Illinois*[11] began a major effort to lessen the disabilities faced by indigent defendants in criminal cases. *Gideon v. Wainwright*,[12] making right to counsel mandatory in all serious criminal cases, was the triumph of his dissent in *Betts v. Brady*.[13] His influence is evident in the pro-

---

Regents, 385 U.S. 589 (1967); on loyalty oaths, see his concurrence in Wieman v. Updegraff, 344 U.S. 183, 192 (1952); Baggett v. Bullitt, 377 U.S. 360 (1964); Elfbrandt v. Russell, 384 U.S. 11 (1966); on membership in subversive organizations and admission to the bar, see his dissent in Konigsberg v. State Bar, 366 U.S. 36, 56 (1961); Baird v. State Bar of Arizona, 401 U.S. 1 (1971).

[3] On libel, see New York Times Co. v. Sullivan, 376 U.S. 254, 293 (1964); Rosenbloom v. Metromedia, 403 U.S. 29 (1971); on obscenity, see Smith v. California, 361 U.S. 147, 155 (1959); Redrup v. New York, 386 U.S. 767 (1967).

[4] Miranda v. Arizona, 384 U.S. 436 (1966).

[5] Gallegos v. Nebraska, 342 U.S. 55, 73 (1951).

[6] 345 U.S. 22, 36 (1953).   [8] 378 U.S. 5 (1964).

[7] 390 U.S. 39 (1968).   [9] 322 U.S. 487, 494 (1944).

[10] See Schmerber v. California, 384 U.S. 757, 773 (1966); United States v. Wade, 388 U.S. 218, 243–46 (1967); Gilbert v. California, 388 U.S. 263, 277 (1967).

[11] 351 U.S. 12 (1956).

[12] 372 U.S. 335 (1963).   [13] 316 U.S. 455, 474 (1942).

tection now available for defendants.[14] And finally, his dissent in
Colegrove v. Green[15] was not only accepted in *Baker v. Carr*,[16] but
has influenced subsequent leading decisions in the reapportionment
field.[17]

It is of course true, as even a casual observance of his last four or
five Terms reveals, that by the end of his career Justice Black was
no longer the leader of the Court. In First Amendment cases he was
chargeable with retreat from absolutism.[18] His later record on
search and seizure,[19] wiretapping,[20] and collateral review,[21] seemed
to be a withdrawal from his earlier willingness to invoke Bill of
Rights guarantees on behalf of persons accused of crime. Restrictive
readings of the Due Process and Equal Protection Clauses raised
doubts about his willingness to continue to extend constitutional
protection to minorities and to the poor.[22] Nevertheless, he continued to articulate his absolutist interpretation of the First and
Fifth Amendments,[23] as well as his strong defense of Bill of Rights
protection for persons accused of crime.[24]

How are these last few years to be understood? Did they reveal
a change toward conservatism, possibly associated with old age?
Did they indicate arbitrary inconsistency? Or did these changes
reveal a basic misconception about the underlying premises of his

---

[14] *Compare* Bloom v. Illinois, 391 U.S. 194 (1968), and Mayberry v. Pennsylvania,
400 U.S. 455 (1971), *with* Justice Black's dissent in Sacher v. United States, 343 U.S 1,
14 (1952).

[15] 328 U.S. 649, 566 (1946).   [16] 369 U.S. 186 (1962).

[17] See Wesberry v. Sanders, 376 U.S. 1 (1964); and Reynolds v. Sims, 377 U.S. 533
(1964).

[18] See, *e.g.*, Brown v. Louisiana, 383 U.S. 131, 151 (1966); Tinker v. Des Moines
School District, 393 U.S. 503, 515 (1969); Cohen v. California, 403 U.S. 15 (1971).

[19] See, *e.g.*, Spinelli v. United States, 393 U.S. 410, 429 (1969); Coolidge v. New
Hampshire, 403 U.S. 443, 493 (1971).

[20] See Berger v. New York, 388 U.S. 41, 70 (1967); Katz v. United States, 389 U.S.
347, 364 (1967).

[21] See Kaufman v. United States, 394 U.S. 217, 231 (1969); Harris v. Nelson, 394
U.S. 286, 301 (1969); Wade v. Wilson, 396 U.S. 282, 287 (1970).

[22] See, *e.g.*, Harper v. Virginia Board of Elections, 383 U.S. 663, 670 (1966); Goldberg
v. Kelly, 397 U.S. 254, 271 (1970); Boddie v. Connecticut, 401 U.S. 371, 389 (1971);
James v. Valtierra, 402 U.S. 137 (1971).

[23] See *e.g.*, Baird v. State Bar of Arizona, 401 U.S. 1 (1971); New York Times v.
United States, 403 U.S. 713, 714 (1971); California v. Byers, 402 U.S. 424, 459 (1971).

[24] See, particularly, Turner v. United States, 396 U.S. 398, 425 (1970).

entire career? In summarizing his colleague's achievements in 1956, Mr. Justice Douglas praised Justice Black for "consistently . . . construing the laws and the Constitution so as to protect the civil rights of citizens and aliens, whatever the form of repression may be."[25] If this assessment is accurate, then Justice Black is, at best, inconsistent. There is much evidence, however, now that his entire career is before us, that he maintained a strong internal consistency and that the popular view of his work is inaccurate. In addition, the fact that Black retained most of his early views—as well as his early passion—to the end in significant areas of constitutional law, suggests that simplistic explanations are inadequate. In this connection, too, it is worth reflecting on Professor Kurland's observation that, although Justice Black was enormously successful in influencing Court positions, he never succeeded in having his basic doctrine accepted.[26] This anomalous fact casts doubt on the validity of the popular understanding of Justice Black's basic doctrine.

A closer look at Justice Black's entire record will support the conclusion that he was consistent. Examination of his last few years will reveal a misunderstanding of his underlying constitutional doctrine rather than inconsistency in his position. This examination will reveal, too, the paradoxical nature of Justice Black's legacy: a general constitutional doctrine of judicial power and protection of individual rights that has had practically no influence on the Court's doctrine, combined with the articulation of positions on specific individual rights that remains of enormous influence.

I. Justice Black's Constitutional Understanding: Limited Government and Absolute Rights

Fostering increasing sensitivity toward human rights and large conceptions of equality under law is not the same thing as always favoring claims of individual liberty against governmental authority. But to foster these ends does necessitate a general openness to such claims which, in the context of American constitutional law, encompasses two broad commitments. The first commitment is to a liberal reading of the Bill of Rights and other limits on governmental powers, particularly the Due Process and Equal Protection Clauses of the Fourteenth Amendment. Implicit in this liberal read-

---

[25] Douglas, *Mr. Justice Black: A Foreword*, 65 YALE L. J. 449, 450 (1956).

[26] Kurland, *Hugo Lafayette Black: In Memoriam*, 20 J. Pub. L. 359, 360–61 (1971).

ing is the assumption that as societal needs change over time, constitutional provisions need reexamination and interpretation in light
of their basic purposes. The second commitment is to a vigorous
use of judicial power—a power accepted as legitimate in a democratic regime. While Justice Black always supported broad protection of individual rights, he never accepted either of these commitments. Nor did he ever focus on protection of individual rights
as a primary political goal, to be sought as a good in itself. For
Justice Black protection of individual rights was always linked to a
specific conception of democratic government. This conception of
democratic government, like the basic qualities of his opinions, is
straightforward and without significant subtlety. Democracy is
conceived exclusively in terms of governmental responsiveness to
popular will. To make this responsiveness effective, government
must be subject to certain limits. Among the more important limits
are those on behalf of individual rights, and, among these, First
Amendment limits are central.

The intellectual freedom secured by the First Amendment insures a thorough canvassing and dissemination of views, the necessary precondition for the emergence of a genuinely free popular
will. Freedom of association joined with constitutionally protected
voting rights implements this intellectual freedom by facilitating
the transmission of popular will into public policy. True responsiveness is incompatible with any exception or qualification of this
process. Critical limits must be absolutely enforced. This absolutism, furthermore, is anchored in the language of the Constitution,
particularly in the unequivocal command of the First Amendment.

Justice Black spoke often of the primacy of the First Amendment. It is the "heart of the Bill of Rights,"[27] and "the foundation
upon which our government structure rests and without which it
could not continue to endure as conceived and planned."[28] More
striking than this, however, was the extent to which he viewed
other limits on behalf of individual rights as subordinate to this same
end of maintaining unfettered intellectual and political exchange:

> For the fears of arbitrary court action sprang largely from the
> past use of courts in the imposition of criminal punishments
> to suppress speech, press, and religion. Hence the constitutional

---

[27] Black, *The Bill of Rights*, 35 N.Y. U. L. Rev. 865, 881 (1960).
[28] Milk Wagon Drivers v. Meadowmoor, 312 U.S. 287, 301 (1941).

limitations of courts' powers were, in the view of the Founders, essential supplements to the First Amendment.[29]

> [Persecution following the attempt to exercise First Amendment rights inevitably involved] secret arrests, unlawful detentions, forced confessions, secret trials, and arbitrary punishments under oppressive laws. Therefore it is not surprising that the men behind the First Amendment also insisted upon the Fifth, Sixth, and Eighth Amendments. . . . If occasionally these safeguards worked to the advantage of an ordinary criminal, that was a price they were willing to pay.[30]

Just as genuine intellectual freedom demands absolute enforcement of the First Amendment, so, too, there must be absolute enforcement of those other provisions which serve this same end. In like manner, the unqualified language of the First Amendment is duplicated in the language of the "essential supplements to the First Amendment," the Fifth and Sixth Amendments.[31]

Absolutism is not only the key to effective limitation of legislative and executive power, but, equally important, it serves to limit the judiciary as well. In a properly run democratic regime, no branch may interfere with the popular formation of public policy. Should the judiciary take upon itself the task of broadly interpreting and updating constitutional provisions, it would, according to Justice Black, be taking upon itself an essentially policy-making role. For the exercise of judicial power to be acceptable, constitutional provisions must be self-executing; their entire meaning must be contained in the text, and be applicable for all time:[32]

> Had the drafters of the Due Process Clause meant to leave judges . . . ambulatory power to declare laws unconstitutional, the chief value of a written constitution, as the Founders saw it, would have been lost. . . . A written constitution, designed to guarantee protection against governmental abuses, including

---

[29] Adamson v. California, 332 U.S. 46, 71 (1947).

[30] Feldman v. United States, 322 U.S. 487, 501–02 (1944). See also Black, note 27 *supra*, at 880; Bartkus v. Illinois, 359 U.S. 121, 150 (1959).

[31] Black acknowledged that the language of the Eighth Amendment, another essential supplement to the First Amendment, is imprecise in that it bans *excessive* fines and *unusual* punishments. Black, note 27 *supra*, at 871–72. During his tenure, there was little Eighth Amendment litigation and thus little opportunity to see how he would interpret the Amendment in particular situations. For his opinion that the Eighth Amendment does not bar capital punishment, see McGautha v. California, 402 U.S. 183, 226 (1971). See also Mishkin v. New York, 383 U.S. 502, 517 (1966).

[32] Goldberg v. Kelly, 397 U.S. 254, 276–77 (1970).

those of judges, must have written standards that mean something definite and have an explicit content.

In addition to the First, Fifth, and parts of the Sixth Amendments[33] only two other major constitutional limits possess the requisite self-executing clarity necessary for absolute enforcement. These
are the Due Process Clause of the Fourteenth Amendment, understood as meaning no less than and no more than the specific guarantees of the Bill of Rights, and the Equal Protection Clause, understood as reaching only certain limited kinds of discrimination.[34]

Other provisions of the Bill of Rights, on the other hand, are
either qualified or imprecise. They cannot be said to carry their
meaning in their words. Limited democratic government demands
judicial deference to interpretation of these clauses made by the
responsible branches. Chief among these are the Fourth Amendment's ban on unreasonable searches and seizures; the Sixth Amendment's guarantee of an impartial jury; the Due Process Clause understood as meaning either less or more than the Bill of Rights; and
the Equal Protection Clause, loosely construed as a mandate to
strike down governmental distinctions:[35]

> Some constitutional provisions are stated in absolute and
> unqualified language such, for illustration, as the First Amend-
> ment. . . . Other constitutional provisions do require courts to
> choose between competing policies, such as the Fourth Amend-
> ment which, by its terms, necessitates a judicial decision as to
> what is an "unreasonable" search or seizure.

Justice Black's constitutional understanding was never presented
as his own interpretation but rather as a faithful rendering of the
Founders' intentions. History and language were the only acceptable standards for interpretation. Standards such as justice, fairness,
or reasonableness were impermissible. The constitutional text, enforced as Justice Black argued its language dictated, *is* fairness and
justice.[36] Failure to follow this standard would be undemocratic.

---

[33] Black treated the "impartial jury" provision of the Sixth Amendment as an imprecise clause, and denied it absolute enforcement. See text *infra*, at notes 116–23.

[34] Black's treatment of the Equal Protection Clause defies easy summation. See text
infra, at notes 151–76.

[35] Rochin v. California, 342 U.S. 165, 176 (1952). See also Berger v. New York, 388
U.S. 41, 74–75 (1967).

[36] Foster v. California, 394 U.S. 440, 448–49 (1969); *In re* Winship, 397 U.S. 358,
377 (1970); Boddie v. Connecticut, 401 U.S. 371, 394 (1971).

In the course of interpreting the words of the Constitution under standards such as justice and fairness, the judiciary would inevitably introduce its own conceptions of justice and fairness, and thus unjustly arrogate to itself the people's policy-making functions:[37]

> It can be . . . argued that when this Court strikes down a legislative act because it offends the idea of "fundamental fairness," it furthers the basic thrust of our Bill of Rights by protecting individual freedom. But that argument ignores the effect of such decisions on perhaps the most fundamental individual liberty of our people—the right of each man to participate in the self-government of his society.

Moreover, acceptance of such standards prepared the way for the kind of judicial abuse which culminated in the New Deal Court crisis.[38] Finally, this "accordion-like" method of adjudication would likely result in a contraction of Bill of Rights protection at some point. It is inevitable that the judicial conception of fairness or justice will, at times, be less strict than the absolutist reading of the First, Fifth, and parts of the Sixth Amendments.[39]

This understanding resolves a good many of the apparent contradictions in Justice Black's judicial career. It explains, for example, how he could argue for both literal adherence to the words of the text, and a liberal, rather than niggardly reading of specific guarantees. It is only for those constitutional provisions whose language is unqualified that judges are to give a liberal or an absolute reading. In practice this means that these limits are to be enforced to the furthest extent that language permits. Individual rights claims are always to take precedence over a demand for governmental action. This is what he meant when he said that the Founders did the balancing for us. All of Justice Black's ringing defenses of individual rights, all of his exhortations to the judiciary to live up to its responsibilities, all of his memorable defenses of minorities and dissidents, occurred in the context of absolutely protected rights, as he defined them. He differed from the libertarian position mainly in Fourth Amendment cases, in due process cases that did not involve specific Bill of Rights guarantees, and in equal protection cases that

---

[37] *In re* Winship, 397 U.S. 358, 384–85 (1970).

[38] Griswold v. Connecticut, 381 U.S. 479, 510–18 (1965); Sniadach v. Family Finance Corp., 395 U.S. 337, 345 (1969).

[39] Rochin v. California, 342 U.S. 165, 177 (1952); Turner v. United States, 396 U.S. 398, 425 (1970).

did not involve confrontation with the criminal process, certain kinds of racial discrimination, or voting rights questions. These departures from the liberal creed are traceable to the beginning of his career.[40]

Justice Black's vision of a free, democratic society was that of a completely automatic and self-regulating mechanism. The heart of the mechanism, the market place of ideas, was to be self-regulating and self-perpetuating. He expected a fully informed populace to reject any political alternative that would destroy the freedom of the market place itself.[41] The real source of danger to the free market place of ideas is the failure to allow it to operate as intended. The judiciary's responsibility is to thwart such attempts by enforcing the clear limits of the Constitution. The judiciary's role is thus also essentially automatic; it exercises no genuine judgment but merely enforces commands whose meanings are manifest from history and the words themselves.

For Justice Black, the constitutional limits provided by the Founders were sufficient to perpetuate this self-regulating system. Should the people conceive themselves threatened by a danger that could not be met by the existing guarantees, the remedy is available through amendment of the Constitution. There is no warrant for the judiciary to arrogate to itself the power to decide what is crucial to liberty, or how to meet a new danger:[42]

> I realize that many good and able men have eloquently spoken and written, sometimes in rhapsodical strains, about the duty of this Court to keep the Constitution in tune with the times. The idea is that the Constitution must be changed from time to time and that this Court is charged with a duty to make

---

[40] On the Fourth Amendment, see Harris v. United States, 331 U.S. 145 (1947); Wolf v. Colorado, 338 U.S. 25 (1949); Ker v. California, 374 U.S. 23 (1963); on due process, see Griswold v. Connecticut, 381 U.S. 479, 507 (1965); Sheppard v. Maxwell, 384 U.S. 333 (1966) (Black's departure from the libertarian position here became evident only after the success of the selective incorporation notions); on equal protection, see Kotch v. Pilot Commissioners, 330 U.S. 552 (1947); Goesaert v. Cleary, 335 U.S. 464 (1948). The charges of inconsistency in his First Amendment adjudication raise more complicated questions. See text *infra*, at notes 195–233.

[41] Carlson v. Landon, 342 U.S. 524, 555–56 (1952); Barenblatt v. United States, 360 U.S. 109, 144–46 (1959); Konigsberg v. State Bar, 366 U.S. 36, 78 (1961); Communist Party v. Subversive Activities Control Board, 367 U.S. 1, 168–69 (1961).

[42] Griswold v. Connecticut, 381 U.S. 479, 522 (1965). See also Harper v. Virginia Board of Elections, 383 U.S. 663, 675–80 (1966); Berger v. New York, 388 U.S. 41, 87 (1967); Boddie v. Connecticut, 401 U.S. 371, 394 (1971).

those changes. For myself, I must with all deference reject that philosophy. The Constitution makers knew the need for change and provided for it. Amendments suggested by the people's elected representatives can be submitted to the people or their elected agents for ratification. That method of change was good for our Fathers, and being somewhat old-fashioned I must add it is good enough for me.

Justice Black frequently expressed his admiration for the Constitution and alluded to the adequacy of the Bill of Rights to protect liberty.[43] At no time did he indicate need for additional protections.

Justice Black's constitutional understanding rested on three dubious propositions: (1) Absolute or liberal enforcement of the precise and unqualified provisions of the Bill of Rights is sufficient to maintain a free regime. (2) This position is a faithful statement of the Founders' intentions and not his own judicial policy-making. (3) The unqualified provisions of the Bill of Rights are, in fact, unambiguous in meaning.

I shall postpone discussion of the first proposition to the end of this paper. To come fully to terms with the historical argument it would be necessary to go over the entire ground. That has already been done well elsewhere. Justice Black's reading of history drew extensive and highly literate criticism, even from those sympathetic to his constitutional interpretation.[44] He never satisfactorily answered his critics, except by repeating his original argument. On this record, he has not made his case. Given Justice Black's stress on the clarity of the text and the single-mindedness of the Founders, the mere existence of reasonable and cogent disagreement over the Founders' intentions weakens his position. At best, it is possible to reach meaningful agreement only on the most general intentions of the original document. The "intentions of the Founders" simply do not lend themselves to the kind of detailed guidance Justice Black claimed for them.

The third proposition deserves lengthier treatment. To do justice

---

[43] Adamson v. California, 332 U.S. 46, 89 (1947); Braden v. United States, 365 U.S. 431, 444–45 (1961). See also Turner v. United States, 396 U.S. 398, 425–26 (1970).

[44] The most thorough examination and criticism of Black's historical argument is found in Fairman, *Does the Fourteenth Amendment Incorporate the Bill of Rights? The Original Understanding*, 2 STAN. L. REV. 5 (1949). Among those clearly sympathetic to Black's constitutional views, see LEVY, LEGACY OF SUPPRESSION (1960); Meiklejohn, *The First Amendment Is an Absolute*, 1961 SUPREME COURT REVIEW 245, 263–64.

to Justice Black's literalism it is necessary to open the larger question of judicial review, democracy, and the activism–self-restraint controversy.

II. DEMOCRACY AND JUDICIAL POWER

Justice Black's literalism reflected his dissatisfaction with the major attempts to reconcile the exercise of judicial review with democracy. In the aftermath of the New Deal–Court controversy there was widespread agreement that vigorous exercise of judicial review entailed judicial policy-making that was incompatible with democratic government. Two main responses arose to this challenge. The first, judicial self-restraint, conceded the basic illegitimacy of judicial review and counseled judicial restraint in all areas of constitutional adjudication. The second, judicial activism, argued that the exercise of Court power in one sphere, individual rights adjudication, did not invade the policy prerogative of the people but actually enhanced it by keeping open the processes of democracy and increasing access to decision-making.[45] The legitimacy of such adjudication was supported with argument that it involved more a legal judgment than a political one. In practice this legal judgment was reduced to linking the democratic exercise of judicial review with a presumption on behalf of the minority litigant.[46] The core of activism, however, remained the proposition that judicial action safeguarding individual rights against popular passion or bureaucratic willfulness enhanced, rather than interfered with, the democratic process.

While Justice Black was clearly the leader of the activist bloc during the 1950s and 1960s, he never accepted this broad proposition exempting individual rights adjudication from the sphere of illegitimate judicial policy-making. His individual rights adjudication rested entirely on activism's subordinate proposition, namely, its legal or technical character. Furthermore, his exclusive reliance on history and language committed him to this proposition more

---

[45] The clearest statement of this position is Rostow, *The Democratic Character of Judicial Review*, 66 HARV. L. REV. 193, 194–203 (1952).

[46] See McKay, *The Preference for Freedom*, 34 N.Y. U. L. REV. 1182 (1959); Frantz, *Is the First Amendment Law?—A Reply to Professor Mendelson*, 51 CALIF. L. REV. 729, 738–44, 753–54 (1963).

fully than was the case for any other member of the Court.[47] Justice Black's literalism constituted a rejection of the dominant justifications for the exercise of judicial power and an attempt to make that exercise more secure by resting it on a revived form of the declaratory theory of law. Difficulties with declaratory theory had contributed to the Court crisis of the 1930s and Justice Black's attempt at revival compounded these difficulties.

To understand this attempt it is helpful to turn first to Chief Justice Marshall, the leading American expounder of the declaratory theory. For Marshall, judicial review rested on the legal character of the Constitution and the judiciary's responsibility to apply and thereby to interpret the law. The text and intent of the Framers were two starting points in Justice Marshall's constitutional interpretation, an interpretation obviously culminating in judicial judgment, which was distinguished from judicial will. He strove to legitimize this exercise of judgment by his efforts to remain faithful to the text and historical intent, by avoidance of overt partisanship, and by the high quality of his judgments.

Over the years the distinction between judicial judgment and will began to lose its force. History and language were increasingly regarded simply as vehicles for the expression of judicial will, and judicial judgment was perceived to be more a reflex of a Justice's values than a thoughtful interpretation of the text to meet important political needs. In the face of the overt partisanship and clear abuse of judicial power by the economic activists, the distinction disappeared completely. Save for the exception made by the libertarian activists, all significant judgment was widely seen as mere will. Justice Black, however, did not find the grounds for this exception persuasive, nor was he willing to relinquish Court power to the extent demanded by the proponents of self-restraint. He sought instead to find something to replace Justice Marshall's judgment, and in so doing returned to history and language alone, asserting their complete clarity and sufficiency for all significant purposes. There was to be no need for any judgment whatever.

This attempt has proved less than serviceable. History is too in-

---

[47] See Justice Murphy's dissent, joined by Justice Rutledge, in Adamson v. California, 332 U.S. 46, 123 (1947); Douglas, Murphy, and Rutledge, dissenting in Wolf v. Colorado, 338 U.S. 25, 40, 41, 47 (1949). The consequences of this divergence were not visible as long as incorporation and First Amendment problems—two areas where Justice Black's literalism served the same ends as those served by activism—dominated the Court's work.

conclusive and words too ambiguous to bear the burden Justice Black would impose on them. Even in statutory interpretation, but certainly in constitutional interpretation, the judicial task is constantly to give new meaning to the same words, in response to changing circumstances. The contention surrounding so many of Justice Black's constitutional positions reflects the breadth of disagreement over the meaning of the text and fatally undercuts his assertion that he is merely enforcing the plain meaning of plain words and agreed-upon intent of the Framers.[48]

Although he never retreated from his position, he was not unaware of the problems it involved. On two occasions he confronted the issue fairly directly, and acknowledged the impossibility of obliterating the need for all judgment. Tacitly accepting the widespread equation of judgment with will, he proposed literalism as the optimal solution for keeping that will within tolerable limits:[49]

> Of course I realize that you can never do away with, or indeed would I want to do away with, an individual justice's judgment. But I think there is something to our people's aspirations for a government of laws and not of men. And I cannot accept a Due Process Clause interpretation which permits life-appointed judges to write their own economic and political views into our Constitution. I earnestly believe that my due process interpretation is the only one consistent with a written constitution in that it better insures that constitutional provisions will not be changed except by proper amendment processes.

Justice Black had made the same suggestion, in a somewhat fuller form, once before, in his *Adamson* dissent:[50]

> Since *Marbury* v. *Madison* . . . was decided, the practice has been firmly established, for better or worse, that courts can strike down legislative enactments which violate the Constitution. This process, of course, involves interpretation, and since words can have many meanings, interpretation obviously may result in contraction or extension of the original purpose of a constitutional provision, thereby affecting policy. But

---

[48] See Justice Harlan's challenge to Justice Black on this score. Griswold v. Connecticut, 381 U.S. 479, 501 (1965). See also the discussion of the declaratory theory of law by Justices Clark and Black in Linkletter v. Walker, 381 U.S. 618, 622–29, 643 (1965); and Justice Black in DeBacker v. Brainard, 396 U.S. 28, 34 (1969).

[49] BLACK, A CONSTITUTIONAL FAITH 41 (1969).

[50] 332 U.S. at 90–92. The internal quotation is from a Black opinion, F.P.C. v. Pipeline Co., 315 U.S. 575, 601, n.4 (1942).

to pass upon the constitutionality of statutes by looking to the particular standards enumerated in the Bill of Rights and other parts of the Constitution is one thing; to invalidate statutes because of application of "natural law" deemed to be above and undefined by the Constitution is another. "In one instance, courts proceeding within clearly marked constitutional boundaries seek to execute policies written into the Constitution; in the other, they roam at will in the limitless area of their own beliefs as to reasonableness and actually select policies, a responsibility which the Constitution entrusts to the legislative representatives of the people."

This explanation, however, did not resolve his difficulties. In the process of "seek[ing] to execute policies written into the Constitution" he strained certain clauses beyond recognition, while downgrading others to the point of virtually eliminating them from judicial scrutiny. It is simply not true that such an approach "execute[s] policies written into the Constitution," or demonstrates a meaningful faithfulness to the Constitution's original language or purpose. Rather, Justice Black's solution became an exercise of judicial will which, within his own framework, he could not justify. This difficulty was particularly acute because of the demonstrated activism of his literal approach. Incorporation, First and Fifth Amendment absolutism, and Justice Black's reapportionment position simply belie any claim that literalism is to be preferred because it serves "to execute policies written into the Constitution." If anything, such activism, coupled with the insistence that this was merely enforcing the clear words of the text, invited cynicism about the judicial function.

Justice Black's position, in fact, failed to win over a single adherent among his colleagues and has been completely bypassed by the changes in both activism and self-restraint that have taken place during the last decade. While the practice of judicial activism has not abated, its underlying justification has undergone a substantial shift. By the late 1960s there was little vitality left in the old categories of activism and self-restraint. This shift evolved in the course of debate over Professor Wechsler's critique of activism[51] and despite the generally negative reception this critique received. While rejecting Professor Wechsler's criticism of leading individual rights decisions, commentators made no serious effort to distinguish the unique character of individual rights adjudication or to link the

---

[51] Wechsler, *Toward Neutral Principles of Constitutional Law*, 73 HARV. L. REV. 1 (1959).

democratic exercise of judicial review with support for minority litigants.[52] Without intending to do so, Professor Wechsler nonetheless made it impossible to deny that protection of individual rights is a problematic, value-laden task, rather than a largely legal or technical one. He thus undermined the libertarian activist position and effectively destroyed its subordinate position, the only one, as we have seen, to which Justice Black adhered. In the process of defending itself from Professor Wechsler's criticism, libertarian activism lost whatever reliance it once placed on the explicitness of the constitutional text, and increasingly rested on the ground that such adjudication is good policy, that it is conducive to worthwhile ends.[53] At the same time, there has also been an increased willingness to defend judicial review without linking it to particular ends, and without apologizing for its supposedly undemocratic attributes.[54]

With Justice Harlan's emergence as leader of the old self-restraint bloc, that bloc too underwent important changes. Self-restraint in Justice Harlan's hands became a necessary instrument of, but not identical with, sound constitutional interpretation. He fully accepted the judiciary's power to make final constitutional determinations and boldly and jealously guarded that power.[55] Justice Frankfurter's agonizing self scrutiny in the flag salute[56] and *Dennis*[57] cases was not repeated. Sounding more like Chief Justice Mar-

---

[52] See Pollak, *Racial Discrimination and Judicial Integrity: A Reply to Professor Wechsler*, 108 U. Pa. L. Rev. 1 (1959); Henkin, *Some Reflections on Current Constitutional Controversy*, 109 U. Pa. L. Rev. 637, 652–55 (1961); Rostow, *American Legal Realism and the Sense of the Profession*, 34 Rocky Mt. L. Rev. 123, 135–46 (1962).

[53] On the bench this shift is most visible in the work of Justice Douglas. He has urged the judiciary to respond to evolving needs, openly eschewing the restraint that original intent might provide. Harper v. Virginia Board of Elections, 383 U.S. 663, 669–70 (1966); Oregon v. Mitchell, 400 U.S. 112, 139–40 (1970). See also Reitman v. Mulkey, 387 U.S. 369, 381 (1967); Walz v. Tax Commission, 397 U.S. 664, 700–06 (1970); Younger v. Harris, 401 U.S. 37, 58 (1971). He makes no serious attempt to distinguish judicial decision-making from legislative decision-making. Off the bench, this position is most clearly stated in Miller & Howell, *The Myth of Neutrality in Constitutional Adjudication*, 27 U. Chi. L. Rev. 661 (1960).

[54] See Mueller & Schwartz, *The Principle of Neutral Principles*, 7 U.C.L.A. L. Rev. 571 (1960).

[55] Katzenbach v. Morgan, 384 U.S. 641, 665–71 (1966); Oregon v. Mitchell, 400 U.S. 112, 204–09 (1970).

[56] Board of Education v. Barnette, 319 U.S. 624, 646 (1943).

[57] Dennis v. United States, 341 U.S. 494, 517 (1951).

shall, Justice Harlan rested judicial review on the judiciary's assigned task of deciding cases.[58] Even when sustaining a challenged exercise of governmental power, the Court placed more stress on its assessment of constitutionality than on the need to defer to judgments made by the responsible branches.[59] Harlan accepted the inevitable need for judgment that grows out of this task, and turned first to history and tradition as guides in the exercise of that judgment:[60]

> [J]udicial self restraint . . . an indispensable ingredient of sound constitutional adjudication . . . will be achieved . . . only by continual insistence upon respect for the teachings of history, solid recognition of the basic values that underlie our society, and wise appreciation of the great roles that the doctrines of federalism and separation of powers have played in establishing and preserving American freedoms. . . . Adherence to these principles will not, of course, obviate all constitutional differences of opinion among judges, nor should it.

In expressing his own constitutional opinions he combined self-restraint with a consistent and successful endeavor to maintain a superior quality of judgment.

The demise of self-restraint has carried over into the Nixon Court. None of the new appointees can be meaningfully described as adherents of that position. In a certain sense everyone on the current Court is an activist. This general activism, of course, is no longer a libertarian activism and it does not carry with it any presumption on behalf of the minority litigant.

The current state of the controversy still leaves major questions unanswered. Neither side can be said to have resolved the dilemma of the legitimacy of Court power in a democracy. For Mr. Justice Douglas's wing this problem involves legitimizing the relatively overt policy-making of the nonelective, nonresponsive Court. For Justice Harlan's successors, it involves, at a minimum, giving credibility to the distinction between judgment and will.

While resolution of such problems remains for the future, Justice Black's theses contribute nothing toward that resolution. He always

---

[58] Mackey v. United States, 401 U.S. 667, 677–81 (1971).

[59] See, e.g., Kaufman v. United States, 394 U.S. 217, 242–43 (1969); Shapiro v. Thompson, 394 U.S. 618, 655 (1969); In re Stolar, 401 U.S. 23, 34 (1971).

[60] Griswold v. Connecticut, 381 U.S. 479, 501 (1965). See also Oregon v. Mitchell, 400 U.S. 112, 152 (1970); Sniadach v. Family Finance Corp., 395 U.S. 337, 342–43 (1969).

was, and remained to the end, an advocate of self-restraint who fundamentally disapproved of extensive constitutional review. It is not surprising that in his last few years Justice Black began to sound increasingly like Justice Frankfurter, as Justice Harlan sounded less so. At the end, Justice Black was the only advocate of self-restraint left on the Court. He found some governmental practices abhorrent but reluctantly saw no judicial remedy.[61] And it was Justice Black who moved to a new position of lonely dissent, on an activist Court willing to use judicial power to go beyond specific guarantees of the Bill of Rights and to give broader meaning to the Due Process and Equal Protection Clauses.[62]

III. LITERALISM AND THE INTERPRETATION OF THE CONSTITUTION

In criticizing Alexander Meiklejohn's absolutist interpretation of the First Amendment, Justice Frankfurter remarked that absolute rules engender absolute exceptions.[63] This is an apt characterization and criticism of all of Justice Black's work. Basically, there was no reasoning process between his rules and his exceptions, because such reasoning involves forbidden judicial judgment. In the absence of a sound reasoning process, and in the face of the need for reasoned support for the distinctions judges draw, Justice Black's definitions of absolute rules and absolute exceptions tended to become highly arbitrary.

A. DUE PROCESS OF LAW: INCORPORATION AND FEDERALISM

Justice Black came to the Court in 1937, at the height of the controversy over the limits which the Due Process Clause placed on governmental power to regulate the economy. He immediately joined those opposed to the Court's use of due process to limit that power. Increasingly, however, the Due Process Clause was invoked

---

[61] Griswold v. Connecticut, 381 U.S. 479, 507 (1965); Harper v. Virginia Board of Elections, 383 U.S. 663, 677 (1966). See also In re Winship, 397 U.S. 358, 385–86 (1970).

[62] Sheppard v. Maxwell, 384 U.S. 333 (1966); Katz v. United States, 389 U.S. 347, 364 (1967); Sibron v. New York, 392 U.S. 40, 79 (1968); Hunter v. Erickson, 393 U.S. 385, 396 (1969); Boddie v. Connecticut, 401 U.S. 371, 389 (1971); In re Winship, 397 U.S. 358, 377 (1970). Chief Justice Burger and Mr. Justice Stewart also dissented in Winship. Their dissents, however, rested on disagreement with In re Gault, 387 U.S. 1 (1967). Neither joined Black's dissent. For a similar assessment of Justice Black's conception of the judiciary see Freund, Mr. Justice Black and the Judicial Function, 14 U.C.L.A. L. REV. 467 (1967).

[63] Dennis v. United States, 341 U.S. 494, 524, and n.5 (1951).

to protect individual rights from legislative and administrative actions. While he was clearly sympathetic to the plea for increased protection of individual rights, he was adamant in his refusal to use the Due Process Clause in a way that sanctioned broad use of judjcial power. This problem presented the supreme challenge of Justice Black's judicial career, a challenge which he resolved in his *Adamson* dissent in 1947.

Justice Black argued in *Adamson*, with the aid of extensive historical material, that the Due Process Clause of the Fourteenth Amendment makes the Bill of Rights, in its entirety, applicable to the states.[64] In his understanding of due process, the clause adds nothing of substance to the Constitution. He treated the phrase "due process of law" as identical with "the law of the land" as used in Magna Carta. For him both clauses were specific: they refer to the written statutory and constitutional provisions already in existence:[65]

> For me the only correct meaning of that phrase is that our Government must proceed according to the "law of the land"— that is, according to written constitutional and statutory provisions as interpreted by court decisions. The Due Process Clause, in both the Fifth and Fourteenth Amendments, in and of itself does not add to those provisions, but in effect states that our governments are governments of law and constitutionally bound to act only according to law.

Due process, for Justice Black, was the chief defense against tyrannical government harassment of the weak, the helpless, and the dissenter through abuse of the criminal law. It provides this defense by constituting a ban on any ex post facto prosecution, and by insuring that where procedural safeguards for the accused had been established, they were to be followed. His fullest discussion of due process as a barrier against tyranny is in *Chambers v. Florida*,[66] an early case striking down convictions based on coerced confessions. He repeated this argument in condensed form in *Adamson*, where he rested explicitly on the intent of the Framers to support the broader argument of full incorporation.[67] This view of due process provided vastly increased protection for individual

---

[64] Adamson v. California, 332 U.S. 46, 68 (1947).

[65] *In re* Winship, 397 U.S. 358, 382 (1970).

[66] 309 U.S. 227, 235–38 (1940).

[67] Adamson v. California, 332 U.S. 46, 68 and historical appendix, 92–123 (1947).

rights in all criminal proceedings without sanctioning case-by-case invocation of judgment. Coupled with Justice Black's suggestion that literal enforcement of the Bill of Rights is adequate protection for liberty, it cemented his conception of the judiciary as enforcer of a self-contained and essentially complete Constitution.

Except for Justice Black, all members of the Court approached the Due Process Clause in terms of the concept of fundamental fairness. For supporters of the incorporation view, at a minimum, all of the Bill of Rights guarantees are necessary components of fundamental fairness. Even those Justices with relatively narrow conceptions of fundamental fairness were open to a variety of due process claims both within and beyond the terms of the Bill of Rights. Consequently, although it never endorsed Justice Black's incorporation doctrine directly, the Court had moved steadily toward that end by a process of selective incorporation that now covers most of the important provisions of the Bill of Rights.[68] Due process questions increasingly call for judgments about the range and meaning of fundamental fairness in the absence of an enumerated Bill of Rights provision. For Justice Black, all such judgments were subjective and hence illegitimate. They invoked "natural law" standards which constitute, as they always have, a mask by which judges supplant popular rule-making.[69]

In every instance where due process protection had been invoked in the absence of a specific Bill of Rights guarantee, Justice Black rejected the claim. Two of these cases involved challenges to administrative procedures. In *Sniadach v. Family Finance Corp.*,[70] the Court struck down a Wisconsin wage garnishment procedure, and in *Goldberg v. Kelly*,[71] it ruled that due process requires a hearing

---

[68] See Duncan v. Louisiana, 391 U.S. 145, 148 (1968), for an enumeration of the Bill of Rights provisions that have been incorporated. The jury trial provision was incorporated in *Duncan* and protection against double jeopardy was added in Benton v. Maryland, 395 U.S. 784 (1969).

[69] "The due process argument which my Brothers HARLAN and WHITE adopt . . . is based . . . on the premise that this Court is vested with power to invalidate all state laws that it considers to be arbitrary, capricious, unreasonable, or oppressive, or on this Court's belief that a particular state law under scrutiny has no 'rational or justifying' purpose, or is offensive to a 'sense of fairness and justice.' If these formulas based on 'natural justice,' or others which mean the same thing, are to prevail, they require judges to determine what is or is not constitutional on the basis of their own appraisal of what laws are unwise or unnecessary. The power to make such decisions is of course that of a legislative body." Black dissenting in *Griswold*, 381 U.S. at 511–12.

[70] 395 U.S. 337 (1969).   [71] 397 U.S. 254 (1970).

before welfare payments could be terminated. In a third case, *Boddie v. Connecticut,* [72] he dissented from the majority holding that court fees required for divorce deprived an indigent of due process of law.

Justice Black's restrictive reading of due process was even more striking in criminal cases. In 1965 he was the sole dissenter from the Court's ruling that a murder conviction in a trial conducted amid grossly excessive publicity violated due process.[73] He dissented without opinion, hoping perhaps that such cases would be rare and that he would not have to probe publicly the limits of due process.

By 1970 he was no longer silent when the Court invalidated a criminal procedure not specifically prohibited by the Bill of Rights. In 1967 the Supreme Court, in *In re Gault,*[74] had ruled that juvenile criminal proceedings were henceforth to be subject to due process protection. Justice Black voted with the majority. Before *Gault,* juvenile proceedings had been considered part of a rehabilitory rather than criminal process and thus lacked the traditional safeguards attached to the criminal process. One consequence of this was that some jurisdictions judged the guilt of juvenile offenders on the basis of proof on a preponderance of the evidence, rather than by the stricter standard of proof beyond a reasonable doubt. In *In re Winship,*[75] which followed *Gault* by three years, the Court was asked to consider whether this standard of proof violated the Due Process Clause. By a large majority the Court ruled that proof beyond a reasonable doubt was a firmly established part of the Anglo-American criminal process and clearly a component of due process of law. Justice Black dissented vigorously, insisting that as there was no constitutional provision requiring proof beyond a reasonable doubt, judges could not consider this standard a mandatory component of due process.

The incorporation controversy also raised important questions about American federalism. The major one was whether Bill of Rights guarantees were to be made applicable to the states with the same meaning applicable in federal cases. Justice Black argued that they should be and again he led a majority of the Court into adopting this view. For Justice Black, however, this position was

---

[72] 401 U.S. 371, 389 (1971).

[73] Sheppard v. Maxwell, 384 U.S. 333 (1966).

[74] 387 U.S. 1 (1967).

[75] 397 U.S. 358 (1970).

an outgrowth of his literalism. The same words can have only one meaning. Resting on this premise, he did not address himself to the substantive issues raised by the adoption of uniform national precedents and standards in the operation of the states' criminal law.[76]

Despite the tremendous impact on federal-state relations implicit in incorporation and other of his positions, Justice Black did not regard himself as an innovator in this field. He did not accept Justice Douglas's assessment:[77]

> [T]he revolution initiated by the adoption of the Fourteenth Amendment . . . involved the imposition of new and far-reaching constitutional restraints on the States. Nationalization of many civil liberties has been the consequence of the Fourteenth Amendment, reversing the historic position that the foundations of those liberties rested largely in state law.

In direct contrast, Justice Black asserted that the "Fourteenth Amendment did not alter the basic structure of our federal system of government."[78] While aptly describing American federalism as neither "blind deference to 'States' Rights' "[79] nor "centralization of control . . . in our National Government," he presumed that this in-between state is somehow clearly delineated in the Constitution. In *Younger v. Harris* he characterized federalism as a system whereby:[80]

> the entire country is made up of a Union of separate state governments, and a continuance of the belief that the National Government will fare best if the States and their institutions are left free to perform their separate functions in their separate

---

[76] For the discussion of these issues see the views of: Justice Harlan, who saw significant difficulties following the imposition of uniform national standards. Malloy v. Hogan, 378 U.S. 1, 14 (1964); Pointer v. Texas, 380 U.S. 400, 408 (1965); Williams v. Florida, 399 U.S. 78, 117 (1970); Justice Goldberg, who supported unqualified use of national standards. Pointer v. Texas, 380 U.S. 400, 410 (1965); Justice Fortas, who, although rejecting Goldberg's call for uniform national standards, was nevertheless willing to support their use in many more situations than was Justice Harlan. Bloom v. Illinois, 391 U.S. 194, 211 (1968).

[77] Walz v. Tax Commission, 397 U.S. 664, 701 (1970). Justice Douglas has gone further than any other Justice in his willingness to use national power. See Younger v. Harris, 401 U.S. 37, 58 (1971); Cameron v. Johnson, 390 U.S. 611, 622 (1968). (In *Cameron*, Douglas joined Fortas's opinion.)

[78] Perkins v. Matthews, 400 U.S. 379, 404 (1971).

[79] Younger v. Harris, 401 U.S. 37, 44 (1971).

[80] *Ibid.* Justice Black's arid discussion of federalism is similar to his discussion of separation of powers in Youngstown Sheet and Tube Co. v. Sawyer, 343 U.S. 579 (1952).

ways. This, perhaps for lack of a better and clearer way to
describe it, is referred to by many as "Our Federalism," and
one familiar with the profound debates that ushered our Federal Constitution into existence is bound to respect those who
remain loyal to the ideals and dreams of "Our Federalism."

While it is of course true that the Constitution provides for some
middle ground, it is also possible to trace much of the course of
American politics in terms of the changes in conception of "Our
Federalism," and the nature of the middle ground.

Justice Black's treatment of federalism illustrates well the tendency toward arbitrariness so characteristic of his work. The claim
of clear constitutional derivation is simply insufficient to support
the distinctions he was continually making. He accepted the entire
post–New Deal Commerce Clause adjudication yet balked at extending national power to a secluded recreation park.[81] He accepted
Brown v. Board of Education and related cases, wrote the majority
opinion in *Oregon v. Mitchell*,[82] and then delivered stern lectures
about the erosion of federalism by national supervision of voting
rights in *South Carolina v. Katzenbach*,[83] *Allen v. State Board of
Elections*,[84] and *Perkins v. Matthews*.[85] And, of course, incorporation itself is a highly controversial and major modification of "Our
Federalism" which Justice Black blithely presented as the clear
command of the Constitution.

B. THE RIGHT TO PRIVACY

Few issues challenged the adequacy of Justice Black's jurisprudence as did the emerging interest in the constitutional status of a
right to privacy, under the growing threats of centralization, bu-
reaucratization, and technological innovation. The issue clearly presents a major test of a nation's "increasing sensitivity toward human
rights," but for Justice Black the "right to privacy" was another
absolute exception to his absolute rules. There was no specific constitutional provision protecting privacy: courts are powerless even
to consider the issue.

The first, and major, judicial discussion of privacy during Justice
Black's tenure was *Griswold v. Connecticut*,[86] the case in which the
Court struck down Connecticut's ban on the use of contraceptives.

---

[81] Daniel v. Paul, 395 U.S. 298, 309 (1969).   [84] 393 U.S. 544, 595 (1969).

[82] 400 U.S. 112 (1970).   [85] 400 U.S. 379, 401 (1971).

[83] 383 U.S. 301, 355 (1966).   [86] 381 U.S. 479 (1965).

The main opinion held that a right to privacy existed in the penumbra of various enumerated guarantees. Justices Harlan and White concurred in the judgment, arguing that restrictions on the use of contraceptives constituted a denial of liberty without due process of law. Justice Goldberg attempted to bolster the constitutional status of privacy by resting, in part, on the Ninth Amendment: "The Enumeration in the Constitution, of certain rights, shall not be construed to deny or disparge others retained by the people."

Justice Black dissented from all these opinions. He rejected the notion that the penumbra of enumerated guarantees can bring constitutional protection to nonenumerated rights. Nor, consistent with his due process understanding, could he accept Justices Harlan and White's discussion of privacy and liberty. Lastly, he opposed Justice Goldberg's attempt to bring the Ninth Amendment into more active use on behalf of nonenumerated individual rights. The Ninth Amendment is similar in potential to the Due Process Clause, and Justice Black restricted the meaning of the former for the same reasons that guided his due process adjudication. In so narrowing the Ninth Amendment, however, he was forced into the awkward position of having to overlook the words of the Amendment itself.

The Ninth Amendment, according to Justice Black, was passed "to assure the people that the Constitution in all its provisions was intended to limit the Federal Government to the powers granted expressly or by necessary implication."[87] The difficulties raised by the acknowledgment of implied powers to one side, this statement bypassed the key problem of the Ninth Amendment. The federal government is to be limited by a constitutional reservation of rights to the people. The definition and interpretation of these rights must be an open question which, under the practice of judicial review, falls to the judiciary to resolve. But to allow the judiciary to undertake such a task would be to sanction forbidden judicial judgment in the virtually limitless area of nonenumerated rights "retained by the people." Justice Black preferred sacrificing the language of the Amendment.

As on so many of the issues that are likely to dominate the Court's work in the future, Justice Douglas, not Justice Black, held the most radical position. On one occasion Justice Douglas suggested that under contemporary conditions the issue of privacy had be-

---

[87] *Id.* at 520.

come as important as First Amendment rights.[88] It is not necessary to accept Justice Douglas's assessment of the priorities in either area to agree that he and not Justice Black spoke to current needs.

C. SELF-INCRIMINATION

The Fifth Amendment's protection against self-incrimination is unqualified, and in interpreting this guarantee Justice Black was "liberal" or absolute. This meant that he was willing to uphold individual rights claims against governmental action to the furthest extent that language would allow. In addition, unlike the broad implications of the Due Process Clause or the Fourth Amendment, the privilege directly concerns court processes and is thus one of the two essential components of limited government—First Amendment freedoms and proper criminal procedures.

Problems of compulsory self-incrimination reach a variety of circumstances: custodial interrogation of persons accused of crime; the use of involuntary noncommunicative evidence such as blood tests, suspects' active participation in line-ups, and suspects' handwriting samples; problems growing out of waivers of the privilege against self-incrimination and the availability of immunity statutes; and legislation involving registration and record-keeping requirements. While the Court drew distinctions among and within these categories, Justice Black urged extension of Fifth Amendment protection to all cases in all these circumstances. The Fifth Amendment provides for the total nonparticipation of an individual in any effort to convict him:[89]

> The defendant, under our Constitution, need not do anything at all to defend himself, and certainly he cannot be required to help convict himself. Rather he has an absolute, unqualified right to compel the State to investigate its own case, find its own witnesses, prove its own facts, and convince the jury through its own resources. Throughout the process the defendant has a fundamental right to remain silent, in effect challenging the State at every point to: "Prove it!"

This protection would cover an individual before he became a suspect in any criminal proceeding, and at all stages in such a proceeding.[90]

---

[88] Wyman v. James, 400 U.S. 309, 330 (1971). See also Schmerber v. California, 384 U.S. 757, 778 (1966); Hoffa v. United States, 385 U.S. 293, 340 (1966).

[89] Williams v. Florida, 399 U.S. 78, 112 (1970).

[90] The one exception to Justice Black's Fifth Amendment absolutism was his acceptance

In support of his absolute interpretation of the Fifth Amendment
Justice Black pointed to the absence of any qualifications limiting
the reach of the Amendment, as some have urged, to testimony
compelled by torture. He pointed out that it is not the manner of
self-incrimination but the use of self-incriminatory evidence that is
prohibited:[91]

> And history supports no argument that the framers of the Fifth
> Amendment were interested only in forbidding the *extraction*
> of an accused's testimony, as distinguished from the *use* of his
> extracted testimony. The extraction of testimony is, of course,
> but a means to the end of its use to punish. Few persons
> would seriously object to testifying unless their testimony
> would subject them to future punishment. The real evil aimed
> at by the Fifth Amendment's flat prohibition against the com-
> pulsion of self-incriminatory testimony was that thought to
> inhere in using a man's compelled testimony to punish him.

This emphasis on the use of the evidence rather than its extraction was consistent with Black's concentration on constitutional
guarantees as defenses against political oppression rather than as
agents for the general guarantee of personal liberty or privacy.[92]
His views were thus in significant contrast to those of Justices
Douglas and Fortas, whose voting record on Fifth Amendment
questions was similar to that of Justice Black. Broad use of the Fifth
Amendment's ban on self-incrimination rested, for Justice Fortas,
on the incompatibility between self-incrimination and individual
dignity:[93]

> The privilege historically goes to the roots of democratic and
> religious principle. It prevents the debasement of the citi-
> zen which would result from compelling him to "accuse"
> himself before the power of the state. The roots of the privi-
> lege . . . go to the nature of a free man and to his relationship
> to the state.

---

of a conviction based on evidence secured through the wartime record-keeping requirement of a federal statute. Shapiro v. United States, 335 U.S. 1 (1948). He did not write an
opinion in this case.

[91] Feldman v. United States, 322 U.S. 487, 499–500 (1944). (Emphasis in original.)
See also Black's emphasis on the use of involuntary confessions in Irvine v. California,
347 U.S. 128, 139 (1954).

[92] Justice Black stated that the Founders' abhorrence of coerced confessions "did not
spring alone from a predilection for personal privacy." Feldman v. United States, 322
U.S. 487, 499 (1944).

[93] United States v. Wade, 388 U.S. 218, 261 (1967).

Although Justice Black occasionally referred to a Fifth Amendment right of silence it is doubtful that he would defend such a right to the degree of Justices Fortas and Douglas. For Justice Black, the right of silence clearly hinged on the possible use of the testimony. In dissenting from the decision sustaining California's requirement that a driver involved in an accident with an unmanned vehicle leave his name at the scene, he indicated that mandatory disclosure was acceptable, although conviction based on this disclosure was not.[94] And it was Justice Douglas, not Justice Black, who wrote the Court's strongest statement on the right to silence, the dissent in *Ullman v. United States*.[95] In this dissent Justice Douglas argued that immunity extending only to the use of testimony in a criminal prosecution was insufficient protection for a witness called before a congressional committee investigating communism. Justice Black joined this dissent, but more likely on First than Fifth Amendment grounds.[96]

It is possible that had Justice Black served longer, this difference over a "right of silence" might have become more manifest. At his retirement, however, he was clearly leading the Court in an expansion of Fifth Amendment protection. Probably the most visible aspect of his influence was *Miranda*.[97] Justice Black did not write in *Miranda*, but starting with *Chambers*,[98] *Ashcraft*,[99] *In re Oliver*,[100] and *Gallegos*, [101] he consistently, and often forcefully, opposed all secret interrogation. His dissent in *Feldman*[102] was accepted twenty years later.[103] *Feldman* sanctioned the use of testimony compelled by a state court, under state immunity, to convict in a federal court. *Garrity*,[104] *Spevack*,[105] and *Gardner*[106] bolstered the Fifth Amend-

---

[94] California v. Byers, 402 U.S. 424, 463–64 (1971).

[95] 350 U.S. 422, 440 (1956).

[96] In Justice Black's discussion of self-incrimination and immunity in Adams v. Maryland, 347 U.S. 179 (1954), there is no suggestion of any basic opposition to conventional immunity statutes.

[97] Miranda v. Arizona, 384 U.S. 436 (1966).

[98] Chambers v. Florida, 309 U.S. 227 (1940).

[99] Ashcraft v. Tennessee, 322 U.S. 143 (1944).

[100] 333 U.S. 257 (1948).

[101] Gallegos v. Nebraska, 342 U.S. 55, 73 (1951).

[102] Feldman v. United States, 322 U.S. 487, 494 (1944).

[103] Murphy v. Waterfront Commission, 378 U.S. 52 (1964).

[104] Garrity v. New Jersey, 385 U.S. 493 (1967).

[105] Spevack v. Klein, 385 U.S. 511 (1967).

[106] Gardner v. Broderick, 392 U.S. 273 (1968).

ment protection of public employees and lawyers when called upon
to testify in relation to their performance in office. *Marchetti v.
United States*,[107] the case in which the federal gambling registration
statute was struck down, was a vindication of Justice Black's dissenting position in *Kahriger*.[108] The Court refused, however, to join
him in extending Fifth Amendment protection to involuntary noncommunicative evidence, such as blood tests, handwriting samples,
and active participation in line-ups.[109]

D. THE SIXTH AMENDMENT

By and large, the Sixth Amendment gave rise, during Justice
Black's tenure, to less controversy than other major provisions of
the Bill of Rights. Clauses calling for assistance of counsel, confrontation of witnesses, speedy trial, and jury trial were all incorporated
into the Fourteenth Amendment.[110] Justice Black agreed with all
these decisions and his opinion in *Gideon v. Wainwright*,[111] making assistance of counsel mandatory in state felony trials, constituted
one of his major triumphs.

Some disagreement existed, however, over the meaning of Sixth
Amendment provisions as applied to the states. One such disagreement was whether the right to a jury trial is applicable for all trials
or only for major crimes.[112] Justice Black refused to recognize a
distinction, citing the absence of any such distinction in the Constitution. He would make the jury trial requirement applicable to
all criminal prosecution.

A second disagreement centered on whether assistance of counsel
is mandatory for aspects of the criminal process outside the trial.

---

[107] 309 U.S. 39 (1968).

[108] United States v. Kahriger, 345 U.S. 22, 36 (1953). See also Grosso v. United
States, 390 U.S. 62 (1968); Haynes v. United States, 390 U.S. 85 (1968).

[109] See Breithaupt v. Abram, 352 U.S. 432 (1957), and Schmerber v. California, 384
U.S. 757, 773 (1966) (blood tests); United States v. Wade, 388 U.S. 218, 243 (1967)
(participation in line-ups); Gilbert v. California, 388 U.S. 263, 277 (1967) (handwriting
samples).

[110] See Gideon v. Wainwright, 372 U.S. 335 (1963) (assistance of counsel); Pointer
v. Texas, 380 U.S. 400 (1965) (confrontation of witnesses); Klopfer v. North Carolina,
386 U.S. 213 (1967) (speedy trial); Duncan v. Louisiana, 391 U.S. 145 (1968) (jury
trial).

[111] 372 U.S. 335 (1963).

[112] See Frank v. United States, 395 U.S. 147 (1969); Baldwin v. New York, 399 U.S.
66 (1970).

The Court held that the line-up[113] and the preliminary hearing[114] are critical stages of the criminal process and therefore require assistance of counsel. Justice Black agreed, emphasizing that his agreement rested on the constitutional text which calls for assistance of counsel for the accused's "defense."[115]

By far the most interesting Sixth Amendment question raised by Justice Black's adjudication concerned the impartial jury clause. Impartial is an imprecise term, and he was willing to give it a liberal interpretation. He also had a long record of reluctance to acknowledge fully the problem of jury bias. While agreeing with the possibility in the abstract, he generally shrank from admitting that a particular jury was not impartial.

In *Groppi v. Wisconsin*,[116] Justice Black argued in dissent that a state law denying change of venue in misdemeanor cases did not violate the Sixth Amendment. His argument rested on the absence of a constitutional provision for change of venue.[117] While granting that the defendant was entitled to an impartial jury, he suggested that other ways could be found to insure that impartiality. He added that it would undoubtedly be difficult to prove that a large area could be so saturated with prejudice that an impartial jury could not be impaneled. He had made a similar suggestion earlier in discussing the free-speech, fair-trial controversy:[118]

> On most of these assumptions that are made with reference to the dangers of the spread of information, I perhaps diverge at a point from many of those who disagree with my views. I have . . . a kind of an old-fashioned trust in human beings. . . .
> I do not think myself that anyone can say that there can be enough publicity completely to destroy the ideas of fairness in the minds of people, including the judges.

This confidence in the jury was not without its problems. On the one hand Justice Black opposed narrowing the scope of jury determinations and the imposition of particular requirements for jury composition. He dissented from the ruling that voluntariness of a confession must be determined by a judge or another jury

---

[113] United States v. Wade, 388 U.S. 218 (1967).

[114] Coleman v. Alabama, 399 U.S. 1 (1970).

[115] United States v. Wade, 388 U.S. 218, 246 (1967).

[116] 400 U.S. 505 (1971).   [117] *Id.* at 515.

[118] Cahn, *Justice Black and First Amendment "Absolutes": A Public Interview*, 37 N.Y.U. L. Rev. 549, 555–56 (1962). See also Sheppard v. Maxwell, 384 U.S. 333 (1966).

before the confession could be heard by the trial jury.[119] He did not regard the unitary trial in capital cases or the jury imposition of capital punishment, without guidance from the trial judge, to be unconstitutional.[120] Nor did he agree that the failure to exclude those who oppose capital punishment from sentence-fixing juries deprived the accused of any constitutional right.[121] The Sixth Amendment declared its trust in juries and thereby decided that a jury trial, providing for confrontation of witnesses, assistance of counsel, and other explicit guarantees, offered a fair trial.[122] There is no other constitutional standard of fairness that the Supreme Court could invoke in its supervision of trial courts.

On the other hand, the Supreme Court could review the record of a conviction and conclude that the confession upon which it was based was involuntary.[123] The Supreme Court would be enforcing the Fifth Amendment's absolute prohibition against self-incrimination. The power that Justice Black was willing to exercise constituted an implied, but only implied, recognition of difficulties with the jury system—difficulties of the kind that underlie attempts to narrow the scope of jury determinations.

E. SEARCH AND SEIZURE

Justice Black's Fourth Amendment stood in stark contrast to his work on the First, Fifth, and Sixth Amendments. It probably accounts for the largest number of his dissents from the libertarian position. The language of the Fourth Amendment, unlike that of the other amendments, is not absolute; only "unreasonable" searches and seizures are prohibited. Moreover, the Fourth Amendment is not "an essential supplement to the First Amendment" and does not deal directly with court processes.

The Fourth Amendment was among the first of the Bill of Rights

---

[119] Jackson v. Denno, 378 U.S. 368, 401 (1964).

[120] McGautha v. California, 402 U.S. 183, 225 (1971).

[121] Witherspoon v. Illinois, 391 U.S. 510, 532 (1968).

[122] The Founders "provided the defendant with clear, emphatic guarantees: counsel for his defense, a speedy trial, trial by jury, confrontation with the witnesses against him, and other such unequivocal and definite rights. The explicit commands of the Constitution provide a full description of the kind of 'fair trial' the Constitution guarantees, and in my judgment that document leaves no room for judges either to add to or detract from these commands." Coleman v. Alabama, 399 U.S. 1, 12–13 (1970).

[123] Jackson v. Denno, 378 U.S. 368, 408 (1964).

guarantees to be included under the due process protection of the Fourteenth Amendment.[124] While incorporation itself did not engender significant controversy, for twelve years the Court was deeply divided over whether the rule adopted for federal courts, excluding illegally seized evidence from the trial, should be applied to state courts. There was general agreement that the exclusionary rule was part of the Supreme Court's supervisory power over the federal court system, not part of the Fourth Amendment.

In deciding whether to apply the exclusionary rule to the states, the Court considered methods of enforcing the ban (on behalf both of persons accused of crime and of victims of illegal searches who are never indicted), the impact of exclusion on federal-state relationships, and the administration of justice in general. The controversy was finally resolved in 1961, with *Mapp v. Ohio*,[125] when the Court held that the exclusionary rule was the only way to enforce the ban, to discipline local police, and to make federal-state relationships more harmonious.

The fact that the exclusionary rule is not "a command of the Fourth Amendment" made it impossible for Justice Black to accept this reasoning. As far back as *Wolf* he had failed to join his libertarian colleagues, Justices Douglas, Murphy, and Rutledge, when they argued in dissent that the exclusionary rule was needed in order to make the constitutional ban effective.[126] Ultimately, however, Justice Black concluded that the Fourth Amendment, combined with the Fifth Amendment, dictated exclusion. Use of illegally seized evidence in a criminal proceeding violates the specific command against self-incrimination.[127] As this suggests, the other purposes served by exclusion—protection of innocent victims of an illegal search, or discipline of local police—were not of concern to him:[128]

> [The Court has made the] repeated statement that the purpose of [the exclusionary] rule is to deter sheriffs, policemen, and other law officers from making unlawful searches and seizures. . . . In passing I would say that if that is the sole purpose,

---

[124] Wolf v. Colorado, 338 U.S. 25 (1949).

[125] 367 U.S. 643 (1961).

[126] Wolf v. Colorado, 338 U.S. 25, 39 (1949).

[127] Mapp v. Ohio, 367 U.S. 643, 662 (1961).

[128] Linkletter v. Walker, 381 U.S. 618, 648–49 (1965).

reason, object, and effect of the rule, the Court's action in adopting it sounds more like law-making than construing the Constitution.

In the course of prohibiting unreasonable searches and seizures the Fourth Amendment set out certain procedures for obtaining warrants. Presumably, searches conducted with properly issued warrants are reasonable, although it has always been recognized that some warrantless searches are necessary. The main body of Fourth Amendment litigation involved determination of the reasonableness of warrantless searches. Justice Black's record was one of general acceptance of policy action and the judgments of reasonableness made by the state courts:[129]

> It is not only wise but imperative that where findings of the facts of reasonableness and probable cause are involved in such state cases, we should not overturn state court findings unless in the most extravagant and egregious errors.

Several categories of reasonable warrantless searches were developed by the Court. One of the most important covers searches incident to a valid arrest. Justice Black originally joined the Court in approving wide-ranging search and opposed the subsequent narrowing of these limits.[130] A second exception covered searches made to forestall destruction of evidence. Justice Black joined the majority in approving such a search which included the unannounced entry by police into an occupied home.[131] A third category touched searches to find weapons and to prevent injury to police, even in the absence of probable cause for arrest. Justice Black upheld these searches, including one where he was the only Justice to accept the police action.[132] The last major category of acceptable warrantless searches was that of automobiles considered reasonable because of the automobile's mobility. Justice Black, writing for a unanimous Court, struck down one such search, made while the owner was in

---

[129] Sibron v. New York, 392 U.S. 40, 82 (1968).

[130] Harris v. United States, 331 U.S. 145 (1947); Chimel v. California, 395 U.S. 752, 770 (1969) (White, J., dissenting); Vale v. Louisiana, 399 U.S. 30, 36 (1970).

[131] Ker v. California, 374 U.S. 23 (1963).

[132] Terry v. Ohio, 392 U.S. 1 (1968); Sibron v. New York, 392 U.S. 40, 79 (1968). Justice Black dissented alone in *Sibron*.

custody on a charge unrelated to the search.[133] Otherwise he continued his pattern of deference.[134]

This same self-restraint characterized his attitude toward judicial supervision of the issuance of search warrants. In a number of cases the Court had set standards to prevent issuing magistrates from being rubber stamps for policemen. Justice Black dissented in each:[135]

> Nothing in our Constitution . . . requires that the facts be established with that degree of certainty and with such elaborate specificity before a policeman can be authorized by a disinterested magistrate to conduct a carefully limited search.
> . . . [T]he Court is moving rapidly, through complex analyses and obfuscatory language, toward the holding that no magistrate can issue a warrant unless according to some unknown standard of proof he can be persuaded that the suspect defendant is actually guilty of a crime.

The problem of wiretapping opened an important new area of Fourth Amendment law. After initially excluding electronic eavesdropping from the reach of the Fourth Amendment,[136] the Court reversed itself, holding that wiretapping and related procedures had to meet the same standards met by other searches.[137] Justice Black dissented from the more recent decisions, arguing that the Fourth Amendment's words relating to "persons, houses, and papers, and effects" cannot be read to include spoken words:[138]

> This literal language imports tangible things, and it would require an expansion of the language used by the framers, in the interest of "privacy" or some equally vague judge-made goal, to hold that it applies to the spoken word. It simply requires an imaginative transformation of the English language to say that conversations can be searched and words seized.

Furthermore, eavesdropping had always been considered a legitimate law enforcement tool; he saw no constitutional difference between conventional and modern techniques of eavesdropping.[139]

---

[133] Preston v. United States, 376 U.S. 364 (1964).

[134] Cooper v. California, 386 U.S. 58 (1967); Coolidge v. New Hampshire, 403 U.S. 443, 502–10 (1971).

[135] Spinelli v. United States, 393 U.S. 410, 429, 435 (1969). See also Aguilar v. Texas, 378 U.S. 108 (1964); Whiteley v. Warden, 401 U.S. 560 (1971); Coolidge v. New Hampshire, 403 U.S. 443 (1971).

[136] Olmstead v. United States, 277 U.S. 438 (1928).

[137] Berger v. New York, 388 U.S. 41 (1967); Katz v. United States, 389 U.S. 347 (1967).

[138] 388 U.S. at 78.   [139] Id. at 72–74.

Justice Black's willingness to accept unsupervised electronic surveillance was, of course, wholly consistent with his general refusal
to recognize a constitutional right to privacy. It was also consistent
with his refusal to accept the widespread interpretation of the
Fourth Amendment as a guarantee of privacy from undue police
intrusion. He argued alternatively that such a reading contracted
the scope of the Amendment by prohibiting only private, rather
than all, unreasonable searches and seizures, and that it expanded the
Amendment by allowing judges to strike down whatever they conceived to be an invasion of privacy:

> But I think it belittles [the Fourth] Amendment to talk about it
> as though it protects nothing but "privacy." To treat it that
> way is to give it a niggardly interpretation, not the kind of lib-
> eral reading I think any Bill of Rights provision should be
> given. The average man would very likely not have his feelings
> soothed any more by having his property seized openly than
> by having it seized privately and by stealth. . . . And a person
> can be just as much, if not more, irritated, annoyed and injured
> by an unceremonious public arrest by a policeman as he is by
> a seizure in the privacy of his office or home.[140]

> It is impossible for me to think that the wise Framers of the
> Fourth Amendment would ever have dreamed about drafting
> an amendment to protect the "right of privacy." That expres-
> sion, like a chameleon, has a different color for every turning.
> In fact, use of "privacy" as the key word in the Fourth Amend-
> ment simply gives this Court a useful new tool, as I see it,
> both to usurp the policy-making power of the Congress and to
> hold more state and federal laws unconstitutional when the
> Court entertains a sufficient hostility to them.[141]

Justice Black's Fourth Amendment adjudication highlights some
of the key problems of his career. The refusal to undertake serious
examination of the term "unreasonable" emphasizes the peculiar
literalism of his approach, and, at the same time, calls into serious
question its adequacy in meeting important problems of individual
rights. Because of the Amendment's purported imprecision, he was
willing to allow a disturbing variety of warrantless searches, to accept unsupervised wiretapping, to downgrade the importance of
privacy against police intrusion, and to dilute standards governing
issuance of search warrants. In contrast to his forceful defense of

---

[140] Griswold v. Connecticut, 381 U.S. 479, 509 (1965).

[141] Berger v. New York, 388 U.S. 41, 77 (1967).

individual liberties, he left the impression that these Fourth Amendment problems need not be a cause for concern.

It is tempting to dispose of Justice Black's Fourth Amendment adjudication as simply another example of his arbitrary absolute exceptions to his concern for individual rights protection. But the arbitrariness disappears upon closer examination of his view of the purposes served by guarantees in the criminal procedures field. In *Feldman*, he drew a distinction between the dissenter or heretic who was caught in the criminal processes as punishment for dissenting views and the "ordinary criminal." He made it clear that constitutional guarantees were intended for the benefit of the former, not the latter: "If occasionally these safeguards worked to the advantage of an ordinary criminal, that was a price [the Founders] were willing to pay for the freedom they cherished."[142] The crucial corollary of this position was that he saw the protections surrounding the criminal process primarily as protection for the innocent rather than as standards to establish, maintain, and continually upgrade the general operation of the criminal law.[143] Justice Black's due process analysis points to this same conclusion. As we have seen, in his hands due process of law becomes a general ban on ex post facto regulations; it is aimed primarily at preventing the courts from becoming agents of political repression, and is only incidentally aimed at an ongoing supervision of the quality of criminal law enforcement.[144]

The Fourth Amendment contributes little toward enhancing the reliability of the fact-finding process or of separating the innocent from the guilty. It could be argued that Fourth Amendment protections aid the guilty without materially aiding the innocent. Whatever the case with the Amendment itself, this was certainly true of the exclusionary rule. For a long time, Justice Black opposed its adoption, and when he finally accepted it, he did so by linking it to the Fifth Amendment's ban on self-incrimination. Improperly seized evidence is not as untrustworthy as other self-incriminatory

---

[142] Feldman v. United States, 322 U.S. 487, 502 (1944).

[143] I am indebted to my colleague, Professor Morton Auerbach, for calling my attention to this point.

[144] Justice Black's discussion of double jeopardy in Bartkus v. Illinois, 359 U.S. 121, 163 (1959), reflected this same concern, as did his emphasis on use, rather than extraction, of self-incriminatory evidence.

evidence, but it was only as part of his Fifth Amendment absolutism that Justice Black could accept the exclusionary rule at all.[145]

This conception of the purpose of Bill of Rights guarantees also explains other troublesome aspects of Justice Black's Fourth Amendment work. His acceptance of wiretap evidence is no longer surprising; such evidence is reliable and unlikely falsely to convict the innocent.[146] To reserve collateral review only for cases where it is likely the conviction was in error would fulfill all constitutional purposes.[147] It also explains the distinctiveness of Justice Black's style in Fourth Amendment, as opposed to other criminal procedure, cases. These opinions often start with detailed descriptions of the crime and give considerable emphasis to the guilt of the accused, as determined by the totality of the evidence.[148] At the same time, in striking contrast to colleagues generally unfriendly to the Warren Court's criminal procedure rulings, he often went beyond the bounds of necessity to make gratuitous comments linking the Court's Fourth Amendment rulings with increased crime:[149]

> I think it is high time this Court, in the interest of the administration of criminal justice, made a new appraisal of the language and history of the Fourth Amendment and cut it down to its intended size. Such a judicial action would, I believe, make our cities a safer place for men, women, and children to live.

As the Court expanded its Fourth Amendment protection, particularly in cases touching the "ordinary criminal," Justice Black was pushed into increasingly stronger dissents. The tension between

---

[145] See Coolidge v. New Hampshire, 403 U.S. 443, 496–500 (1971), for Justice Black's insistence that the only constitutionally cognizable exclusionary rule is that of the Fifth Amendment. In two other instances Justice Black treated due process and Fourth Amendment problems in terms of the privilege against self-incrimination. In the process the issues were distorted, while full recognition of the implications of Justice Black's literalism was delayed. See Rochin v. California, 342 U.S. 165, 174 (1952); Irvine v. California, 347 U.S. 128, 139 (1954).

[146] See Berger v. New York, 388 U.S. 41, 73–74 (1967).

[147] Kaufman v. United States, 394 U.S. 217, 234 (1969); Wade v. Wilson, 396 U.S. 282, 287 (1970). Compare Justice Black's opinion in *Kaufman with* the majority opinion of Justice Brennan, at 228–29, *and* the dissenting opinion of Justice Harlan, at 242.

[148] See, *e.g.*, Kaufman v. United States, 394 U.S. 217, 231 (1969); Bumper v. North Carolina, 391 U.S. 543, 554 (1968); Davis v. Mississippi, 394 U.S. 721, 729 (1969); Coolidge v. New Hampshire, 403 U.S. 443, 493 (1971).

[149] Davis v. Mississippi, 394 U.S. 721, 730 (1969). See also Kaufman v. United States, 394 U.S. 217, 240–41 (1969); Sibron v. New York, 392 U.S. 40, 81 (1968).

his deference to police and lower court judgments and the Supreme Court's willingness to give a liberal reading to the entire Bill of Rights had, by the end of his career, produced ironic results. In his last search and seizure case Justice Black converted this limit on governmental power into a grant of power:[150]

> The Fourth Amendment provides a constitutional means by which the Government can act to obtain evidence to be used in criminal prosecutions. The people are obliged to yield to a proper exercise of authority under that Amendment.

F. EQUAL PROTECTION

Justice Black's understanding of the Equal Protection Clause provides still another example of apparently anomalous aspects of his work—his arbitrariness and his lack of leadership in the movement forging "large conceptions of equality under law." Faced with the open-endedness of the words of the Equal Protection Clause, his premises allowed practically no alternative but self-restraint. This self-restraint, however, was tempered by three major exceptions: some race relations cases, cases involving indigency and the criminal process, and reapportionment. The absence of sound reasoning in distinguishing some of these equal protection claims from similar ones that he rejected underlie the arbitrary character of his work.

It was only within the last decade or so that the Court became receptive to a liberal reading of the Equal Protection Clause. For a long time the Court was virtually unanimous in its self-restraint; only invidious distinctions could be struck down, and any distinction that could reasonably be defended could stand. Justice Black always voted with the majority in these early cases, in both upholding and denying equal protection claims.[151]

This deference to the legislature's assessment of reasonableness gave way in the last fifteen years of Black's tenure. The first major expansion of the scope of equal protection took place in the race relations field, where, for a long time, the Court was unanimous in its decisions. Justice Black, of course, was part of this unanimous

---

[150] Coolidge v. New Hampshire, 403 U.S. 443, 498 (1971).

[151] Skinner v. Oklahoma, 316 U.S. 535 (1942); Kotch v. Pilot Commissioners, 330 U.S. 552 (1947); Takahashi v. Fish and Game Commission, 334 U.S. 410 (1948); Goesaert v. Cleary, 335 U.S. 464 (1948); Railway Express v. New York, 336 U.S. 106 (1949).

Court and shared in the widespread agreement that the general intent of the framers of the Fourteenth Amendment was to end discrimination based on race. Notwithstanding this agreement, as race relations issues became more complex, particularly with respect to state action, the Court's unanimity broke down. Justice Black was among those opposed to liberal extension of the Equal Protection Clause.[152]

By the late 1960s the Court had moved beyond race relations in broadening the reach of equal protection. It began to open the vast potential inherent in the clause by delineating what it called certain "suspect categories" and "fundamental rights," whose qualification demanded a compelling governmental interest in order to be sustained. Poverty and race were the chief suspect categories; voting rights and free speech were the chief fundamental rights.

Justice Black never accepted this new understanding. In *Harper v. Virginia Board of Elections*,[153] he reaffirmed his adherence to the old standard:[154]

> [D]istinctions drawn and even discriminations imposed by state laws do not violate the Equal Protection Clause so long as these distinctions and discriminations are not "irrational," "irrelevant," "unreasonable," "arbitrary," or "invidious.". . . The restrictive connotation of these terms . . . are a plain recognition of the fact that under a proper interpretation of the Equal Protection Clause States are to have the broadest kind of leeway in areas where they have a general constitutional competence to act.

His voting record, however, did not simply reflect adherence to the old standard. Both in cases dealing with the poor and in voting rights cases, he made certain exceptions to his general support for the reasonableness standard, strictly understood.

Justice Black rejected the notion that the poor constitute a "suspect category" for purposes of legislative or executive discrimination. He denied that a poll tax,[155] a one-year residence requirement

---

[152] See Bell v. Maryland, 378 U.S. 226, 318 (1964); Evans v. Newton, 382 U.S. 296 312 (1966); Reitman v. Mulkey, 387 U.S. 369 (1967); Hunter v. Erickson, 393 U.S. 385, 396 (1969); Evans v. Abney, 396 U.S. 435 (1970). See also Daniel v. Paul, 395 U.S. 298 (1969); James v. Valtierra, 402 U.S. 137 (1971); Palmer v. Thompson, 403 U.S. 217 (1971).

[153] 383 U.S. 663 (1966).   [154] *Id.* at 673–74.

[155] Harper v. Virginia Board of Elections, 383 U.S. 663 (1966).

for welfare recipients,[156] filing fees for indigents seeking divorce,[157] or mandatory local referenda to approve public housing sites,[158] violated the Equal Protection Clause. On the other hand he always supported equal protection claims of indigents in the criminal process. He wrote the majority opinion in the leading case, *Griffin v. Illinois*,[159] holding that the state must provide the transcripts for an indigent's appeal. In every case thereafter, in which indigency was a bar to vindication of rights in a criminal proceeding,[160] or where inability to pay a fine resulted in a criminal sentence,[161] he supported the equal protection claim. He drew attention to this distinction between rights of indigents in criminal proceedings and the broader relationship between indigency and equal protection. His voting pattern, however, is clear and the distinction is wholly consistent with his conception of constitutional limits as barriers to false conviction of the innocent.

Justice Black's record on voting rights and equal protection is more complicated. He consistently held that malapportionment constituted a denial of equal protection, while upholding the constitutionality of related voting rights claims. Justice Black first argued that malapportionment was a violation of equal protection in 1946.[162] His only major reapportionment opinion, *Wesberry v. Sanders*,[163] dealt with congressional districting, and rested on Article I of the Constitution, not the Equal Protection Clause. But he concurred in all the state reapportionment cases which rested on equal protection grounds, and which extended the basic one-man, one-vote principle in a variety of circumstances.[164]

The only other major voting rights case in which he extended equal protection was *Williams v. Rhodes*.[165] Here stringent state

---

[156] Shapiro v. Thompson, 394 U.S. 618 (1969).

[157] Boddie v. Connecticut, 401 U.S. 371 (1971).

[158] James v. Valtierra, 402 U.S. 137 (1971).

[159] 351 U.S. 12 (1956).

[160] See, *e.g.*, Douglas v. California, 372 U.S. 353 (1963); Burns v. Ohio, 360 U.S. 252 (1959).

[161] Williams v. Illinois, 399 U.S. 235 (1970); Tate v. Short, 401 U.S. 395 (1971).

[162] Colegrove v. Green, 328 U.S. 549, 566 (1946).

[163] 376 U.S. 1 (1964).

[164] Reynolds v. Sims, 377 U.S. 533 (1964); Avery v. Midland County, 390 U.S. 474 (1968); Hadley v. Junior College District, 397 U.S. 50 (1970). Justice Black wrote the majority opinion in *Hadley*.

[165] 393 U.S. 23 (1968).

requirements for third parties seeking to qualify for the ballot were struck down. Justice Black, writing for the Court, argued that the stringency of the requirements favored the two established parties and thereby interfered with the right of qualified voters to cast their votes effectively. At the same time, however, he denied that a poll tax violates equal protection.[166] He accepted a voting restriction in school district elections to owners or lessees of taxable realty in the district, or to parents or custodians of children enrolled in those schools.[167] He upheld Georgia's electoral law which provided for election of the governor by the legislature should no candidate win a popular majority.[168] The most striking aspect of this case is the similarity between this provision and the county-unit system struck down, with Justice Black's approval, in *Gray v. Sanders*.[169]

In discussing the limits on states' power over voting rights Justice Black drew his familiar distinction between specific constitutional limitations and the "generalities of the Equal Protection Clause."[170] While willing to enforce the former,[171] he warned against using the latter to infringe on rightful state power. The only Fourteenth Amendment restriction on this power is the traditional one of an invidious or arbitrary discrimination, without relevance to a valid state purpose.

Justice Black's reapportionment and ballot requirement decisions rested on this standard. Malapportionment discriminates arbitrarily against otherwise qualified voters on the basis of residence.[172] As I have indicated, his position in *Williams v. Rhodes* rested on the ground that voters who support minority parties were victims of arbitrary discrimination. He found, on the other hand, that the distinctions in *Harper* and *Kramer* were reasonably related to valid

---

[166] Harper v. Virginia Board of Elections, 383 U.S. 663, 670 (1966).

[167] Kramer v. Union School District, 395 U.S. 621, 634 (1969) (Stewart, J., dissenting). But see Cipriano v. City of Houma, 395 U.S. 701, 707 (1969); Phoenix v. Kolodziejski, 399 U.S. 204 (1970).

[168] Fortson v. Morris, 385 U.S. 231 (1966).

[169] 372 U.S. 368 (1963).

[170] Oregon v. Mitchell, 400 U.S. 112, 125–26, 135 (1970).

[171] These would seem to be the Fifteenth, Nineteenth, and Twenty-fourth Amendments. See Oregon v. Mitchell, note 170 *supra*. He would undoubtedly have included the Twenty-sixth Amendment, granting the vote to eighteen-year-olds, ratified in 1971.

[172] Colegrove v. Green, 328 U.S. 549, 570–71 (1946); Hadley v. Junior College District, 397 U.S. 50, 52, 54–55 (1970).

state purposes. In *Fortson v. Morris*[173] he denied that any voting rights question was involved. The case concerned provisions for electing a governor, and such provisions did not have to pass scrutiny under the Equal Protection Clause.

Justice Black's voting rights decisions reach the apex of arbitrariness. If a poll tax is reasonably related to a valid state purpose, it is hard to understand why deviation from the one-man, one-vote principle in state legislative apportionment, particularly where this deviation is not the result of willful failure to reapportion, is not.[174] If the county-unit system violates the Equal Protection Clause, why not the related claim in *Fortson v. Morris?*

The arbitrariness in Justice Black's voting rights decisions stemmed from his refusal to accept "the generalities of the Equal Protection Clause" as providing an evolving standard of equality with respect to electoral choice, while he remained committed to the reapportionment decisions. He sometimes implied that the Equal Protection Clause barred discrimination against otherwise qualified voters but did not call for review of voting qualifications themselves. While this distinction is serviceable for a certain range of cases, it ultimately breaks down.[175] It is impossible, without becoming arbitrary, to escape the central question of all the voting rights cases: To what extent does the Equal Protection Clause demand an approximation of the one-man, one-vote principle as the basis of all our electoral law? For the others on the Court, including those who opposed as well as those who supported the reapportionment and related decisions, this was the central question. The isolation and untenability of Justice Black's position was most clearly revealed by his and Justice Fortas's opinions in *Fortson*. Writing for a majority of five, composed of himself and all those who had consistently opposed the Court's work in the reapportionment cases, Justice Black upheld Georgia's electoral law and denied that any voting rights issue was at stake. Justice Fortas, in dissent, replied:[176]

> I respectfully submit that this, too, is a "voting case."...
> ... This Court's apportionment and voting rights decisions

[173] 385 U.S. 231 (1966).

[174] By the same token, it is also hard to reconcile the state reapportionment cases with Justice Black's position in *Kramer*.

[175] Kramer v. Union School District, 395 U.S. 621 (1969); Fortson v. Morris, 385 U.S. 231 (1966).

[176] 385 U.S. at 246, 249–50.

soundly reflect a deepening conception . . . of the meaning of
our great constitutional guaranties. As such, they have re-
invigorated our national political life at its roots so that it may
continue its growth to realization of the full stature of our
constitutional ideal. Today's decision is a startling reversal;
a belittling, . . . of our Constitution's dynamic provisions with
respect to the basic instrument of democracy—the vote.

The Court brushes off *Gray* v. *Sanders* by saying that it has
to do only with the "equal right" of all voters to "vote and
have their votes counted without impairment or dilution."
That is so. But that is precisely the issue in the present case.
We have not heretofore been so beguiled by changes in the
scenery that we have lost sight of principle.

Again, it is not necessary to accept Justice Fortas's evaluation of
the particular issues to agree that he posed them properly, while
Justice Black's formulation strained our understanding.

G. THE FIRST AMENDMENT

Before the process of gradual incorporation began in earnest in
the middle 1960s, Justice Black's most significant work had been his
absolutist interpretation of the First Amendment. And although
incorporation is likely to be his most enduring achievement, First
Amendment analysis remains basic for understanding Justice Black.
At every stage of his judicial career he reaffirmed his belief in the
centrality of First Amendment guarantees.[177]

Justice Black's last years seemed to mark a retreat from his earlier
First Amendment absolutism, just as they seemed to mark a retreat
from a general libertarianism. The issues in First Amendment cases
are especially complex. Certainly there is no inconsistency in the
sense that precedents exist for all the holdings of his later years.
Yet, in another, more important sense, there is an inconsistency.
There was a definite and meaningful shift in emphasis in First
Amendment cases, and the reasoning in some of Black's opinions
began to undermine his basic premises about the process of democracy and the sufficiency of procedural safeguards to maintain
liberty.

The central theme of Justice Black's First Amendment adjudication always rested on the necessity for the completely unabridged

---

[177] Milk Wagon Drivers v. Meadowmoor, 312 U.S. 287, 301 (1941); Feldman v.
United States, 322 U.S. 487, 500–02 (1944); Adamson v. California, 332 U.S. 46, 70–71
(1947); Black, note 27 *supra*, at 880–81; BLACK, note 49 *supra*, at 44.

airing of views on public questions. This full freedom is necessary to meet two intimately related and equally important ends, self-government and progress.[178] Threats to the achievement of these goals could take many forms, besides the direct attack on dissidents, represented by legislation such as the Smith Act.[179] Consequently, Justice Black always opposed such governmental actions as publication of the Attorney General's list of subversive organizations;[180] legislative investigation of suspected subversives;[181] and penalties for Communist party association, such as removal from labor union office,[182] disbarment,[183] denial of tax exemptions,[184] and denial of passports.[185] These actions jeopardized freedom and inhibited innovation while invading protected areas of belief and association. Only overt acts violating valid laws could rightfully be subject to punitive governmental action.

Absolutism was presented in response to the contending position that, basic as First Amendment rights are, they have to be balanced against other interests. In the Communist cases, this interest was national security. An integral part of Justice Black's absolutism was the denial of the propriety of such balancing. The Founders, in their initial balancing, made the correct assessment that national security was not likely to be threatened by this kind of dissent. The market place of ideas, if left unfettered, was self-regulatory. The people could be trusted to distinguish and reject speech which jeopardized future freedom.[186]

For Justice Black, this relationship between freedom of speech, self-government, and human progress governed all First Amendment problems. In certain respects, his argument calls to mind the

---

[178] Speiser v. Randall, 357 U.S. 513, 532 (1958); Barenblatt v. United States, 360 U.S. 109, 134, especially at 145–46, 149–53 (1959); Black, note 27 *supra*, at 880–81; Communist Party v. Subversive Activities Control Board, 367 U.S. 1, 137, especially at 167–69 (1961).

[179] See Dennis v. United States, 341 U.S. 494, 579 (1951); Yates v. United States, 354 U.S. 298, 339 (1957).

[180] Joint Anti-Fascist Refugee Committee v. McGrath, 341 U.S. 123 (1951).

[181] Barenblatt v. United States, 360 U.S. 109, 134 (1959).

[182] American Communications Assn. v. Douds, 339 U.S. 382, 445 (1950).

[183] Schware v. Board of Bar Examiners, 353 U.S. 232 (1957); Konigsberg v. State Bar, 366 U.S. 36, 56 (1961).

[184] Speiser v. Randall, 357 U.S. 513, 529 (1958).

[185] Kent v. Dulles, 357 U.S. 116 (1958); Aptheker v. Secretary of State, 378 U.S. 500, 517 (1964).

[186] See text *supra* preceding note 40.

absolutist analysis of Alexander Meiklejohn.[187] But he went beyond
Professor Meiklejohn, who had originally attempted to delineate
two spheres of speech: public or political speech, which was to
have absolute First Amendment protection, and private speech,
which was to be safeguarded by less stringent due process standards.
Justice Black, as did others sympathetic to Professor Meiklejohn's
aims, questioned the adequacy of this proposal. The fact that all
speech has public aspects raises the prospect that Professor Meiklejohn's resolution would not be able to provide sufficient protection.
Justice Black overcame this problem by ignoring the "private" aspect of all utterances. In all First Amendment categories, he focused
on the dissemination of views on public questions and, accordingly,
extended absolute protection. The vice of laws regulating obscenity, for example, is not that morality or literary tastes should be
beyond public regulation. Rather, he foresaw that proscription of
what is called obscenity could culminate in proscription of dissident
political views. *Smith v. California*[188] remains Justice Black's fullest
statement on obscenity, and in it he argued:[189]

> While it is "obscenity and indecency" before us today, the ex-
> perience of mankind—both ancient and modern—shows that
> this type of elastic phrase can, and most likely will, be synony-
> mous with the political and maybe with the religious unortho-
> doxy of tomorrow.

Industrial picketing over the practice of cut-rate milk distribution
merited First Amendment protection because it was "an attempt to
persuade people that they should look with favor upon one side of
a public controversy."[190] A general ordinance forbidding door-to-
door solicitation was unconstitutional because such solicitation "is
essential to the poorly financed causes of little people."[191] A ban on
loud and raucous amplifying equipment "thereby favor[s] competing channels of communication."[192] A newspaper cannot be re-

---

[187] Professor Meiklejohn's original statement is in FREE SPEECH AND ITS RELATION
TO SELF-GOVERNMENT (1948). He qualified his position somewhat in *The First Amendment Is an Absolute*, 1961 SUPREME COURT REVIEW 245.

[188] 361 U.S. 147 (1959). See also Cahn, note 118 *supra;* BLACK, note 49 *supra*, at 46–48.

[189] 361 U.S. at 160.

[190] Milk Wagon Drivers v. Meadowmoor, 312 U.S. 287, 305 (1941).

[191] Martin v. Struthers, 319 U.S. 141, 146 (1943).

[192] Kovacs v. Cooper, 336 U.S. 77, 102 (1949).

strained from commenting on a public trial because "anyone who might wish to give public expression to his views on a pending case involving no matter what problem of public interest, just at the time his audience would be most receptive, would be . . . effectively discouraged."[193] The requirement that malice be proved before a libel judgment can be awarded is "at best an evanescent protection for the right critically to discuss public affairs."[194]

The absolutist position was not fully articulated until the early 1960s. While it is arguable that some of Justice Black's original First Amendment opinions departed from the demands of absolutism, it is not clear that there was ever any serious departure.[195] Toward the end of his career, however, some genuine inconsistencies seemed to develop, particularly in cases dealing with picketing and public demonstrations.[196] In 1969, Justice Black published an extensive defense of the consistency of his work on the Court,[197] and in it he reaffirmed his allegiance to absolutism and to the limitations which, he argued, were always part of that absolutism. While he was certainly correct in pointing to these limitations, there has been, nevertheless, an unmistakable change in the way he has used them, for which he did not account.

The qualifications and distinctions that Justice Black drew are firmly rooted in libertarian analysis. The major one is the distinction between speech and conduct. While the former merits absolute protection, the latter is subject to regulation. Recognizing, however, that speech and conduct are often intertwined, he repeated in 1967 what he had long advocated. If a regulation of conduct produced an indirect effect on speech, the Court could balance the need for the regulation against the indirect effect on speech. Governments have the right to regulate the times, places, and manner of speech, subject to the requirement that such regulation be

---

[193] Bridges v. California, 314 U.S. 252, 269 (1941).

[194] New York Times Co. v. Sullivan, 376 U.S. 254, 293 (1964).

[195] See Reich, *Mr. Justice Black and the Living Constitution*, 76 HARV. L. REV. 673, 680–81, 687–90 (1963).

[196] See Bell v. Maryland, 378 U.S. 226, 318 (1964); Cox v. Louisiana, 379 U.S. 559, 575 (1965); Brown v. Louisiana, 383 U.S. 131, 151 (1966); Adderley v. Florida, 385 U.S. 39 (1966); Amalgamated Food Employees Union v. Logan Plaza, Inc., 391 U.S. 308, 327 (1968); Tinker v. Des Moines School District, 393 U.S. 503, 515 (1969); Cohen v. California, 403 U.S. 15, 27 (1971) (Blackmun, J., dissenting).

[197] BLACK, note 49 *supra*.

nondiscriminatory and not based on the content of speech. While freedom of speech is absolute, protection extends only to those places where speakers have a right to be for such purposes.[198]

Justice Black's refusal to extend First Amendment protection in a variety of contemporary picketing situations rested on these distinctions. He emphasized, toward the end of his career, that he always regarded picketing as conduct, not speech. As such it is subject to regulation, including, conceivably, complete prohibition.[199] In reviewing earlier cases he indicated that he did not read *Thornhill*, the leading case in which the Court overturned a general anti-picketing statute, as equating speech and picketing, or as extending First Amendment protection to picketing itself. For him, the vice in *Thornhill* was the law's vagueness and overbreadth.[200] Justice Black also cited *Giboney v. Empire Storage Co.*,[201] decided in 1949, in which, writing for a unanimous Court, he upheld the conviction of picketers in an industrial dispute. The picketers were members of an ice peddlers' union who were picketing a wholesale ice distributor in an effort to induce the distributor to stop selling ice to nonunion peddlers. Such an agreement, however, constituted violation of the state's antitrust law. Justice Black's opinion reflected the widely held view that when speech is intertwined with illegal action, the First Amendment cannot bring protection to the illegal action.

The more contemporary picketing cases, however, did not elicit the unanimity of *Giboney*. Dispute centered on the status of the laws being broken. For here the Court was not dealing with statutes aimed at agreed upon ends, such as antitrust but with trespass laws making public protest itself illegal conduct. Justice Black strenuously defended the validity of these laws, emphasizing that the places covered by them were not proper ones for public speaking. His first reference to such a limit to absolutism came in 1959,[202] and he discussed the problem again in greater detail in 1962. In a

---

[198] *Id.* at 44–63.

[199] Labor Board v. Fruit & Vegetable Packers, 377 U.S. 58, 78–79 (1964); Cox v. Louisiana, 379 U.S. 559, 577, 581 (1965).

[200] Labor Board v. Fruit & Vegetable Packers, 377 U.S. 58, 77, n.1 (1964); BLACK, note 49 *supra*, at 57.

[201] 336 U.S. 490 (1949).

[202] Barenblatt v. United States, 360 U.S. 109, 142 (1959).

statement unlikely to generate disagreement, Justice Black drew a line around the privacy of a home:[203]

> I would feel . . . badly if somebody were to try to come into my house and tell me that he had a constitutional right to come in there because he wanted to make a speech against the Supreme Court. I realize the freedom of people to make a speech against the Supreme Court, but I do not want him to make it in my house.

Disagreement begins, however, over where precisely "a speaker has a right to be" in places other than a private home, and has manifested itself in the course of litigating two kinds of cases: those dealing with demonstrations on private property open to the general public and those on public property devoted to particular uses. The Court, during Black's last eight years, reviewed convictions of demonstrators in a private restaurant,[204] on a public street,[205] on a street opposite a courtroom,[206] in a public library,[207] on jailhouse grounds,[208] on a privately owned shopping center parking lot,[209] and in an elementary school classroom.[210]

Justice Black voted to sustain all but one[211] of these convictions, denying that the places involved qualified as places open for public speaking. The fact that private property is open to the general public does not alter the rights of ownership, which include full right to bar unwanted speakers. Public property is devoted to particular uses, and neither the public character of the place nor the First Amendment itself takes precedence over the need to maintain the intended functions of the place. Justice Black made no attempt to

---

[203] Cahn, note 118 *supra*, at 558. In the same interview he underscored the importance attached to the proper place for public speech with this comment on Justice Holmes's statement on the availability of First Amendment protection for a person falsely shouting fire in a crowded theater: "If a person creates a disorder in a theater, they would get him there not because of *what* he hollered but because he *hollered.* They would get him not because of any views he had but because they thought he did not have any views that they wanted to hear there." *Id.* at 558–59.

[204] Bell v. Maryland, 378 U.S. 226 (1964).

[205] Cox I v. Louisiana, 379 U.S. 536 (1965).

[206] Cox II v. Louisiana, 379 U.S. 559 (1965).

[207] Brown v. Louisiana, 383 U.S. 131 (1966).

[208] Adderley v. Florida, 385 U.S. 39 (1966).

[209] Amalgamated Food Employees Union v. Logan Plaza, Inc., 391 U.S. 308 (1968).

[210] Tinker v. Des Moines School District, 393 U.S. 503 (1969).

[211] Cox I v. Louisiana, 379 U.S. at 575. The conviction was for obstructing public passages.

invoke his balancing test to see if these valid regulations of conduct had an indirect effect on speech. On the contrary, he defended the trespass laws in exceedingly strong and virtually absolute language, stressing the connection between such laws and maintenance of the democratic process. If private property cannot enjoy the ready protection of the law, owners of that property will be pushed to the point of taking the law into their own hands.[212] If public places are to suffer disrupting demonstrations, government by mob rather than law will be the likely outcome.[213]

When trespass laws touch demonstrations on public streets, Justice Black did recognize the possibility of an unacceptable indirect effect on speech.[214] He never sanctioned complete prohibition of street picketing without referring to his balancing test.[215] In this case Justice Black voted with the majority to overturn a conviction for obstructing public passages. The statute upon which this conviction was based, however, exempted labor demonstrators from its prohibitions, and this clear discrimination invalidated the conviction without the need to discuss any "indirect effect" on speech.

There was another series of cases growing out of the same civil rights movement that produced most of the trespass cases, in which concededly protected public speech was challenged under general breach of the peace statutes. Typically, in such cases police stopped a speaker in order to prevent a disturbance and the Court was called upon to pass judgment on the ability and commitment of the police to control the crowd rather than to stop the speaker. Again, Justice Black maintained his legal consistency. He never sanctioned silencing the speaker.[216] In his later opinions, particularly *Gregory v. Chicago*,[217] he introduced concerns that were new in his work:[218]

---

[212] Bell v. Maryland, 378 U.S. 226, 327–28, 346 (1964).

[213] Brown v. Louisiana, 383 U.S. 131, 167–68 (1966); BLACK, note 49 *supra*, at 62–63. See also Tinker v. Des Moines School District, 393 U.S. 503, 524–26 (1969).

[214] Labor Board v. Fruit & Vegetable Packers, 377 U.S. 58, 77–78 (1964); Cox I v. Louisiana, 379 U.S. 536, 577 (1965).

[215] 379 U.S. 536, 577–78 (1965).

[216] Milk Wagon Drivers v. Meadowmoor Co., 312 U.S. 287, 299 (1941); Terminiello v. Chicago, 337 U.S. 1 (1949); Feiner v. New York, 340 U.S. 315, 321 (1951); Edwards v. South Carolina, 372 U.S. 229 (1963); Cox I v. Louisiana, 379 U.S. 536 (1965); Gregory v. Chicago, 394 U.S. 111 (1969).

[217] 394 U.S. 111 (1969).   [218] *Id.* at 117.

The facts disclosed by the record point unerringly to one conclusion, namely, that when groups with diametrically opposed,
deep-seated views are permitted to air their emotional grievances, side by side, on city streets, tranquility and order cannot be maintained even by the joint efforts of the finest and
best officers and of those who desire to be the most law-abiding
protestors of their grievances.

Never before had he acknowledged the complexity of the problems
growing out of some public demonstrations, nor had he suggested,
as he did here, that these complexities might not be amenable to
resolution by some basically automatic process.[219]

It is hard to find a single case where Justice Black did not satisfactorily explain his vote. Yet his later opinions, starting with *Bell
v. Maryland*, deviated from his earlier work in emphasis and implication; they form the single greatest inconsistency of his judicial
career. His earlier opinions were noteworthy for the priority given
to freedom for the dissemination of views on public questions, often over appeals for public convenience and civic order.[220] There
was then an unmistakable openness and encouragement of diverse
forms of public discourse, which gave way to a clear animus toward public demonstrations. This animus was reflected first in his
refusal to consider whether a variety of valid regulations of conduct
might have an indirect effect on speech and the spread of ideas. In
the past the stress lay with the need for balancing in the face of valid
regulations in order to avoid even an indirect restriction on the
spread of ideas.[221] At the end not only were trespass laws treated
with the respect formerly accorded the First Amendment, but in a
variety of controversial circumstances the question of indirect effect was not even acknowledged as legitimate. The exact extent to
which particular demonstrations actually interfered with the intended functioning of an institution was not considered relevant.[222]

---

[219] Compare his dissent in Feiner v. New York, 340 U.S. 315, 323 (1961), in which he
labeled the decision sanctioning police action to stop a speaker "a long step toward
totalitarian authority."

[220] Milk Wagon Drivers v. Meadowmoor, 312 U.S. 287, 299 (1941); Martin v.
Struthers, 319 U.S. 141 (1943); Kovacs v. Cooper, 336 U.S. 77, 98 (1949); Beauharnais
v. Illinois, 343 U.S. 250, 267 (1952). See also Terminiello v. Chicago, 337 U.S. 1 (1949).

[221] See Barenblatt v. United States, 360 U.S. 109, 141–42 (1959); Konigsberg v.
State Bar, 366 U.S. 36, 68–70 (1961).

[222] See, especially, Brown v. Louisiana, 383 U.S. 131, 151 (1966); Adderley v. Florida,
385 U.S. 39 (1966); Tinker v. Des Moines School District, 393 U.S. 503, 515 (1969).

Nor would Black address important questions such as the relationship between private property, the changing patterns of land use, or the dissemination of views on public questions.[223]

Even where Justice Black was willing to balance, there was a shift in his priorities. Earlier, he fostered acceptance of public streets and parks as not merely appropriate but desirable places for the dissemination of views on public questions.[224] Later, the unavoidable acknowledgment that public streets are proper places for public protest came as a grudging acknowledgment, while emphasis shifted to the streets' primary purpose as avenues of transportation. At the same time, reminders of the constitutionality of a total ban on street demonstrations[225] and a call to limit picketing in residential areas[226] took on new prominence. To be sure, a total ban on street picketing was subjected to balancing, and a statute limiting picketing in residential areas would have to be narrowly drawn. But where once the times, places, and manner regulations were introduced as part of the extension of First Amendment protection in a variety of controversial circumstances, they were later invoked to limit such extensions. In *Kovacs v. Cooper*, Justice Black opposed a municipal ban on "loud and raucous amplifying equipment," stressing the importance of such equipment as a means of communication of the poor. His concession that volume and hours might be regulated was clearly incidental to his obvious encouragement of this means of communication. Similarly, his concession that individual home owners could bar a door-to-door solicitor barely detracted from the force of his *Struthers* opinion, forbidding a municipality to make such a ban, while invoking the need for "vigorous enlightenment to triumph over slothful ignorance."[227] While his *Struthers*

---

[223] Amalgamated Food Employees Union v. Logan Plaza, Inc., 391 U.S. 308, 327 (1968).

[224] Marsh v. Alabama, 326 U.S. 501 (1946); Kovacs v. Cooper, 336 U.S. 77, 98 (1949); Poulos v. New Hampshire, 345 U.S. 395, 421 (1953). See also Martin v. Struthers, 319 U.S. 141 (1943); Breard v. Alexandria, 341 U.S. 622, 649 (1951).

[225] Cox II v. Louisiana, 379 U.S. 559, 577 (1965).

[226] Gregory v. Chicago, 394 U.S. 111, 117–26 (1969).

[227] In this connection see Kalven, *Upon Rereading Mr. Justice Black on the First Amendment*, 14 U.C.L.A. L. Rev. 428, 449–50 (1967). Fowler V. Harper, in his biography of Justice Rutledge, Justice Rutledge and the Bright Constellation 54–55 (1965), revealed that Justice Black had originally supported the ban on door-to-door solicitation in *Struthers*, on the ground that such solicitation was conduct amenable to regulation. Black changed his mind after seeing draft opinions of Justices Stone and Rutledge. This

and *Kovacs* opinions brushed aside all concern for the effects of the practices in question on privacy, Justice Black later defended trespass laws by arguing: "Were the law otherwise, people in the streets, in their homes and anywhere else could be compelled to listen against their will to speakers they did not want to hear."[228] These differences are all the more striking in light of the fact that the issues in the later litigation more clearly involved attempts "to persuade people that they should look with favor upon one side of a public controversy" than did those involved in the earlier cases.

Justice Black's concern for public order and institutional integrity was by no means unwarranted. What is startling, considering his earlier stance, was his concentration on these goals without an equal concern for the role of picketing as a means of communication by the poor, or the use of trespass laws to suppress unpopular demonstrations. Not only was such a balanced inquiry conspicuously absent, but there was instead a striking and wholly new concentration on the possibility of mob violence and the need to preserve public order. At the beginning such fears were either ignored completely or disparaged in relation to the need for full dissemination of views on public questions. There is virtually no difference between Justice Black's opinions in contemporary picketing cases and Justice Jackson's dissents from Justice Black's positions in *Struthers* and *Terminiello*.

This late fear of mob violence was matched by a new disparagement of protest groups and their leaders. Earlier, Justice Black studiously avoided making negative reference to even the most offensive causes. Later, he deprecated groups as "clamorous and demanding,"[229] who "think they have been mistreated or . . . have actually been mistreated."[230] While dissenters once were treated

---

original openness to both sides of the issue, the *Struthers* opinion itself, and Justice Black's work in later picketing cases constitute perhaps the most graphic expression of the changes in his use of the times, places, and manner proviso. It also reveals as much about Justice Black's conception of the judicial role as it does about his First Amendment understanding. Once committed to a particular result, he introduced no qualifications into his argument. (I would like to thank Professor Edward N. Beiser, for calling my attention to Harper's references to Justice Black.)

[228] Cox II v. Louisiana, 379 U.S. 559, 578 (1965).

[229] BLACK, note 49 *supra*, at 63.

[230] Brown v. Louisiana, 383 U.S. 131, 162 (1966). See also Cox I v. Louisiana, 379 U.S. 536, 584 (1965).

by Black as heroes, the leaders of dissent became ambitious politicians guilty of fomenting hatred and riot:[231]

> [Our] laws do not provide that elected officials . . . will act
> in response to pre-emptory demands of the leaders of tramping,
> singing, shouting, angry groups controlled by men who,
> among their virtues, have the ordinary amount of competing
> ambitions common to mankind. A control of this kind by such
> particularized groups is directly antagonistic to a control by
> the people's representatives chosen by them to manage public
> affairs. In other words, government by clamorous and de-
> manding groups is very far removed from government by the
> people's choice at the ballot box. What we have in this country
> is a government of laws, designed to achieve justice to all, in
> the most orderly fashion possible, and without leaving behind
> a deluge of hate-breeding divisions and dangerous riots.

The fact that the later protests took place "where protestors do
not have a right to be for such purposes" can hardly explain this
degree of hostility, or the differences in thrust between *Meadowmoor, Beauharnais, Kovacs,* and *Struthers* on the one hand, and
Bell v. Maryland, Brown v. Louisiana, and *Tinker v. Des Moines,*
on the other.[232] Nor is this distinction sufficient to explain why
contemporary advocacy is likely to degenerate into mob violence
and a subversion of democracy, while analogous fears about labor
organizing, racial agitation, or the consequences of Communist
party activities were not worth serious attention.

It was not only Justice Black's votes, but the forcefulness of his
argument subordinating concerns such as privacy and possible violence to the dissemination of views on public questions that led to
his emergence as the dominant figure in the era of "freedom of
expression." Although this emphasis completely disappeared in
cases dealing with protest demonstrations, it is important to note
that it remained in all other First Amendment areas. On such issues
as freedom of association and communism, prior restraint and the
press, libel, and the publication of obscenity, Justice Black did not
depart at all—by vote or implication—from his early positions.[233]

---

[231] BLACK, note 49 *supra,* at 62–63.

[232] See also Jones v. Board of Education, 397 U.S. 31 (1970).

[233] See Baird v. State Bar of Arizona, 401 U.S. 1 (1971) (freedom of association);
New York Times Co. v. United States, 403 U.S. 713, 714 (1971) (prior restraint); Curtis
Publishing Co. v. Butts, 388 U.S. 130, 170 (1967) (libel); Ginzburg v. United States,
383 U.S. 463, 476 (1966) (obscenity).

IV. Conclusion

Justice Black always strove for internal consistency in his work, and he was far more consistent than a superficial review of his record would indicate. Most of the charges of inconsistency arise from a misconception of his basic position. He never supported Court intervention on behalf of individual rights in general. Although he contributed enormously toward its realization, he cannot rightfully be regarded as the leader in the movement for "increasing sensitivity toward human rights, and large conceptions of equality under law." The goals of this movement are far broader than those of Justice Black. He always sought to restrain the Court from abusing power while enabling it to give significant meaning to the Bill of Rights. In practice this meant a liberal interpretation only of the specific guarantees of the Constitution, particularly the First, Fifth, and parts of the Sixth Amendments, and incorporation. He never supported liberal interpretations of the Due Process or Equal Protection Clauses, the two key clauses for implementing expanding conceptions of human rights and equality.

For the overwhelming number of cases in Justice Black's last five years in which he agreed with his former opponents, there are sufficient precedents for his work. By far the largest number of such cases involved Fourth Amendment questions, and his record here was never on the civil libertarian side. His unwillingness to extend due process protection beyond the specific provisions of the Bill of Rights was clearly stated in *Adamson* in 1947. As the incorporation struggle abated with the success of selective incorporation, new due process problems beyond the confines of the Bill of Rights were brought to the Court. In his positions in *Goldberg, Sniadach,* and *Winship,* as well as in his refusal to recognize a constitutional right to privacy, Justice Black was wholly faithful to his *Adamson* position.

Equal protection and First Amendment problems were the only areas that put a strain on Justice Black's internal logic. While incorporation allowed him to overcome the openness of the Due Process Clause without seeming to violate his own strictures on the appropriate use of judicial power, it was far more difficult to give any meaning to the Equal Protection Clause without being forced into the kind of strained distinctions he made, for example, between reapportionment and other voting rights cases. On First Amendment questions his tone and emphasis changed more than his votes.

There are, however, two aspects of Justice Black's work which raise important questions of consistency beyond the technical consistency already discussed. One was an obvious shift in tone and language reflecting a changed attitude toward political reform and society's obligations to, and the responsibility of, dissidents and minorities. The second, and more far-reaching, touches Justice Black's premises concerning the essentially self-regulating democratic process, which needs a judiciary only to enforce clear, written limits on governmental power in order to sustain itself.

The major part of Justice Black's career was marked by a passionate concern for the "poor, the ignorant, the numerically weak, the friendless, and the powerless."[234] In his last years this strong concern clearly abated. In some instances it seems to have disappeared entirely. He certainly did not view what he called, "the ordinary criminal," for example, in these terms, nor did he regard him in any way as a victim of society. He was also unreceptive to accepting poverty as a suspect category in equal protection cases and showed himself unsympathetic to calls for judicial protection of welfare recipients.[235] As we have seen, his disparagement of protest movements and their leaders was without parallel in his long career.

Justice Black's official statements offer few clues to understanding these changes. In the end he claimed full support for his positions in the clear commands of the Constitution, without offering adequate explanation for the changes in his work or the genuine differences that clearly exist over constitutional interpretation. We may thus go beyond his writing to review his overall political views, in an attempt to gain additional understanding.

Justice Black was, in decisive ways, a product of the New Deal and of one strand of populism that fed into the New Deal. He was heir to that component of American reform which, while opposing concentrated power and wealth, never had any basic objection to capitalism, to competition as the central mechanism in economic relationships, or to individualism as the key to personal advance

---

[234] Chambers v. Florida, 309 U.S. 227, 238 (1940). For similar statements, see Feldman v. United States, 322 U.S. 487, 500–01 (1944); Bartkus v. Illinois, 359 U.S. 121, 163 (1959).

[235] Justice Black's equation of welfare with charity was also contrary to the implications of his earlier work. Goldberg v. Kelly, 397 U.S. 254, 275 (1970).

and satisfaction.[236] Opposition to concentrated power was aimed essentially at fostering competition and individualism rather than at replacing or qualifying it. Governmental regulation of the economy was encouraged as a necessary instrument in providing genuine equality of opportunity and in maintaining a competitive and productive economy in the face of new technology and new forms of economic organization.[237]

When Justice Black talked of political oppression he often conjured up an image of a distinct and powerful minority, divorced from society, oppressing the many.[238] An integral part of this conception was the supposition that the many are decent, hard-working, honest, and patriotic.[239] When government ceases to be a tool of the few, the need to concentrate on the underdog is vastly diminished; the underlying virtues of self-discipline, hard work, and individualism can be expected to come to the fore.

Justice Black's work during the last decade of his career suggests that he considered the New Deal and the postwar years successful in taking government out of the hands of the few and putting it at the service of the many. Equality of opportunity had been made a reality, thus ending the need for major political reform. Incorporation and the extension of Fourteenth Amendment protection to end de jure discrimination fulfilled the true promise of the Consti-

---

[236] FRANK, MR. JUSTICE BLACK: THE MAN AND HIS OPINIONS (1949), especially chap. 4; STRICKLAND, ed., HUGO BLACK AND THE SUPREME COURT: A SYMPOSIUM 279–80 n.11 (1967). For a statement of Justice Black's commitment to the competitive mechanism, see Northern Pacific Railway v. United States, 356 U.S. 1, 4 (1958).

[237] See the defense of the thirty-hour work bill made by Justice Black when he was a senator in 1933. 77 CONG. REC. 1115, 1126–27 (1933). His argument centered on the interdependence of employer and employee and on the need to reduce the work week as a consequence of the increased productivity of modern machinery. He stressed the desirability of stripping away the "spirit of avarice" that unfortunately attaches itself to the spirit of commerce, in order to "preserve for the people the beneficent advantages that a fair trade and commerce can afford a nation."

[238] Feldman v. United States, 322 U.S. 487, 501 (1944); Adamson v. California, 332 U.S. 46, 88–89 (1947); Black, note 27 supra, at 880; Communist Party v. Subversive Activities Control Board, 367 U.S. 1, 149–63, 167–69 (1961).

[239] See, e.g., Konigsberg, v. State Bar, 366 U.S. 36, 78 (1961); BLACK, note 49 supra, at 63, 65–66. In defending the thirty-hour work bill, Senator Black spoke of the rights of ownership of property "honestly acquired and fairly used," and the rights of workers to enjoy "health, happiness, and security justly theirs in proportion to their industry, frugality, energy, and honesty." 77 CONG. REC., at 1115. See also, text infra, at notes 241–43.

tution and symbolized the conversion of the judiciary from a tool of the few into the agent of the many. No longer did he link poverty and ignorance with numerical weakness, friendlessness, or powerlessness. Justice Black's often noted patriotism, an extension of his own experience, was an expression of satisfaction with the course of American democracy: [240]

> I am a typical example of this highly successful experiment in government. I was born in a frontier farm home in the hills of Alabama in the troublesome times of Reconstruction, after the Civil War, and my early life was spent in plain, country surroundings. There I became acquainted with the "short and simple annals of the poor," among plain folks who learned most of their law and sound philosophies from the country schools and churches. In due course the people of Alabama chose me to be their United States Senator. I served in the Senate until appointed Associate Justice of the United States Supreme Court in which position I have now served for more than thirty years. It is a long journey from a frontier farmhouse in the hills of Clay County, Alabama, to the United States Supreme Court, a fact which no one knows better than I. But this nation, created by our Constitution, offers countless examples just like mine. My experiences with and for our government have filled my heart with gratitude and devotion to the Constitution which made my public life possible. That Constitution is my legal bible; its plan of our government is my plan and its destiny my destiny.

Anthony Lewis, in reporting a memorial ceremony for Justice Black, related the following anecdote, which focuses more sharply on the Justice's expectations: [241]

> A former law clerk [to Justice Black,] Louis F. Oberdorfer, read out to the assembled members of the Supreme Court Bar a tribute that they adopted as a memorial resolution. He spoke at one point of "The Greening of America," the book by Prof. Charles Reich of Yale, another one-time Black law clerk.
>
> Justice Black had read the book, Mr. Oberdorfer said. In one passage Mr. Reich said dismissively that "Consciousness I," his term for the original American view of society, "believes that the American dream is still possible and that success is determined by character, morality, hard work and self-denial." Justice Black wrote in the margin: "I still do."

---

[240] BLACK, note 49 *supra*, at 65–66.

[241] N.Y. Times, 22 April 1972, p. 33, col. 1.

In upholding the rights of Communists, Black made it clear that he expected them to fail:[242]

> I think this fear [that the American people can be alienated from their allegiance to our form of government] is groundless for I believe that the loyalty and patriotism of the American people toward our own free way of life are too deeply rooted to be shaken by mere talk or argument from people who are wedded to totalitarian forms of government.

This expectation rested on a trust in popular devotion to this country, a devotion not unlike his own. His support for freedom of speech and his linking of it to self-government and human progress —notwithstanding any of his comments about accepting whatever wins out in the free market place of ideas—rested not so much on his willingness to accept whatever did emerge as on his expectation of the compatibility of those results with his own goals:[243]

> Where rights of communication, assembly, and protest are made secure, which is what our First Amendment is intended to do, people develop a sturdy and self-reliant character which is best for them and best for their government.

The protest movement starting in the middle 1960s served, in effect, to try Justice Black's equation of human progress and the workings of the unregulated market place of ideas. In 1944 when he linked freedom of speech, protection of dissidents, and human progress, it was in terms of combatting "vested interests":[244]

> This amendment reflects the faith that a good society is not static but advancing, and that the fullest possible interchange of ideas and beliefs is essential to attainment of this goal. The proponents of the First Amendment, committed to this faith, were determined that every American should possess an unrestrained freedom to express his views, however odious they might be to vested interests whose power they might challenge.

By 1965, however, he no longer talked of American government in terms of vested interests. His descriptions began instead to touch

---

[242] Konigsberg v. State Bar, 366 U.S. 36, 78 (1961). For similar statements, see Carlson v. Landon, 342 U.S. 524, 555–56 (1952); Barenblatt v. United States, 360 U.S. 109, 146 (1959); Communist Party v. Subversive Activities Control Board, 367 U.S. 1, 167–68 (1961).

[243] BLACK, note 49 supra, at 63.

[244] Feldman v. United States, 322 U.S. 487, 501 (1944).

on the government's representative character.[245] Human progress, as he had always thought of it, meant the kind of reform already in existence and not a continually new and open-ended process. In turn, dissident groups of the late 1960s began to be portrayed as sectarian and unconcerned for the general welfare.[246] While most of the public demonstration cases in the later years involved black protest, Justice Black's attitude was not so limited.[247]

Justice Black did not lead the judicial effort on behalf of the black minority as he led the fight for protection of Communist dissenters. He was, however, part of the unanimous Court that overturned the "separate but equal" doctrine. With the success in ending de jure discrimination, more complicated issues of state action and de facto discrimination arose. It was no longer clear that government power was being used as the agent of oppression. In *Gregory*, Black indicated that the protestors in question had already won the law over to their side: "In 1954 our Court held that laws segregating people on the basis of race or color in the public schools unconstitutionally denied Negroes equal protection of the laws."[248] While he extended First Amendment protection to the protestors in this case, his support was not, as we have seen, as unequivocal as similar support had been in the past. There is no indication in any of his work that he regarded American racial problems as not amenable to solutions that had been successful in enhancing the status of other groups, once official discrimination had ceased. Thus it is not surprising that he was not sympathetic to different conceptions of private and public responsibility involved in broadened conceptions of state action. In addition, the fear of riot that is so evident in his work on black protest represented a genuine fear that was absent in other situations. In the face of the black protest movement of the late 1960s, he was no longer certain that shared values, common goals, and inner self-restraint would work to insure the good society as he understood it.

Justice Black's lack of sympathy with the protest of the 1960s

---

[245] BLACK, note 49 *supra*, at 63. See also Brown v. Louisiana, 383 U.S. 131, 160–61 (1966); Hunter v. Erickson, 393 U.S. 385, 397 (1969).

[246] See text *supra*, at notes 229–32.

[247] See Tinker v. Des Moines School District, 393 U.S. 503, 515 (1969); Cohen v. California, 403 U.S. 15, 27 (1971) (Blackmun, J., dissenting). See also Turner v. New York, 386 U.S. 773 (1967). All these cases involved antiwar demonstrations.

[248] Gregory v. Chicago, 394 U.S. 111, 114 (1969).

was only one manifestation of his lack of sympathhy with many trends in contemporary society. His discomfort with large-scale economic organization, for example, has been frequently noted.[249] His vigorous enforcement of antitrust laws, as well as his receptivity to state economic regulation revealed not only an antipathy to the contemporary large-scale, nationally integrated economy but a disinclination to accept contemporary realities in seeking remedies for economic problems.[250] At the same time, however, he had nothing in common with the most vocal protest against contemporary trends, with its massive rejection of individualism and competition.

In *Tinker v. Des Moines*, Justice Black dissented from the extension of First Amendment protection to elementary school children who demonstrated against American involvement in Vietnam by wearing black arm bands to class. In the course of this dissent he stated:[251]

> And I repeat that if the time has come when pupils of state-supported schools, kindergartens, grammar schools, or high schools, can defy and flout orders of school officials to keep their minds on their own schoolwork, it is the beginning of a new revolutionary era of permissiveness in this country fostered by the judiciary.

What he saw and condemned in today's permissiveness was a rejection of the virtues of "character, morality, hard work, and self-denial." This same rejection underlay his lack of sympathy for some underdogs whom he regarded as failing to live up to their responsibilities in a society that he saw as basically just.

It also becomes easier to understand his exclusion of rights of

---

[249] STRICKLAND, note 236 *supra; Antitrust in a Coonskin Cap*, 74 FORTUNE 65–66 (July, 1966); United States v. Von's Grocery Co., 384 U.S. 270, 288–89 (1966) (Stewart, J., dissenting).

[250] Justice Black's antitrust policy has been criticized for erroneously focusing on the number of competitors in a given field rather than on the actual impact of a given merger on competition itself. FORTUNE, note 249 *supra*. Justice Stewart's dissent in *Von's*, accused Justice Black's opinion of being "hardly more than a requiem for the so-called 'Mom and Pop' grocery stores . . . that are now economically and technologically obsolete in many parts of the country." 384 U.S. at 288. For similar commentary on *Von's*, see *The Supreme Court, 1965 Term*, 80 HARV. L. REV. 245–47 (1966). Justice Black's opinions in Hood & Sons v. DuMond, 336 U.S. 525, 545 (1949), and Dean Milk Co. v. Madison, 340 U.S. 349, 357 (1951), upholding state regulations of commerce, show little concern for what Justice Jackson, in Duckworth v. Arkansas, 314 U.S. 390, 400 (1941), referred to as the "balkanization of American commerce" by state regulation.

[251] Tinker v. Des Moines School District, 393 U.S. 503, 518 (1969).

privacy from his conception of constitutionally protected individual rights. Protection of individual rights was always, for Justice Black, intimately linked with populist notions of the few and the many and the opportunity to foster needed political reform. There was always a presumption that the dissident in need of constitutional protection was acting on behalf of "the people" and that other dissidents could be safely endured, as they would lose out in the market place of ideas. The individualism associated with Justice Black's conception of individual rights was a community centered, patriotic individualism, grounded not in individual differences but in shared moral virtues of hard work and self-denial. For the same reasons, his concern for individual rights never embraced the "ordinary criminal."

In *Bumper v. North Carolina*,[252] Justice Black had occasion to comment on the constitutionality of a police search of a private home. In discussing whether the owner had given the requisite consent for the search, he remarked:[253]

> Mrs. Leath's readiness to permit the search was the action of a person so conscious of her innocence, so proud of her own home, that she was not going to require a search warrant, thus indicating a doubt about the rectitude of her household. There are such people in this world of ours, and the evidence in this case causes me to believe Mrs. Leath is one of them.

This attitude reflected his indifference to the privacy issue, in the context of search and seizure, self-incrimination, and general privacy. His description of Mrs. Leath also stands out in striking contrast to his disparaging descriptions of many protestors, and to his description of another protestor, the father of the Tinker children: "Their father, a Methodist minister without a church, is paid a salary by the American Friends Service Committee."[254] He obviously preferred Mrs. Leath.

Justice Black's long-standing concern for the poor, the weak, the heretic, and the dissenter always rested on a clear conception of moral virtue and its connection with the political good. With that conception shaken, there was bound to be some change in his work, even though he was able to maintain an internal, technical consistency.

---

[252] 391 U.S. 543 (1968).

[253] *Id.* at 556–67.   [254] 393 U.S. at 516.

The second inconsistency in Justice Black's judicial career casts doubt on the core of his doctrine: that democracy is essentially an automatic, self-regulating process that needs only judicial enforcement of clear, written limits in order to maintain itself. His fear of protest and its potential for degeneration into mob violence challenged his earlier confidence in the self-regulating market place of ideas. It challenged his expectation that successful democratic life is the by-product of enforced absolute limits on governmental power. In his earlier years Justice Black had pushed the market place concept virtually to absurdity. Yet the spoken premise of *Gregory* is that First Amendment cases present difficult problems that may not be subject to satisfactory resolution simply by applying the general principle embodied in the constitutional text. There emerged the recognition that there are—at least—two sides to First Amendment issues, and that the resolution of particular problems is difficult. Furthermore, the unspoken premise of *Brown* and *Gregory* is that more speech may not necessarily defeat bad speech and that the unregulated market place of ideas may not necessarily produce progress but may end in self-destruction.

In a sense, Justice Black never did rely on an automatic process to maintain liberty. If the foregoing analysis is correct, his fundamental reliance rested not with absolute limits but on the expectation that certain shared standards were operative in society and that these standards guided the market place and the nation toward salutary choices. It is impossible to know the extent to which he acknowledged the primacy of these standards to himself. He certainly never did so in his opinions. It is clear, however, that the difficulties with his First Amendment adjudication grew out of this conflict over the relative importance of underlying societal standards and values on the one hand, and constitutional limits on the other. In his First Amendment inconsistencies, seeking to maintain the primacy of judicially enforced guarantees while losing confidence in the accompanying values, Justice Black unwittingly began the critique of his own work.

The First Amendment states a general and important political principle. Supreme Court enforcement of that guarantee helps to reinforce the principle. But despite Justice Black's best efforts, it is obvious that all important provisions need continual interpretation in their application to particular circumstances. Part of that interpretation involves consideration of the conditions needed for the successful operation of the general principle.

Perhaps the most crucial condition for successful enjoyment of First Amendment freedoms is the existence of common standards by which various speech is judged. No intelligible discourse can take place without the capacity to distinguish honest inquiry, no matter how basic or exaggerated, from such attacks on meaningful public discussion as demagoguery, calculated slander, or systematic subversion. When this capacity is present, legal restraint becomes largely superfluous. When this capacity is absent, the law can contribute to its cultivation; when it is weak the law can help envigorate it. But if the law consistently denies validity of such distinctions, the public's capacity to make them can disappear. It is unrealistic to rely on the continual vitality of private choices while the standards for making these choices are publicly undermined.

Yet this is precisely where Justice Black's absolutism pointed, with its equation of all speech and its strident refusal to make judgments on the content of any speech. The problem is well illustrated in the current debate over libel of public figures. Until *New York Times v. Sullivan*, falsehood was punishable as libel. With the *New York Times* case, the requirement of actual malice was added. Statements made with the knowledge that they were false, or with reckless disregard for truth, were actionable; honest error was not. The decision reflected the judgment that to hold all falsehood libelous overly inhibits the cautious and subjects the careless but honest commentator to excessive restraint. These evils were considered more serious than the impact of honest error on political debate.

Justice Black concurred in the decision but advocated the extension of First Amendment protection to all speech, including the malicious and deliberate lie. Yet the distinction that he rejected is crucial for the vitality of First Amendment freedoms. It is an integral part of the public's capacity to maintain a democratic, to say nothing of a decent, society. Were Justice Black successful, it is at least as likely that "bad speech"—demagoguery, slander, subversion—would eventually drive out honest discourse.

All major First Amendment problems encompass similar considerations. It cannot be blandly assumed that all challenges to a democratic order will prove as ineffective as did the Communist challenge, the major national security issue during Justice Black's tenure.

American economic conditions, coupled with basic political traditions, probably precluded a successful Communist appeal. But other
such movements may meet more receptive conditions. The most
obvious one at this time would be some antidemocratic movement
exploiting racial fears and antagonisms. When needed most, "more
speech" can succeed in curbing "bad speech" only if public appeals
to distinctions between worthwhile and worthless speech have genuine meaning. Other First Amendment problems would also be
easier to handle if there were more acceptance of the legitimacy
of judgments about the quality of speech and if there were more
overt assessments of the threat of particular speech to other interests, such as fair trial, public peace, or institutional integrity.

If there is one underlying problem in all of Justice Black's work
it is precisely his denigration of this kind of judgment. His literalism was fashioned to avoid recourse to it. First Amendment absolutism avoided the need for judgment. Justice Black's continual
attack on the judiciary's attempt to give specific meaning to concepts of reasonableness, fairness, and justice extended the attack on
judgment to other constitutional guarantees. He derided all such
attempts, indicating that they involved "natural law" concepts,
clearly a term of abuse as he used it. All departures from strict enforcement of explicit constitutional commands are lumped together
as unacceptable exercises of judicial will.

In the same way, however, that standards for the popular evaluation of speech are a necessary condition for the successful operation of First Amendment freedoms, so too, societal acceptance of
reasonableness, fairness, and justice as meaningful standards for political action is a precondition for the enjoyment of other rights.
The vision of a purportedly neutral Court interposing itself in an
otherwise automatic democratic process to safeguard liberty by upholding the written text is as unrealistic as Justice Black's vision of
a completely self-regulating market place of ideas. For the constitutional guarantees to have genuine vitality there must first be a
society willing to listen to its courts, and to the judicial resolution
of a significant area of political conflict. This in turn rests on a general societal commitment to the principles of reasonableness, fairness, and justice, on the quality of debate in interpreting these commitments, and on the popular responsiveness to such debate.

American courts, in the process of constitutional adjudication,
play an enormous role in this debate, articulating and shaping basic

values. In so doing they make as significant a contribution to a healthy society as they do in enforcing particular provisions of the Constitution. Whether or not *Miranda* remains law, for example, is less important than how the public and the police respond to the call for higher standards in law enforcement. The Equal Protection Clause cannot bring racial equality in the absence of sufficient popular commitment to racial justice. There can be no hope for maintaining workable and decent criminal procedures without ready acceptance of such judgments that proof beyond reasonable doubt is an essential part of fundamental fairness,[255] and that a conviction in a trial permeated by excessive publicity and a "carnival-like" atmosphere is a denial of justice.[256] If not related to meaningful conceptions of justice, judgments of constitutionality will not be able to survive.

Justice Black, of course, feared that a judiciary giving confident voice to such judgments would endanger liberty. He would have us believe that we have only two choices in constitutional adjudication—either to abandon ourselves to unrestrained subjective judgments or to uphold absolute rules whose meaning is irrevocably fixed by history and language. But Justice Black's choice is Hobson's choice. First, as we have seen, history and language do not fix the meaning of the constitutional text, and exclusive reliance on these standards results in arbitrariness, not objectivity. Secondly, Justice Black shifted our gaze away from the true political choice—it is not, as he said, between no standards or clear standards but between better or worse standards for public life.

The susceptibility for abuse inherent in the search for better standards has given strong appeal to any attempt to avoid recourse to such standards. The rule of law itself is testimony to the need for a system of rules, rather than case-by-case resolution of problems in light of abstract principles. Yet no system of rules can anticipate and provide for all situations. Justice Black went as far as possible in making an attempt to do just that. But he failed. No set of rules can provide in detail for the multiplicity of changing needs that must be judged as they arise. In addition to rules there must always be judgment. With respect to the necessarily broad rules of the Constitution, the need for judgment is even greater. That there

---

[255] See *In re* Winship, 397 U.S. 358 (1970).

[256] See Sheppard v. Maxwell, 384 U.S. 333 (1966).

is little likelihood of agreement on the worth of all judgments does not mean that no judgments are possible. Societies must continue to argue over and strive toward better judgments if they are not to succumb to the worst judgments. No judicial determination need end debate on the merit of a distinction that has been drawn. Public argument over alternative standards is far preferable to the denial of the possibility of defending any meaningful standard and the retreat to a legal objectivity and neutrality that is illusory.

There are some negative consequences of Justice Black's approach. We have already seen how overt reliance on the words of the text, in the face of obvious disagreement over the meaning of such words, resulted in arbitrariness. This, in turn, led to cynicism about the judiciary's work. In addition, there is simply no evidence for Justice Black's confidence that the Bill of Rights, as drafted by the Framers, meets all the needs of limited government. His incapacity to give satisfactory treatment to the problem of electronic surveillance, and of privacy in general, are major examples of the serious limitations of his approach.

Professor Kurland, in noting Justice Black's success in bringing the Court to his position, without thereby gaining converts to his basic doctrine, noted that this could not be pure coincidence.[257] It cannot be and it is not. What linked Justice Black with the majority he led was a concern for a limited government solicitous of individual rights. But for Justice Black, this goal was overwhelmed, as it never was for others, by a staggering fear of judicial abuse of power and a simplistic conception of the democratic process. Serious as these defects are, their danger is mitigated by their lack of power to compel. They also contain a negative virtue in that they clearly show the dead end that awaits the attempt to banish judgment from political life.

Despite the genuine problems in his work, however, Black shaped the major trends in contemporary constitutional law. He was the architect of incorporation, which has served to nationalize higher standards of police conduct. Although First Amendment absolutism is not likely to triumph, Justice Black was instrumental in narrowing the scope of libel, in tightening restraints on obscenity, and in generating greater acceptance of public protest, even over his own dissent. In addition, loyalty oaths, disbarment, and various penalties

---

[257] Kurland, note 26 *supra*, at 362.

ind disabilities for alleged subversion will undoubtedly have to survive stricter scrutiny than in the past. He is also the author of
leading decisions, such as *Gideon* and *Griffin*, which, while they
do not, as perhaps they cannot, eliminate the disadvantages of poverty in the criminal process, go far toward mitigating them. If not
always for the soundest reasons, he made it more difficult to accept
glib justifications for such practices as convicting a person in one
jurisdiction for evidence compelled in another, and for making
failure to disclose information a crime in one jurisdiction while
that information is incriminating in another.

   Justice Black achieved these ends through the forcefulness,
power, and single-minded clarity of purpose of his opinions, rather
than through exceptional analytic ability or subtle treatment of the
many complexities of constitutional adjudication. His rhetorical
force and consistent voting record, for the major part of his career,
were instrumental in focusing attention on the Bill of Rights as legal
protection for individual rights against undue governmental power.
Even with all his shortcomings, the power of his opinions is such
that it is still accurate to think of the judicial era just ended as that
of "The Black Court."

   In Justice Black's law school yearbook, as he once recalled, it was
said of him, "This fellow seems to possess but one idea, and that is
a wrong one."[258] Justice Black's one idea is not so much wrong as
incomplete. Insisting on judicial enforcement of the constitutional
text can only be the starting point in making the Bill of Rights a
legal limit on political power. But his insistence on fidelity to the
text, with all its unresolved problems and incompleteness, has served
to enhance the importance of basic constitutional guarantees. This
same insistence on fidelity to the text can serve another worthwhile
end, too. Justice Black's literalism constitutes a reminder of "our
people's aspirations for a government of laws and not of men."
While his literalism is an unsatisfactory and oversimplified attempt
to fulfill this aspiration, it can serve a useful purpose amid stress on
the openness of the constitutional text, the political character of
the Court's work, and the suggestion that we accept the inevitability of the rule of men. For this too is an oversimplification, as is
the contrast between a government of laws and one of men. A government of laws represents a singular achievement of men, while the

---

[258] Quoted in Black, *Reminiscences*, 18 ALA. L. REV. 8 (1965).

Supreme Court's practice of judicial review is a unique manifestation of the rule of law. On the whole it has been successful in providing legal resolution for a significant area of political controversy
and in elevating the quality of American political life. Constitutional law calls for a range of talent well outside that of traditional
legal analysis and easily accommodates—if not demands—greater
freedom in interpreting the legal text than do other branches of the
law. Yet is remains one branch of legal analysis, and the Court's
success in its unique endeavor is intimately tied to its performance
as a court of law. This makes fidelity to the text—for all its openness—a necessary part of constitutional adjudication.